Landscapes of
Capital

Landscapes of Capital

Representing Time, Space, and Globalization in Corporate Advertising

Robert Goldman and Stephen Papson

polity

The right of Robert Goldman Stephen Papson to be identified as Authors of
this Work has been asserted in accordance with the UK Copyright, Designs and
Patents Act 1988.

First published in 2011 by Polity Press

Polity Press
65 Bridge Street
Cambridge CB2 1UR, UK

Polity Press
350 Main Street
Malden, MA 02148, USA

ISBN-13: 978-0-7456-5207-8
ISBN-13: 978-0-7456-5208-5(pb)

A catalogue record for this book is available from the British Library.

Typeset in 10.5 on 12 pt Plantin
by Servis Filmsetting Ltd, Stockport, Cheshire
Printed and bound in Great Britain by MPG Books Group Limited, Bodmin,
Cornwall

The publisher has used its best endeavors to ensure that the URLs for external
websites referred to in this book are correct and active at the time of going to
press. However, the publisher has no responsibility for the websites and can
make no guarantee that a site will remain live or that the content is or will remain
appropriate.

Every effort has been made to trace all copyright holders, but if any have been
inadvertently overlooked the publisher will be pleased to include any necessary
credits in any subsequent reprint or edition.

All images in this book have been created by the authors from digitized versions of
the advertisements discussed.

For further information on Polity, visit our website: www.politybooks.com

Dedicated to

R. Danielle Egan
&
Tillie

Contents

Images

Chapter 1, page 1, © General Electric 2010; pages 5–6, © Cisco 2007; page 16, © Merrill Lynch 1995; page 16, © MCI WorldCom 1998.

Chapter 2, page 19, © MCI WorldCom 1998; page 26, © First Union 1999; page 41, © Conoco 2004; page 41, © CDW 1999; page 41, © UPS 1999; page 41, © Norfolk Southern 2002; page 41, © UPS 1999; page 41, © Norfolk Southern 2002; page 45, © IBM 2009.

Chapter 3, page 47, © Merrill Lynch 2000; page 51, © Wachovia 2002; page 54, © Merrill Lynch 2008; pages 61–2, © MCI WorldCom 1998.

Chapter 4, page 64, © Neon 2000; page 70, © Bank of America 2005; page 73, © AT&T 2006; page 73, © Smith Barney 2004; page 73, © Verizon 2006; page 73, © Scudder 2000; page 73, © SBC 2004; page 73, © New York Stock Exchange 2001; page 77, © Smith Barney 2004; page 82, © WorldCom 2001; page 85, © Akamai 2001; page 93, © Honda 1999; page 93, © SAP 2001; page 93, © Nasdaq 1999; page 95, © WalMart 2006; page 97, © Thingamajobs 2006; page 100, © Council for Biotechnology Information 2001.

Chapter 5, page 105, © Qwest 1999; page 113, © Cisco 2001; page 124, © Computer Associates 2000; page 124, © SBC 2004; page 124, © US West 1997; page 124, © Akamai 2001; page 128, © Northern Light 1999 digital room; page 129, © Harbinger 2000.

Chapter 6, page 133, © New York Stock Exchange 2000; page 135, © Verizon 2006; page 139, © Sun Microsystems 1997; page 139, © Epic Imaging 2007; page 139, © Nasdaq 1999; page 139, © Computer Associates 2000; page 139, © Siemens 1999; pages 141–2, © New York

Stock Exchange 2000; page 145, © SAP 1999; page 151, © Nuveen 2000; page 151, © New York Life 2000; page 151, © MCI WorldCom 1999; page 151, © Cabletron 1999; page 151, © MCI WorldCom 1999; page 151, © First Union 1999; page 154, © Boeing 2000; page 154, © MCI WorldCom 1998; page 154, © General Electric 2010.

Chapter 7, page 156, © Hewlett Packard 2000; page 160, © Boeing 2000; page 160, © Cisco 1999; page 160, © Hewlett Packard 2000; page 160, © General Electric 1998; page 160, © Siemens 1999; page 161, © Boeing 2001; pages 164–5, © Chevron Texaco 2003; page 170, © Cisco 1999; pages 175, 177, 179 © Cisco 2007.

Chapter 8, page 183, © IBM 2009; page 188, © AT&T 2006; page 192, © Morgan Stanley 2007; page 192, © Cisco 2007; pages 194–5, © Dow 2006; pages 200–1, © Morgan Stanley 2007; page 202, © Council on Biotechnology Information 2000; page 202, © GlaxoSmithKlein 2005; page 203, © New York Stock Exchange 2001; page 203, © Boeing 2004; page 203, © New York Stock Exchange 2001; page 203, © Siemens 1999; page 203, © IBM 2009; page 203, © IBM 2010.

Acknowledgements

This research project began in 2000 as a web-based book, an attempt to demonstrate that long-form scholarship could not just be done via the Internet, but that dynamic hyperlinking could enable a form of scholarship permitting new ways of integrating multimedia source materials into textual analyses. The website included the creation of a database that allowed readers access to all of the textual materials included in the study. That version was written for use with students in classrooms. The website sought to foreground the video aspect of the project. As the project continued to evolve we decided to write a more theorized book version – hereafter referred to as "version 2.0." Inevitably, writing books about audiovisual objects demands a different way of telling the story when the audiovisual object is absent. The transition from writing for the Internet to writing on paper was ironically prompted by writing for the electronic journal *Fast Capitalism*. Previous versions of chapters four and five appeared in *Fast Capitalism*. We are grateful to Ben Agger for creating a space for writing critical theory with new modes of storytelling. Of course, the volatile history of Capital during this period has made for shifts in storyline and so the rewriting has been continuous, and perhaps will continue to be because the full story has not yet been told.

We owe much to Mary Haught who transcribed the 2400 commercials. Thanks to Joe Goodman for conversations exploring conceptualizations of rhizomatic labor and for his work on the database. Students at Lewis & Clark College have contributed to a climate of thoughtful engagement: a shout-out in particular to Gabe Wynn, Guy Dobyns, Ruth Buchanan, Amber Case, Maraya Massin-Levey, Alyssa Conley, Oliver Brandt and Kat Klopp. Shayna Lignell and Shanndara McNamara assisted in preparing the index. Thanks to Jim Proctor for his geographer's perspective, and to Joe Goldman for his unconventional perspectives; they have proven to be useful grist for the mill. Also thanks to R. Danielle Egan for her support and critical readings. Doug Kellner never fails to be on target with his criticisms, and we appreciate that. Special thanks to Debby Gould for her indefatigable spirit of optimism; Cindy Coleman for her friendship and patient listening, and to Liz Safran for her friendship, critical readings, and uniquely complementary form of meshugaas.

Our most significant debt is to Noah Kersey, our friend, colleague and sometimes co-conspirator. Noah has at various times worn the hats of website designer, webmaster, graphic designer, information architect, and database guru. Noah also created the cover art for this volume. Above all we thank Noah for his generosity of spirit.

The memory of Hilton David Goldman and Marguerite Papson, who each passed during the writing of this project, will forever be with us.

This book began with our studied interpretation of roughly 2,400 television ads covering the period from 1995 to 2010. Of those 2,400 ads, a smaller subset figured in the actual writing of this volume. We have prepared a companion website to this volume, a digital archive of those television ads that we referenced in the book. Since finishing this written volume, the stream of corporate advertising has, of course, continued; so we have tossed into the archive a representative slice of 2010 ads. The archive is searchable by ad names and keywords. We have also made additional information, including written transcriptions of many ads, available on the website. This digital archive is intended as a resource for students and scholars of advertising in its cultural forms. The website address is www.landscapesofcapital.com.

1

Mapping the Symbolic Landscape of Corporate Capital

Geographies of sign value

Writing against the backdrop of the early stages of modernity's decomposition, C. Wright Mills noted the difficulty of making sense of modern life in which people's visions of the social were "bounded by the private orbits in which they live" (1959:3). In the half-century since Mills wrote, the pace of change has accelerated and there is a widening gap between the orbits of personal life and the forces and transformations that shape our epoch. As the decades have passed, our ways of seeing the world have grown increasingly dependent upon discourses that originate outside the immediate contours of daily life – discourses that originate with the state, the corporation, and the mass media. Whether called advertising, propaganda, or public relations, these discourses play a prominent role in framing shared understandings of how a global society might bear upon our lives.

Spurred along by the computerization of the planet and the spread of vast, integrated, electronic networks, both the cultural frames and the institutions that structure our lives are less likely to be hinged to geography than at any time in our history. The orienting signposts that once gave us direction amidst the dizzying volatility of images and values have also become unhinged. How, today, are we to situate ourselves in a global economy, in a networked society, when our accounts of the world themselves consist of fleeting combinations of images and stories? Under such circumstances the meaning of place and the meaning of identity can no longer be strictly confined to what we confront in our personal geographies. Where in everyday life do people find the means of imagining the scales and structures of globalization that shape their day-to-day existence? Amongst contemporary narratives, the maps drawn by corporate television advertisements offer some of the most visible and recurrent imaginings of what globalization looks like, and in doing so they give us a language for making sense of today's economy and society.

Skewed by the agendas of corporate branding and legitimation, the landscapes of Capital painted by corporate advertising offer utopian settings characterized by continuous and unrestricted flows of information, communications, goods, and services through spaces that bear no evidence of borders, boundaries, or limits. Most striking about these scenes of frictionless and instantaneous circulation through time and space is the apparent absence of power relations.

The centerpiece of the new economy is the transnational corporation positioned in circuits of networked relations, seeking to direct flows of capital to its advantage. The transnational corporation traverses national economies and territorial borders, while symbolically dressing itself to fit the prescripts of a multicultural environment. Flexibility and integration are the primary code words used to characterize corporate practices that outsource production processes to the peripheries of the world system, while retaining a managerial capacity to respond as quickly as possible to the mood of the market. As new organizational forms emerged to respond to this new economic environment of high-tech information flows and rapidly changing niche markets, corporations needed to conceptualize, brand, and legitimize themselves to both investors and the public. They have painted a portrait of themselves and contemporary capitalism that is both distorted and true.

We began this project with an eye towards understanding how Capital conceptualized the geography of the high-tech global economy from 1995 to the present. We were interested in how the televisual media represented one key feature of globalization – "time–space compression": the increasing speed and ease of business travel and transactions, which take place as if geography and distance no longer matter. When a currency transaction can be conducted between New York and Singapore in a matter of seconds, for all intents and purposes both space and time have been overcome as barriers to commerce.

Corporate capital has pursued this and other transformations at a furious pace, sometimes through merger and acquisition, sometimes by virtue of new technologies, always by expansion. Our study examines the public self-representations that corporations offer as they transform themselves and the societies in which they exist. The transformations are of several orders – one is towards globalization; one is towards a new economy of high-tech firms; one is towards the widespread populist incorporation of the middle classes into retail investing; one is towards the Internet and wireless telecommunications. And the transformations left out of their accounts will prove no less significant – e.g., the steadily widening gap between rich and poor, the erosion of the middle classes, exploitation, third world labor, hunger, war, environmental degradation, the disappearance of a regulatory state, and the absence of panoptic authority and power.

As a discourse that seeks to brand and legitimize each specific corporation, corporate advertising gives an ideological face to the global informational economy associated with transnationalism, post-Fordism, and flexible accumulation. Though the landscapes depicted in these advertisements are rarely unified – their meanings are multiple, and often self-contradictory – nevertheless, when taken in aggregate, recurrent patterns of signifiers, frames, and narratives lend an overall appearance to Capital.

Before continuing we should say something about our use of the concept of Capital. By capitalizing "Capital" we run the risk of reifying it, imposing a false unity on it. The term we would prefer to use would be plural – "Capitals" – but that reads awkwardly in sentences. We capitalize "Capital(s)" to emphasize that, taken collectively, the discourse of corporate advertising corresponds to a cohesive way of seeing the world, and a way of organizing thinking about it. Just as when sociologists speak of Society, we know full well that it is only a useful analytic fiction. We understand that in its material and symbolic forms Capital does not share a universal set of interests, nor possess a unitary "spirit"; in fact it is the unity of self-contradictions that we are calling Capital.

No less than those of the eighteenth-century landscape artists, television advertisers' landscapes have been carefully crafted to convey spatial and social narratives. Television advertising constructs montages out of disparate signifiers, which are often joined together without regard to history or geography. Though isolated markers of history remain scattered here and there in the form of carefully situated signifiers, historical relationships have been flattened and forgotten, reduced to a universal present that sometimes becomes indistinguishable from a universal future. On television, landscapes appear free to roam, no longer constrained by the fixity of old-school geography, nor by the train of historical events and animosities, nor even by the borders of nation-states. Instead, the flux of landscapes is now regulated by the aims of corporate branding. These landscapes reveal a "postmodern confusion of time and space, in which temporal continuity collapses into extension and spatial dimension is lost to duplication" (Olalquiaga 1992:19). In the world of television advertising, landscapes float. In both form and content, this geography of floating landscapes seems an apt representational accompaniment to a system of flexible accumulation.

When landscapes are assembled out of shifting combinations of signifiers, the glue that holds these disparate signs together is commodity
aesthetics. Within a framework of universal commodification, all spaces
and all surfaces within these landscapes undergo aesthetic makeovers.
Each branded unit of capital seeks to stylistically identify and differentiate its landscape from those of competitors. Aesthetically redefining the
appearance of landscape surfaces distills out historical tensions between
workers and owners, between nations, and between the powerful and
the dispossessed. The formal composition of camera shots overwhelms
content, redirecting us away from a critical interrogation of the messi-
ness of history. As we shall see, the landscapes of Capital bear none
of the blood of history; they suggest a societal *tabula rasa* that leaves
"history behind" (Baudrillard 1990:14).

These advertising representations of market landscapes are certainly
not those of our forebears. They bear no trace of the Hobbesian impulse
to possess at the expense of others. Rather, these are markets apparently
fueled by perfect and transparent knowledge and thus lack the critical
feature of past markets – relations of power, conflict, and exploitation.
As seen on TV, Capital appears to have abandoned its more brutal
forms of surplus extraction, even though

> If . . . capital is a mode of domination, then we are always in its midst.
> This is because the structural law of value is the purest, most illegible form
> of social domination, like surplus-value. It no longer has any references
> within a dominant class or a relation of forces, it works without violence,
> entirely reabsorbed without any trace of bloodshed into the signs which
> surround us, operative everywhere in the code in which capital finally
> holds its purest discourses, beyond the dialects of industry, trade and
> finance, beyond the dialects of class which it held in its "productive" phase
> – a symbolic violence inscribed everywhere in signs, even in the signs of
> revolution. (Baudrillard 1990:10)

When corporate advertising narrates our world today, it does so with
what John Berger describes as "a change in the mode of narration."
A 2007 Cisco commercial offers a grand global vision not by telling
a "story sequentially unfolding in time," but by telling a lateral story
sequentially unfolding across spaces and between places. Cisco's ad
creates a narrative landscape defined by "the simultaneity and extension
of events and possibilities," where the mode of narration is conceptualized around a series of lateral transitions from one signifying cluster to
another – moving across space rather than over time (Berger 1974:40).

We have extracted frames from the Cisco ad (composed of 111 shots)
and arranged them linearly to stress the absence of a temporal relationship between the ad's frames. The ad flattens time into a universal

instant. The order of these landscapes has nothing do with real material historical and geographical relationships. The mix and match of landscape frames and scales is predicated on our acceptance of the advertising form and its logic of correlatives, that is to say, the correlation and transfer of meaning from one image frame to another (Williamson 1978). The apparently arbitrary sequencing of these landscape images is in fact organized by the logic of the advertising form and its structural (semiotic) law of value, rather than by the unfolding of historically situated relationships. Across the whole of these landscapes, economic relations (Capital) merge with an undifferentiated generic Society. The Corporation and Society appear to become one. The differentiated institutions that formed modern society lose their specificity, and everyday life appears as an amorphous whole, tied together not by locale or by culture but by the overarching presence of corporate capital – in this case, Cisco's voiceover unifies the otherwise incommensurate landscape signifiers. Corporate ads that seek to convey a global, unifying presence do so by editing together chains of signifiers arranged in a lateral stream that flows past a stationary viewing subject. Though the presuppositions of modern geography lurk vaguely behind these scenes, actual locations are made immaterial because their real significance lies in their distributedness, in the fact that they can be represented as connected via the unifying presence of the corporate brand throughout the world. A shifting, variable geography becomes an effect of signifier chains. The importance of location shifts from the referent world to location within the signifying chain. Put another way, as a set of landscapes, geography based on actual referents dissipates. Capital's self-portrait landscapes depict it as coextensive with civil society. No distinction can be made between the spheres of production and those of social reproduction; no distinction can any longer be made between the sphere of production and the sphere of symbolic articulation.

> The current phase, where "the process of capital itself ceases to be a process of production," is simultaneously the phase of the disappearance of the factory: society as a whole takes on the appearance of a factory. The factory must disappear as such, and labour must lose its specificity in order that capital can ensure the extensive metamorphosis of its form throughout society as a whole. (Baudrillard 1990:18)

welcome to   ｜｜｜｜｜｜
the human network cisco

To reinforce this illusion, representations of production have nearly disappeared from these symbolic landscapes, as the act of labor in production has been subsumed by technologies that operate on their own. Production has been absorbed and diffused into the associated activities that surround it: communication, trading, marketing, financing, transportation. But perhaps even more significantly, these landscapes less immediately associate Capital with production than with the generalized social reproduction of civil society. The Cisco ad encompasses all spheres of civil society within its network – personal and familial relationships, schooling, traditional marriage, leisure activities, even the merger between everyday life and the society of the spectacle. There seems no longer to be a distinction between political economy and civil society. Correspondingly the State disappears from these landscapes until we are left with the imagery of a civil society under the umbrella of Capital's organization of markets and technologies. A global society defined by corporately mediated spaces, rather than nation-states, is a world defined by an absence of barriers – the freedom of unregulated transactions flowing through unconstrained open spaces. These landscapes also give visual form to the transformations of economy and society due to the invisible agents of the Internet and networking.

The portrait of Capital developed in these ads suggests a deterritorialized global network that operates on a commitment to maximum efficiency, flexibility of organization, instantaneity, innovation, global integration, and multiculturalism. It seems perfectly appropriate that these landscapes often resemble self-portraits of each corporate brand of Capital, because in the post-Enlightenment era the subject is no longer the individual, but Capital itself.

At the historical moment in which the commodity seems to have become the universal form of value, it also seems that values have become ever more volatile and unstable. This translates directly from the market's premise of value as a fluctuating index of moods and sentiments, grounded in just-in-time production and delivery systems. The goal of markets – as they become ever more refined by the instrumentation of technology – is to reflect "real-time" (that is, instantaneous) valuations. Proponents of real-time valuation herald a new era of democratic transparency and consensus. The varied landscapes sponsored by corporate capital stress consensual, power-free relationships, and neglect to chart the new constellations of power that accompany the volatility and instability of market relationships.

What is the relationship between the corporate landscape narratives and the political economy of sign value? *Circa* the millennium, we examine these landscapes of Capital as expressions of a political economy of sign value entangled with the logic of Capital. What is the relationship between commodity culture and the dynamics of capitalist development? Jean Baudrillard argued that the political economy of sign value signaled an end of production. By contrast we interpret the economy of sign value as a necessary corollary of global production in which the goal has been to break the limits of time and space in order to boost the rate of profit. The cultural economy of signs has become every bit as significant as the more traditional political economy of Capital which precedes it and underlies it. The relationship between the construction of sign value and the current stage of capitalist development is nowhere more immediate and obvious than in the corporate branding process. Every ad is an investment in brand value, and every landscape is an expression of that brand value.

How does the cultural economy of signs motivated by the logic of Capital condition the representation of landscapes? In the sense that "signs are exchanged against each other rather than against the real" (Baudrillard 1993a:7) the construction of landscapes as signs has the implication that landscapes no longer refer to material geographies, but rather gain meaning from the signs that have been substituted for them. If Cisco's geographies are locatable, it is because they are constructed out of stereotypic signifiers that have circulated through other media forms: cinema, tourist advertising, and news promos, etc. Retrieved from image banks these stereotypical signifiers work as a universal visual language, the shorthand of advertising discourse.

A brief history of the recent economic past

The fall of the Berlin Wall not only heralded the crumbling of the Soviet bloc, it figuratively marked the twilight of the landscapes of heavy modernity. In the US the 1970s and the 1980s had been marked by the travails of deindustrialization and the diminished competitiveness of US capital. The political-economic malaise had its counterpart in a deepening culture of cynicism and a diminished sense of future horizons. The crumbling of the Soviet alternative coupled with the unfolding of neo-liberal globalization spurred a renewed optimism among capitalist elites about investment opportunities in emerging markets. If the 1970s and 1980s had elicited speculation about the decline of the grand narratives of truth, science, and progress, the 1990s witnessed a resurging confidence in those grand narratives, this time abbreviated in the form of brand signifiers. Taking a broad view of corporate advertising since 1995, it can be described as the church of the so-called "new economy"

– a conceptualization itself premised on the utilitarian union of markets and technological innovation in computers and telecommunications.

By the late 1990s, surging growth in computer technologies and the Internet, coupled with the advent of rhetorically populist investment services, prompted a collage of global narratives that streamed together themes of universal humanism and multiculturalism, technological progress and advancement, and personal empowerment through access to digital information flows, all sponsored by branded capital operating in an apparently barrier-free market economy. This type of advertising envisioned the future as a technotopia made possible by applied technoscience directed by capital investment.

Adherents of the "new economy" argued that digital technologies gave incentive to innovation by boosting productivity and thus competitive advantage. By the same token, the supposed dynamism of this new economy, predicated on the vigor of private sector investment in digital technologies, sounded the ideological death knell of bureaucratic hierarchy. Most importantly, the "new economy" designated an affirmative shift from manufacturing to a knowledge and idea-based economy. Advertising rhetoric mirrored the discourse of the new economy in its embrace of risk and constant change – creative destruction became glamorous as a motivation for venture capital. The 1990s' stock market boom centered on technology companies, and the growth of the NASDAQ stock market index rode a renewed enthusiasm for the narratives of science and technology that promised to conquer the material world of scarcity, while continuously driving forward productivity rates to permit an ever-increasing quality of life, even if millions of jobs had left the country. Technology and economic growth became synonymous, wrapped in rhetoric of market innovation and competition as secular salvation. Even after the high-tech bubble collapsed and the NASDAQ valuations returned to less speculative levels, mythologies of inevitable technological progress still drove corporate dreams.

Technological competition has pushed the integration of high-tech products into the fabric of everyday life. The diffusion of the Internet, wireless connectivity and computer technology changed investing, consumption, politics, education, the pleasure of game playing, and virtual communities. Airbrushed technological innovations connect easily with desires for greater convenience, efficiency, and livability. Even without the ad glitz, such narratives connect with prevailing paradigms of common sense. Cell phones, plasma television screens, DVD-recorders, digital video cameras are no longer stand-alone technologies but integrated systems.

In the financial sector the older boundaries between banking, insurance, and investment fell, spurred by deregulation and a proliferation of financial tools, thus speeding up both investment and profit-taking. New forms of capital were given a boost as technologically mediated e-brokerage firms such as e*trade, Suretrade, and Ameritrade courted small investors. Reducing fees to a few dollars per trade expanded the numbers of working people who could join in what Susan Strange (1986) called "casino capitalism." Retirement and pension programs broadened a sense of being aligned with Capital's interests, and as friends, families, neighbors, and colleagues formed investment clubs, speculative capital poured into the tech economy. Where the old television networks (CBS, NBC, and ABC) largely neglected daily coverage of stock markets, cable television and the logic of niche audience markets opened possibilities for financial news. Television could do what traditional print media could not – report in close to real time. The medium changed the very nature of what it reported on by joining the push towards immediacy with the structural tendency to reduce stories into effective visual signs. Television financial news channels spectacularized the relationship between Capital and Wall Street, hourly marching forward analysts to offer stock picks. Celebrity analysts emerged, as did celebrity stocks. The stakes ratcheted up as expectations grew. CEOs and corporate officials appeared on air to toot their company horns. The quarterly earnings' seasons became a blur, a steady tension on which to build stories. Which companies could meet the analysts' earnings estimates? Who had presented the best stories regarding their company's growth potential? And it was certainly of interest to the television news channels to grow the market for their shows – to grow their ratings. Corporate advertising fit perfectly into this genre – promoting the corporation itself to an investment-oriented audience. Within this context, the branding of corporate capital grew in importance.

After 2000, dramatic changes of circumstances became manifest, some rooted directly in the contradictions of Capital and others in the political hostilities bred by histories of domination and exploitation within an imperial global system. The NASDAQ and dotcom bubbles burst, sending the market averages plummeting. A continuous stream of less-than-stellar earnings reports in the technology sector suggested a technology plateau where proprietary intellectual property seemed to turn in an almost law-like fashion into commoditized technologies, and price competition negated the promise of always-expanding future earnings. With price competition came a process of intensified emphasis on branding.

A frenzy of mergers and acquisitions bred new corporate giants, some of whom claimed to have discovered how to do business in more innovative and profitable ways. For good reason, the financial scandals and subsequent collapse of Enron, WorldCom, Global Crossing, and Arthur Andersen shook the corporate world, reopening the entire subject of "valuation." Was the "new economy" nothing more than smoke and mirrors? Capital's legitimacy took a hit as a steady stream of sound bites wove together imagery of financially strapped workers who had lost jobs and retirement savings with investors who helplessly watched their share values dissolve into the ether, with tales of corporate officers shamelessly engulfed in greed and excess. But minus any structural critiques, coverage became reduced to the theme of just a few bad apples. Frames such as "corporate crime wave" may appeal to populist sentiments about punishing the rascals who done wrong, but they also tend to absolve the capitalist system by making "human nature" the focus rather than how our system is structured. Predictably, for a short period after these scandals, advertising messages relied heavily on themes of reliability and honesty.

The destruction of the World Trade Center, a monument of capitalist globalization, rattled the investment community. Perhaps more importantly, it reinvigorated the nation-state. In the post-Reagan era many had hailed the withering away of the bureaucratic nation-state, in which "regulatory authority" was delegated and outsourced to other organizations (Busch 2007:439). But 9/11 and the politics of terrorism dramatically revived the State's role as protector. The World Trade Center attack was not interpreted as an attack on Capital but on the Nation, and became, of course, part of the Bush administration's pretense for wars in Iraq and Afghanistan. The cost of those wars, the growing cost of Homeland Security, the massive US debt, the mushrooming trade deficits, and weakening of the dollar all point to difficult days ahead for the US economy. For a brief period after 9/11 patriotic ads flourished, mostly in commodity advertising, e.g., "Let's get America rolling again. 0% financing." While a few corporate advertisers (Boeing, Lockheed, Chevrolet, and the NYSE) changed the landscape imagery of their advertising immediately following 9/11, the return to patriotic (nationalist) rhetoric did not last long; after a suitable period of mourning, corporate advertising resumed the emergent visions of global economies independent of the symbolic presence of States. The landscapes of Capital tend to register secular economic and social trends (longer-term trends like the development of the Internet; the importance of supply chains; the aging of baby boomers), rather than responding to the immediacy of political events, no matter how significant those events are. Where once corporate ads sought to bolster legitimacy by drawing on the value of nation-state symbols, now the consequences of being identified with the State go in the opposite direction. Whereas television news focuses on institutions of governance and the conflicts, disorder, and crises associated with States, corporate advertising depicts a remarkably homogeneous and non-divisive world.

Suddenly, in 2008, a global financial crisis of still unknown magnitude unfolded. Capitalist economies abruptly began to disintegrate, driven by a housing mortgage crisis that stemmed from the reckless, and unregulated, use of derivative financial devices that allowed banks to buy loans by leveraging debt rather than assets. Indeed, as the absence of underlying assets became more apparent with every passing hour, enormous corporate banks began to fail. Minus assets to cover the trillions and trillions of dollars of debt, market liquidity vanished, and in 2008 the Dow Jones Industrial Average dropped from a June high of 13,197 to an October low of 7,392. The interdependencies of a global capitalist system were immediately evident and the crisis rippled out across emerging economies. After Bears Stearns and Merrill Lynch collapsed and financial markets froze, the US government stepped in to bail out financial institutions and then the US automobile industry. These programs were followed with a promise of a federal government stimulus package from the Obama administration. CNBC newscasters nostalgically debated the end of free-market capitalism, or rather, the illusion of free-market capitalism. Nevertheless, even the most ideologically driven free-marketers pointed out the need for some government regulation of the financial industry. In 2009 the loss of consumer confidence, a saturated credit economy, and rising unemployment rates continued to weigh down the economy. But even as this crisis deepened into global recession, corporate advertising continued to paint images of a harmonious global landscape.

Questions about how these advertisements are used to build popular hegemony for the current approach to business and government pervade the collected scenes that make up the landscapes of Capital. The dominant ideas of our epoch continue to be those sketched out by the class that has access to the means of communication. These ads present the view from above, choosing to focus on supply chain innovations rather than the outsourcing that has restructured manufacturing worldwide; stressing the freedom of investing from home rather than the structural adjustment programs that have pushed millions off the land into a "planet of slums"; or fetishizing the privatized bubbles of everyday life cut off from the resource extraction and "heavy duty transport of natural and biological resources" that form the backbone, and massive carbon footprint, of the global economy (Davis 2006; Brennan 2003:5).

The advertising texts

The emerging sign economy has dislodged from national economies and has begun to reflect the circuits of global capital. Over the past decade, corporate television advertising for Fortune 500 companies has become pervasive, migrating beyond the business and news channels to sports and entertainment channels, while spreading across national borders via satellite broadcast and global media networks. We have gathered 2,400 television ads covering the period from 1995 to 2010. This collection overweights corporations in telecommunications, computer technologies (semiconductors and software), finance (investment, banks, insurance), Internet, biotechnology and the life sciences, and energy sectors, but also includes autos, aerospace and defense, pharmaceuticals, and corporate consulting. We also have broadened the category to include States (e.g., Michigan, Ontario, Korea) because their ads also brand and define a larger entity in terms of the ingredients of Capital – infrastructure, labor force, education – as they compete to recruit capital to their regions.

All the ads have been digitized, entered into a database, coded for key concepts and key signifiers, and a transcript of the spoken text included. That database, complete with the ads themselves, is available for study online. Our writing dwells upon readings of selected advertising texts, but these readings invariably followed from a first draft that charted in more aggregate ways the patterns we saw in the ads. While, historically, corporate ads generally aimed at identifying a company and what it stood for rather than offering a particular commodity for sale, these distinctions are no longer as clear-cut as firms advertise their products and services to other businesses. What unites all corporate ads is that they aim at "branding" the company. In our rubric, this "branding" process contributes (by building, reinforcing, or defending) to a corporation's "sign value."

Brand building works to create an association between a recognizable commodity or corporation and the imagery of a desirable quality. The brand itself is assigned a recognizable, but differentiated, representation: the logo. Then, that representation is attached to a series of layered signifiers that point to a specific set of meanings: the signified. The goal is to harmoniously blend layers of signifiers to support the branding message. Vectors are created across elements (visual, audio, textual) so that a sound signature might bind a narrative to a logo as well as signifying something in its own right. Global scapes are turned into second-order signifiers hurled through these vectors of equivalence exchange – global scapes are transformed into currency that might add value to corporate logos (Barthes 1972).

Branding aims at boosting value in markets that are cluttered with both goods and images. Though competitive branding aims at differentiating products and firms from one another, companies tend to rely on signifiers that have worked for others. The result ironically is that competitive branding generates more clutter than it resolves.

While the intended audience may vary somewhat with each particular campaign, corporate ads tend to address the wider business community, investors, regulators, purchasing managers, and a firm's own employees. Their primary audience is the business community and investors – defining capital for those who have a self-interest in capital. They provide glimpses of how corporate finance, technology, organization, and practice ought to work. They idealize not only the processes of capital but also their business-oriented audience. Just as the bucolic landscapes commissioned by the English landholding classes artfully concealed all semblance of impoverished labor from the eye of the sponsoring spectator owner, so too the landscapes of corporate capital are defined as much by what they veil as what they stress.

Two factors might explain the expanded domain of these ads – first, the investor class expanded dramatically in the 1990s to include a wider portion of the middle class, and second, these ads also serve a broader public relations initiative. A remarkably large subset of these ads seem designed to represent corporations as good citizens and ethical actors: environmentally concerned, responsible neighbors supporting local communities. These legitimation ads are often a response to public criticism directed at corporations through other media forms such as news and documentaries. Almost all energy sector ads, for instance, proclaim environmental concern.

Some portion of corporate advertising thus aims to defend (or legitimate) the value of Capital. In truly severe circumstances, advertising is unable to stem the tide – the most salient examples were the valuation crises of Enron and WorldCom – and the loss of confidence resulted in the evaporation of capital. But just as significant are those ads that seek to build capital investment. Here investment in the sign – in the brand – aims to boost the value of capital via its stock price or its return on investment. In the world of investing, perception is reality – what better tool to mobilize therefore than the simulacra of sign values?

Reading a symbolic landscape

How do units of Capital represent themselves during the historical period of transition into high-tech globalization? Corporate ads can be read to reveal how Capital represents itself and the world that is being wrought – in terms of the signifiers used and the stories told. We have tried to assemble the map, to find the pieces and link them together with the intention of providing a rough guide for navigating the representational world of Capital.

If we think at all of maps of Capital we picture graphs showing statistical measures of economic data – such as GNP, retail sales, new-home constructions, employment, trade, income, and the range of visually represented financial data that appear in newspapers and on TV. Such maps, like stock charts, help to visualize the routine flows – the ups and downs – of a capitalist economy. While such maps can easily be made to reveal distributions of power and wealth, they rarely do. In contemporary society, "mapping has become an activity primarily reserved for those in power, used to delineate the 'property' of nation states and multi-national companies" (Aberley 1993:1) – or it was until the appearance of Google Maps. Capital and the Nation-state are not just subjects of the mapping process but also the authoritative producers of the mappings that frame our understanding of a complex world. The relationship between maps and power is not insignificant.

> Because [an Interested party] selects from the vast storehouse of knowledge about the earth what the map will represent, these interests are embodied in the map as presences and absences. Every map shows this but not that, and every map shows what it shows this way but not the other. Not only is this inescapable but it is precisely because of this interested selectivity – this choice of word or sign or aspect of the world to make a point – that the map is enabled to work. (Wood 1992:1)

And yet, unless one is looking for it, one rarely sees in maps these tracings of political-economic and cultural power. This is because maps offer us cooked representations of raw data. In their cooked form maps seem to objectively chart territories – whether these are economic territories or spatial territories. Mapping offers a way of seeing that appears factual, realistic, and proportional. However, mapping is a representational process that distorts through selectivity and omission, emphasis and combination, exaggeration and simplification. While conventionally we think about mapping from a geographer's perspective, we might also speak of mapping from a cultural studies perspective. Capital not only produces flows of goods and monies but also flows of signs. Capital has been pressing into new spaces for about three centuries. At each new stage of expansion, there is a cultural dimension as well – and this is the matter of the representation of Capital in its landscapes.

Mapping ads requires a metaphorical leap. While a conventional map is a rendition of a geographical space that situates its various elements so that they appear to constitute a natural whole, TV commercials are less neat and tidy. TV ads appear at different times on different channels, are in constant flux (campaigns may last only a couple of weeks), and represent a variety of sometimes competing interests. To complicate matters further, the intention of ads is branding and selling. In spite of these many difficulties, when ads that address questions of global capital are brought together, a visual constellation, a landscape, begins to emerge. Though any single commercial may lack the representational breadth, taken as a totality, corporate ads do constitute a symbolic landscape of time–space relations.

While we look at how specific corporate campaigns work to brand corporations, our goal is to move to higher levels of abstraction. By identifying recurring themes, images, and narratives, we attempt to produce a picture of how Capital itself is branded. Here we must entertain questions of the hegemonic nature of corporate branding. How does this body of corporate discourse naturalize a particular set of economic, political, and social relations that we refer to as transnational corporate capitalism? To what extent does it justify the processes that we associate with globalization as necessary and inevitable? To what extent does this discourse exclude and obscure and mask relations that are destructive to the cultural and social life of particular social groupings and classes?

We have taken the metaphor of landscape and pushed it to embrace almost all that can be represented spatially. There are close to 2.5 million frames in the ads that comprise our data set and these include an abundant variety of landscapes – from a surprisingly few traditional agrarian landscape scenes, to the architectural abstractions of hyper-modern cityscapes, to the micro landscapes of circuit boards and nanospaces, to mappings of telecommunication connectivity, and even the glamour landscapes of nature photography, to mention but a few. Each corporation strives in its advertising and branding to identify itself with differentiated imagery, but competition amongst them also invites mimesis and clutter – the result is a tendency towards overlapping tropes and signifiers and an overall aesthetic of corporate capital.

Cultural analysts have long employed the strategy of reading landscapes for clues into the social and cultural make-up of a time and place. "The visual conventions we use to understand" socially constructed landscapes "emerged from painting and photography and were made universal by advertising and film" (Nye 1997:5). A "landscape is a natural scene mediated by culture. It is both represented and presented space, both a signifier and a signified, both a frame and what a frame contains, both a real place and its simulacrum, both a package and a commodity in the package" (Mitchell 1994:1). Landscapes can thus encapsulate broad cultural understandings of the ways we live and the ways in which we have imposed ourselves upon nature.

We have lifted and joined two seemingly disparate landscape scenes from television ads. The landscape on top suggests a tranquil bridge scene – patterned perhaps after a venerable Japanese print; it has been lifted from a montage arranged to idealize Merrill Lynch's (1995) global investment strategies in Asia. The photographic imagery of orange-robed Buddhist monks became a late 1990s favorite amongst corporate advertisers, who perhaps saw the orange-robed monk as a signifier of diversity's inclusion in the "new world order." Or perhaps they chose such imagery to connote Eastern wisdom, or to convey a sense of balance between enduring traditions and energetic modern Capital (Merrill Lynch). What might decontextualized images of orange-robed monks be made to tell us about capitalist cultures *circa* the millennium?

We ripped the second image from an MCI WorldCom (1998) ad, where it was meant to signify the speed of data transfer over the Internet. Whereas the first landscape scene might testify to continuity amidst the forces of globalization that are penetrating and transforming Asia, the second landscape speaks not to place but to space, an abstraction that more and more seems to lie at the core of the capitalist world-system. If we interpret this radically decontextualized image as pointing to the inside of a fiber-optic cable, it can be viewed as a cyberscape of the moment, not simply a symbol of a future that is upon us, but a functional conduit, the veins of a network that, like a river, flows through us, connecting us.

As different as these landscape images may appear, consider the way in which each raises the relationship between a *mindscape* and Capital/ Technology. Shrouded in a colorfully beatific aura, the fiber-optic cable does more than merely indexically point, it evokes a symbol of a heaven made possible by the discoveries of science – beams of light radiate the power to liberate us, leading us to the infinite that lies before us as a result of the marriage of technology and capital. Similarly, the apparent tranquility of Buddhist signifiers does more than point towards a spiritual presence in a hyper-modern world of investment, invoking the conservation of cultures practiced by forward-looking capital. As Slavoj Žižek (2005) observes, the newfound popularity of Buddhism within corporate culture may have to do with how it can be harnessed to global capital – the "Taoist Ethic and the Spirit of Capitalism." Žižek suggests that Buddhist-tinged philosophies "actually function as the perfect ideological supplement" of global capitalism insofar as the Buddhist "attitude of inner peace and distance" discourages attachment and supports the necessary economic tactics for contemporary global capitalism built on perception, speculation, and the rapid circulation of capital itself. Where attachments of any kind to anything or anyone put one at a competitive disadvantage in global markets characterized by "dizzying change," the Buddhist stance of a fleeting objective reality can be seen to parallel the ephemeral markets built on the hit and run of speculative investments.

The digital, electronic integration of markets across the planet requires a paradigm shift in the way we imagine the world fitting together. Sometimes elegant, sometimes distorted, the stories and imagery fashioned via corporate ads give popular audiences a set of conceptual tools for imagining the scope of corporate globalization. As Hardt and Negri note, "Contrary to the way many postmodernist accounts would have it, the imperial machine, far from eliminating master narratives, actually produces and reproduces them . . . in order to validate and celebrate its power" (2001:34). Grand narratives have not vanished from the contrived stories constructed via the ads, but their form has changed. Grand narratives have transitioned from discursive arguments to the blunt force of isolated and floating grand signifiers, condensed reenactments that tightly compress and abbreviate the residue of formerly complex narratives into images of desire. How these narratives can survive as tacit understandings in such compressed form remains something of a mystery.

Capitalism is represented in corporate advertising as an unobtrusive container, a spatiality open to all possibility because it is absent from all forms of restrictive authority. In claiming to universally open up all spaces, the spirit of Capital appears to fully occupy all spaces, negatively appropriating all space so that nothing can be imagined outside it: "The capitalist axiomatic closes and defines – in the sense of fully inhabiting . . . yet it is also in motion, providing a space of becoming, of undecidability" (Gibson-Graham 2006:89). These ads, which aim at legitimation, depict capitalist relations not as they are, nor even as they have been, but as they might be – full of openness, hope, and possibility. Though big companies might wish to be seen as integrated and fully rationalized totalities, fully committing to that imagery forecloses on the spaces of becoming. And so, we see in the landscapes of Capital a representational contradiction that runs deep: they are simultaneously landscapes of hegemonic immanence and landscapes that dream of transcendence. The same images that hail the victory of global capitalism picture its transcendence.

Though one agenda in fashioning these landscape representations may be to evoke stable values in a volatile and unstable environment of peripatetic capital markets, the very processes of simulation contradict that agenda. Corporate landscape representations seek to address both legitimation and accumulation imperatives, but reconciling these imperatives is not easy. In the landscapes of Capital we witness the collapse of space between cultural contradictions and economic contradictions. This is because, in order to continually expand the domain of commodity exchange values, there has been a corresponding move to turn culture into a commodity, a turn to chewing up cultural forms – mining them – so that they can be converted into sign value. Advertising produces ideological simulations, but those simulations have become "material" in their impact on the processes of globalization. Advertising discourse is neither an epiphenomenon nor a false simulacrum. It embodies, as it represents, the contradictory core of capital's unfolding in its present form. The desperate search to hype value through the continuous construction of sign values imperils the very category of value. Signing (branding) globalization represents the most advanced stage yet of universal commodification, even as it also signals an emergent universal crisis of value not just within the commodity form, but also within the corporate stage of capital itself.

2

Dreamworks of the New Economy

How do branded units of Capital represent their place in a system of corporate globalization organized by global networks of investment, markets, and computers? Catch phrases such as flexible accumulation, just-in-time production, post-Fordism, casino capitalism, neo-liberal market economy, network society, and global cultural economy all aim to make sense of emergent global economic systems. As globalization and high technologies converged to restructure the  world of business, companies rushed to frame themselves relative to a new hierarchy of value defined by codewords such as "innovation" and "flexibility" and a vision of an always-flowing global electronic market network that puts a premium on integrated subsystems to compress time–space relations.

Flexibility and swiftness of response became prized organizational attributes in a global marketplace characterized by flux. Innovation made possible by high technologies became treasured as the key to profitability, while innovations of financial instruments (swaps and derivatives), contracts, licensing, and partnerships became key drivers of what seemed to be a boom. This chapter explores the most prominent self-portraits rendered by Capital from 1995 to 2008 beginning with the cultural constructions of Capital – the notion of a "new economy" and the permutations of finance capital that grew out of it. We consider how Capital distinguished itself from its earlier form of industrial capital, by calling attention to its own restructuring as "creative destruction" and renewal. Information and communication technologies were cast as linchpins of a new kind of economy that values novel ideas, depicting the pursuit of these ideas as endless vistas of opportunity. We examine how ads translate claims about the new economy – the stress on flexibility, innovation, productivity, and integration – into branded landscapes.

The dream of Capital is a friction-free network in which information and commodities flow at unlimited rates. Advertising representations of a world created by Capital strip away the messy consequences of a political economy of globalized Capital and replace these relationships with utopian Capital – an image, a reinvented Capital, that imagines itself as the realization of accelerated market forces and advanced technologies. This new Capital, as represented in its advertising, envisions itself presiding over an inevitably smarter future made possible by its direction of autonomous technology and ubiquitous financial capital. The advertisements assemble landscapes of utopian social life by stitching together decontextualized, abstracted signifiers of desire. Hence, the promise of a friction-free economy and society can be constructed around images of light beams framed by sensuous invitations such as Qwest's "Ride the light." In general, beams of fiber-optic light heralded a new era of peace, prosperity, and possibility at our children's fingertips.

In the next chapter we examine these "new economy" representations in relation to the spectacular shocks, scandals, and structural crises that have shaken the world of Capital during the last decade. To situate this in a wider historical perspective, we see a chronic tendency towards overcapacity and declining rates of profit within global capitalism over the past four decades. We consider the 2008 global financial crisis in relation to "fictitious capital" and the emergence of "hyperreal capital" – the tendency for financial instruments to become decoupled from underlying (referential) assets. We also analyze the campaigns of Merrill Lynch (financial capital), Enron (deregulated energy), and WorldCom (deregulated telecommunications) as a way of further thinking about the relationship between crisis tendencies of capital today and their representation in the political economy of sign value. We view corporate advertising and the utopian landscapes it produces as investments in brand (sign) values – itself an exercise in hyperreality – that have come to be considered both as the public face of the corporation, and as an "intangible asset" on corporate balance sheets.

The landscapes of Capital assembled throughout corporate ads correspond to a political economy that has become dominated by the circulation of signs. On the scale of the political economy, capital has drifted towards the ungrounded circulation of simulated values – that is, value has become detached from an economy of asset-based referents.

More often than not, ads imagine global landscapes that float unconstrained by the logic of referents located in time and place. As the "structural play of value" becomes ascendant, it calls forth "the emancipation of the sign" from its referents (Baudrillard 1993a:6–7). It is precisely this emancipation of the sign, the desire to extend the structural play of value, that lies at the heart of the supposed emancipation from the rules of the older capitalist economy.

While the landscapes of Capital may substitute utopian fantasies for the harsh realities of inequality, exploitation, and resource degradation, there is another deeper sense in which these landscapes provide a faithful representation of the coming-to-existence of simulated Capital – these representations seem to have transcended the dirty materialism of capitalism as it was. The utopian advertising landscapes of Capital highlight the pure flow of unrestricted circulation, and thus express the fondest fantasy of Capital – that it can surmount its own crisis tendencies and overcome its own limits by generating value through its own "pure circulation." This dream of self-replicating money values hinges upon the idea that surplus value could itself be emancipated from its origins in labor.

The economically determined new economy

One quasi-utopian vision of capitalism *circa* the millennium held that a supposedly "new economy" was overturning the old rules of capitalism. Proponents of the "new economy" or the "wired economy" asserted that a high-tech revolution made possible unlimited increases in productivity, and with such increases there could be ever-rising markets minus inflationary pressures. The dream of accelerating productivity would permit the seemingly impossible – the continuous expansion of value while diminishing labor costs. The new economy also promised the rebirth of the entrepreneurial spirit and of the upstart with a better idea, because the advantage in a cyber-economy would not automatically go to size. Especially during the dotcom era, ads stressed the lean and mobile upstarts – unmoored in either time or space – that vanquished the vertically fixed infrastructure of corporate titans.

The historical shift in capitalism from Fordist production to just-in-time production entailed globally decentralized production processes alongside a corresponding concentration in the mode of consumption – e.g., the proliferation of superstores like Wal-Mart and Costco. The transition involves a reliance on integrated information flows coupled with continuous pressure on overcoming the limits of space and time in order to profitably integrate global systems. Competition encourages the pursuit of speed and the latter has become a prime goal of corporate business systems. Frequently associated with agility, speed of transaction became counterposed against rigid bureaucratic machinery. The business media thus hailed the advent of less hierarchical organizations marked by flexibility, multitasking, and non-bureaucratic initiatives. Speed translates into a metaphor for fluidity and efficiency and greater consumer satisfaction. Rather than focusing on the disruptive aspects of speed and flexibility, the media dwelt on how innovation serves the consumer (the contemporary notion of "everyman") with lower prices.

Advertising during this period represented new economic formations *as* mobile, horizontal, modular, networked, and sleek – unburdened by the weight of massive physical plants, bureaucratic infrastructures, or even the gravity of fixed location. Replacing industries of scale weighted by ponderous bureaucracies with streamlined operations ostensibly enables capital to achieve higher levels of productivity because management can respond more rapidly to market fluctuations and opportunities. Discursively, this presumes that higher rates of productivity lead inevitably to higher standards of living. Yet, except during the heyday of "new economy" rhetoric (1996–2000), productivity in recent decades has empirically increased at less than robust rates.

Ads show just-in time-production eliminating warehousing, and new informational technologies coordinating a global system of supply chains. In these scenarios, when managed by the ultra-rational imperatives of software rather than the heavy hand of an interventionist state, markets prosper, delivering a cornucopia of dividends and satisfactions. Missing from these representations are the disruptive consequences of rule by Capital – the outsourcing of manufacturing, downsizing organizations, technologically eliminating jobs and deskilling others, the abandonment of pension obligations, and a widening burden of inequality and poverty.

The ideological exclusion of this dark side also suppresses other features of the new political economy. The now decades-long transition from Fordism to the current regime of production, consumption, and financing has been accompanied by changes in the political landscape – most importantly, the forces unleashed by deregulation of corporate markets and the loss of power by organized labor. Just as the predictability of consumers is an unspoken requisite of this system, so too the dislocation and relocation of labor in the global system has been kept out of sight. In the last decade, human rights advocates contested this invisibility by drawing attention to how corporate labor practices have moved the nexus of exploitative labor practices into the third world.

Ideologues of the "new economy" were positively giddy; their inflated rhetoric about an end to alienated labor made possible by a hyper-efficient market democracy hyped the economic interests of the high-tech industry and investment capital, while diverting attention from the growing concentration of capital and the deteriorating conditions of workers (Henwood 2003).

When we talk about the new economy, we're talking about a world in which people work with their brains instead of their hands. A world in which communications technology creates global competition – not just for running shoes and laptop computers, but also for bank loans and other services that can't be packed into a crate and shipped. A world in which innovation is more important than mass production. A world in which investment buys new concepts or the means to create them, rather than new machines. A world in which rapid change is a constant. A world at least as different from what came before it as the industrial age was from its agricultural predecessor. A world so different its emergence can only be described as a revolution. (Browning and Reiss 1998)

The "new economy" was a "rhetorical fabrication" amongst stakeholders who worked "the cultural circuits of capital" (Thrift 2005; Henwood 2003). Advertising and marketing formed key relay stations in these "cultural circuits of capital," constructing the "new economy" as a *sign value* that reframed Capital as a provider of an ultra-rational global system of information technologies enabling people to freely pursue their goals. "New economy" narratives stressed the role of creativity and unalienated labor as a result of information-driven neo-entrepreneurialism. Thrift (2005:423) writes, "another way of understanding the new economy is as a ramp for the financial markets, providing the narrative raw material to fuel a speculative asset price bubble which was also founded on an extension of the financial audience."

Redefinitions of the "new economy" altered accepted conventions about assessing value. Judgements of value shifted away from analyses of fundamentals to models of risk. The fiascos with Enron, WorldCom, AIG, and Citigroup raised anew questions about what constitutes value? Under a system that assigned extraordinary discursive power to stock analysts to estimate equity valuations, the gap between assets and valuation grew wider as dividend yield models were tossed aside in favor of expanding price/earnings ratios. Issuing additional shares of price-inflated stocks became the preferred currency for empire building. WorldCom rode this strategy to a market cap of $120 billion before plunging to bankruptcy after its $11 billion accounting fraud was revealed. In the world of high finance where arbitrage and derivatives became the preferred method of making money, Citigroup plummeted from an imaginary market cap of $260 billion in 2007 to assets of $6 billion in 2009; at its peak AIG claimed a $280 billion market cap that evaporated into the distilled remains of $4 billion. Enron CEO Jeffrey Skilling's enthusiastic defense of an "asset-light" strategy came straight out of the "new economy" playbook. Following deregulation of natural gas markets, Enron moved from the natural gas business to trading in the wholesale energy market in the search for more lucrative returns.

Thus Enron argued that it should not be judged by conventional valuation rules regarding hard assets; since it had remade itself as a trading
company, it should be evaluated as an "asset-light" portfolio of securities and futures contracts. Stock analysts seemed to find the argument
convincing, but it fueled a fast and furious burnout from a supposed
$66 billion market capitalization to bankruptcy.

Creative destruction and myths of the new capitalism

If each corporate ad campaign were a ballot, then Joseph Schumpeter
might be considered the preferred economic theorist of a corporate
world devoted to an ideology of market-driven innovation as the proper
driver of change. Echoing Schumpeter, Beaud argues capital must peri-
odically purge what it has built in order to create anew and expand.

> The social logic of capitalism destroys other productive forms, and
> destroys formerly existing activities, social forms, and resources. At the
> same time, this logic creates new activities, new markets, and new needs.
> It gives rise to a totality which is simultaneously productive, trade-based,
> and monetary. This totality is both territorialized and worldwide, and is
> in a state of constant change; in addition, it demonstrates an increasing
> autonomy relative to the societies in which it has been formed. This is the
> totality we call "capitalism." (Beaud 2002:309)

For Schumpeter (1975), "creative destruction" in a capitalist economy
required the liquidation of institutional practices and organizations
to make way for new economic formations. In corporate advertising,
such a view translates into a landscape of entrepreneurial innovation
that propels Society as a whole upward and forward. But the narrative
of innovation and "creative destruction" also turns risk, anxiety, and
uncertainty into defining subtexts of the economic landscape.

"Two distinct worlds" encompass contemporary globalization. "In
one of these worlds, the disintegration of the social is so absolute –
misery, poverty, unemployment, starvation, squalor, violence and
death – that the intricately elaborated social schemes of utopian think-
ers become as frivolous as they are irrelevant" (Jameson 2004:35).
Advertising as a corporate discourse envisions a utopian social sphere
as the outcome of market innovations, while avoiding the disorder and
dislocations that unfold from rapidly shifting market relationships.
Exploitative relationships towards either labor or nature disappear, so
growing disparities of wealth and resource access become non-issues,
as does a continual state of regional wars, and warnings about global
warming cannot be conceptualized in relation to Capital's practices.

Population dislocations and resource antagonisms triggered by shifting patterns of capital investment in the unending search for cheaper labor costs become mere externalities, as are the normative uncertainties and hyper-anomic social conditions that accompany rapid and continuous economic change (Beck 1999; Bauman 1998).

Under the regime of globalization new formations continuously erupt, presenting both possibility and disruption, intensifying Schumpeter's account of the simultaneous creative and destructive power of Capital: "This process of Creative Destruction is the essential fact about capitalism. It is what capitalism consists in and what every capitalist concern has got to live in" (1975:84).

The juggernaut of capital renovation

First Union Bank's 1999 ad campaign featured elaborately executed commercials that visually symbolized the turbulent, chaotic, and corrosive forces of a financial world in upheaval, in order to cast itself as the new champion able to master and transcend tendencies towards volatility, decay, greed, peril, and uncertainty that meet us when we enter the financial world. Their exaggerated aesthetic style stood out amid the clutter of bank advertising, helping to "brand" a bank that had swiftly transitioned from regional obscurity to national stature through stock merger and acquisition. Each ad opened with a scene of the sun rising over the curved horizon of planet Earth. As the camera zooms in, the hegemony of the dollar sign is imprinted across the surface of the planet, to signal that we are entering the topographic world of Capital.

During the 1999 Super Bowl, First Union debuted an ad depicting "creative destruction" on a monumental scale that encompasses the built environment of the global financial city. The ad narrated the restructuring of financial capital as a visual story about restructuring the architectural landscape of the global financial center. Framed by music heralding the dawning of a heroic new epoch, a corporate leader – a commanding male figure with vision and purpose – stands astride a team of massive mechanical juggernauts (pulling together like draft horses) driving these enormously powerful forces and institutions to enact the renovation and transformation of financial landscapes.

Male voiceover: In the financial world, nothing is permanent but change.
The landscape is constantly shifting.
Everyday companies are downsizing.
Seeking the right merger. Looking for acquisitions that make sense.
Even deceptively simple corrections like debt restructuring can take months, and demand a variety of financial products.

Today companies searching for solutions in the changing world are finding them in a place of stability and experience.
Come to the financial mountain called First Union.
Or if you prefer the mountain will come to you.

Exaggerated representations of dynamic purpose create a meta-phor for the energy of capital as it restructures. Keyed to "The landscape is constantly shifting," the driver of change removes a bowler hat attached to his head, and replaces it with a younger head attached to a hardhat. This new visionary master wields a giant bullwhip to direct a team of colossal tractors pulling a sky-scraper, moving it from one location to another. Symbolically, the power, command, and direction exercised by his figure are visually extended into the imagery of the corporate tower and icon of First Union – the new "Financial Mountain" of Capital. The commanding presence of these hybrid characters – bankers turned men-of-action – is dramatically played out as they super-vise the restructuring of capital's architecture. This is the stuff of legend, titanic figures in sweeping waistcoats whose actions suggest a vision (a plan) they intend to enact. This *labor of capital* refashioning the financial landscape is an extraordinary trope that fundamentally inverts much of what was actually taking place in the political economy of finance.

Keyed to the verbal reference to "debt restructuring" is a visual reference to "derivatives" etched deep into a girder as a banker turned laborer swings a giant sledgehammer. Ironically, the reliance upon derivatives evolved precisely because processes of material production that rely on labor-power to produce value have, since the late 1980s, been deemed to be too slow, and too low, in return on equity.

Derivatives – a financial tool – are by definition derived from other assets and, as the biggest banks all competed vigorously in the derivative business, derivatives became more and more removed from any underlying assets, until the assets vanished as material substance. So it seems ironic to identify "derivatives" as a steel girder that structures the new building/financial system. Here the ad makes evident an inadvertent meaning – that the new system of financial capital is in fact based on a structure of thin air. Bauman's metaphor about the transition from heavy to liquid modernity/capitalism must be pushed along here to the next state of matter – gaseous capitalism.

Helicopters are mobilized as a pivotal piece of technology in this fairy tale about restructuring the material cityscape of finance capital. These helicopters suggest a flexible and mobile technology, yet one still capable of doing the heavy lifting necessary to drop into place the new "architectural face" of capital. Bearing the name "First Union," the powerful helicopter is positioned as the moving force of this transformation, symbolically representing the fusion of capital and technology to remake our world.

First Union's imagery negates the early modern, mid-twentieth-century, corporate bank, while making it over to fit into an architectural pastiche that better suits First Union's contemporary presentation of itself – as a new center of consolidated Capital. First Union ads imagined a postmodern skyline of Capital, a skyline replete with architectural ornamentation keyed to symbols of money and capital. This pastiche appropriates postmodern architectural styles that recombine allusions to various historical styles and traditions along with decorative elements that playfully identify the commodity function of this landscape, capped in the end by dropping into place a façade of a simulated Parthenon to mark (as it does already) the front of the New York Stock Exchange (NYSE).

Even as the ad distorts the relationships between capital, labor, and value production, one dramatic scene graphically symbolizes how the everyday lives of men and women are affected by the wrenching transformations of "downsizing." As the narrator states that "Everyday companies are downsizing," the corresponding scene shows a giant boring machine tunneling into the side of a building, cutting away and extracting massive debris from the building. Beneath this dramatic imagery miniature figures of employees can be seen fleeing the building. As a metaphor for downsizing, these figures carry umbrellas to protect themselves from the wreckage and debris of capitalist restructuring that rains down on them, leaving them unemployed and their lives in ruins.

This ad gives visual substance to Schumpeter's view of the imperative that capital must continually negate what it has created in order to continually create and expand: "the same process of industrial mutation – if I may use that biological term – that incessantly revolutionizes the economic structure *from within*, incessantly destroying the old one, incessantly creating a new one" (1975:84).

Decay and renovation

Another First Union ad highlighted the need for new economic formations by addressing the decay of modern banking institutions. The campaign's self-conscious use of landscape reflected changes that had altered the financial sector, such as new digital technologies, nearly instantaneous electronic currency exchanges, and the increased reliance on financial instruments such as swaps and derivatives, as well as shifts in regulatory rules. Commercial banking had been in decline for some time, facing increasing competition from non-bank competitors:

> *In the financial world, banking as we have known it has become a thing of the past. Brokerages, insurance companies, all of our financial institutions are in transition. Teller windows have become electronic gateways, the savings book is now the investment portfolio and financial products, which once could only be obtained from a vast number of different sources, can now be obtained from one. Stocks, bonds, mutual funds, planning, insurance, all have moved to a single place, to the financial mountain called First Union.*

Visually, First Union depicts the ruins of modern banks to address the banking environment in transition. The ad opens by noting that banking capital, thanks to the 1999 repeal of the 1933 Glass–Steagall Act, is no longer regulated by what bankers considered Byzantine rules that separated commercial banking from investment banking, and banks from brokerages. Early scenes depict something like the collapse of an empire as a decaying building identified as a "Brokerage" institution is shown crumbling, while signage for an "Insurance" company lies broken on the ground. History is invoked here as a negative that has crumbled under its own weight. By contrast First Union shows itself superseding outdated and inefficient financial institutions by becoming a one-stop banking center capable of providing everything that mutual funds, brokerage houses, and insurance companies offer. In the new banking landscape, these are now the companies with whom banks must compete to attract cash.

The text describes how the banking landscape has changed with the development of electronic computer technologies. "Teller windows have become electronic gateways, the savings book is now the investment portfolio." Banking institutions that dominated during earlier decades lie in ruins and can no longer be considered modern – they are inefficient, dusty, dilapidated, and poorly lit. The passbook is an antiquated relic, a dusty, weighty reminder of a past spent in lines. Ghostly images recall an earlier era of sleepy prosperity when customers had a personal, but slow-moving, relationship with the bank teller. Out of the ruins a sleekly modern tower appears amidst a postmodern financial skyline.

The political-economic impact of concentrated and centralized capital also receives mention, as banks grow bigger, more streamlined, and more integrated. Combined with the regulatory shift mentioned above, the combination of corporations into ever larger units paves the way for the surviving giants of the merger and acquisitions game to compete in offering one-stop shopping for consumers, and to try to dominate their markets from their mountaintop. This ad implies a dramatic ontological shift with the transition to the world of First Union: the sky brightens, revealing a glistening skyline, illuminated by a shining golden beacon, while money floats about on wind currents.

Transcending the dark side of capital

Other First Union ads (1999) thrust viewers into a world of surplus commodification, a densely filled urban space marked by imperatives to BUY and SELL. Borrowing from films like *Blade Runner*, the futuristic feel of flying devices coupled with oversaturated colors evokes the lurid excesses of an unregulated dystopian market. The First Union "Launch" commercial assaulted viewers with extravagantly fantastic and surreal scenes of a dystopian financial world filled with mechanical two-faced heads shilling the "mutual fund of the month," false idols of golden bulls, giant coins rolling through densely packed financial districts, scenes of a carnival side-show and a Vegas-like money market full of hucksters, con-men, scam artists, and illusionists ready to sell their snake-oil to gullible patrons. Another ad similarly opens in "chaos and confusion" where a glut of choices confronts investors in the noise and swirling clutter of a helter-skelter capitalist market space. Entering "a world of risk and uncertainty" that combines a decadent carny atmosphere with unscrupulous greed, a businessman falls and smashes his head like a piggybank, coins rolling out.

This landscape reveals no signs of the Protestant Ethic or the virtuous capitalism that it supposedly spurred. Instead these scenes evoke "casino capitalism" where betting replaces investing. Everywhere there are visual allusions to gambling, imperatives to "Play! Synthetic index" are suggestive of a Lotto universe, and the one-armed bandits that visually correspond to references to "hot stocks" and "bonds, t-bills, commodities, precious metals" confirm the casino capitalism thesis. On this dark side of capitalism, where everything is starkly for sale and no one can be trusted, a harsh blizzard of signs – enticements, seductions, commands, and imperatives – define the landscape. Amidst these signs are more nightmarish images, garishly surreal, drawn again from the carnival midway – storefront neon signs offering "credit lines" or "treasury notes" while barkers shill mutual funds, and the money-go-round promises the illusion of the brass ring. In such a world the market "can take you to success and prosperity, or sometimes to no place at all." The lure of easy money breeds risk. This is a world where new financial instruments constantly multiply to take advantage of the market – but the more arcane and elaborate these instruments become, the greater the speculative risk.

First Union's "Market mania" ad depicts the financial world as dark, dissonant, and fast-moving. Market mania becomes a metaphor for rapid fluctuation and change, and a coercive sense of urgency that sweeps investors along. In this foreboding world of jacked-up markets, everything is built out of signs. Signs, signs, everywhere there's signs – buy, sell, currency swaps, hot stocks, advances, naked options, synthetic derivatives. "Market mania" evokes the late 1990s market boom, day-trading, and the myth of deregulation. These forces intensified the street-level chaos among the nickel-and-dime players where fraud and deception are rampant, while the "big boys" raced to outbid and outmaneuver one another. This market mania generated "asset bubbles" – first in tech stocks and then in housing.

A towering wall of flickering monitors represents the way too many choices daily bombard consumers and investors – visual and aural clutter and noise. The wall of television screens represents total media saturation – semiotic overload. But it also represents television hype – "Wall St. Go!" and "HIGH" "HIGH" "HIGH." This is a world without substance, a world where sales pitches have been fully abstracted and disconnected from what is being pitched. Welcome to the carnival of the simulacrum where rational discourse has been pushed aside. While the simulacrum may have initially been subject to the laws of the market, it is the market that is now driven by the structural forces of the simulacrum. Especially interesting here is the bricolage-like electronic midway monstrosity that visually corresponds to synthetic commodity instruments that comprise derivatives markets. The spectacular monster built out of electronic signs and lights symbolizes commodification run amok, as well as that other devil that corrupts our world – the media. As the chaos of the market builds and the viral proliferation of "unfamiliar choices" becomes "overwhelming," the entire system reaches a crisis point as the wall of monitors short-circuits, an electronic overload, leaving the world abruptly still and dark. The darkness gives way to the soft light of First Union, a new "beacon" offering financial "comfort" and salvation. Also referred to as "the Mountain," this beacon represents the heritage of disciplined and rationally continuous capitalism (Weber 1947). In stark semiotic contrast to the crass commercialism of the spectacular midway, the "Mountain" is calm and serene, a place where sensible, rational choices can be made away from the hype and noise. Whereas risk is correlated with the world of noise and confusion, where too many possibilities screaming for attention can disorient, First Union represents the security of expert knowledge and profit.

The contrast between the carnival of excess and the beacon of light and mastery makes this allegory reminiscent of biblical stories as well. Interpreted as a moral tale, this spectacle represents the false gods and idols of Mammon. But unlike the old-testament God, the First Union beacon is calmer and gentler as it restores order via its singularity – the steadying force of a powerhouse that encompasses one-stop banking, all your financial needs taken care of by one bank. In contrast to the false gods and idols spurred by the forces of greed and opportunism, First Union, "the Mountain," represented the unified, universal God of the New Economy.

But such hubris never goes unpunished and First Union's moment as the unifying force of the new economy was brief indeed, a nanosecond in world history. In 2001 Wachovia acquired First Union in what was called a merger of equals. The pressure towards consolidation in the bank industry had been continuous. The 1994 Interstate Banking and Branching Efficiency Act spurred movement towards nationwide combinations. Throughout the banking industry aggressive competition motivated dual responses of cost-cutting measures (downsizing, outsourcing) and expansion by merger and acquisition to gain "efficiencies." The same desire to achieve one-stop shopping continued to drive the wave of bank consolidations. Traditional bank services – deposits and loans – could now be secured through a range of other financial institutions and competition ate into profit margins. More lucrative markets beckoned, prompting banks to sell mutual funds to lower-middle income groups, and to develop complicated risk-management products such as derivatives and swaps for wealthier clients. Branching out into these newer and more lucrative businesses favored banks with greater resources to cover the costs of new computer technologies and the greater risks that came with the more complicated financial instruments. Wachovia's 2003 acquisition of Prudential Securities made it the fourth-largest bank holding company and the third-largest full-service brokerage firm in the US. This push can be seen reflected in advertising that hailed the wealthier clientele seeking greater returns on investment.

In 2006 Wachovia bought Golden West Financial, among the nation's largest mortgage lenders, for $26 billion and then swallowed up A.G. Edwards. In 2006, only Merrill Lynch and Citigroup underwrote more collateralized debt obligations (CDOs) than Wachovia. By November 2007 Wachovia took a $1.3 billion write-down on collateralized debt obligations, in addition to previously reported "market disruption-related losses" that included $347 million of subprime-related valuation losses (Spence 2007). At the same time, Morgan Stanley, Citigroup and Merrill Lynch reported losses in the billions (and analysts put Citigroup's subprime CDO exposure at $55 billion).

The lust for acquisition boomeranged, as the Golden West Financial takeover swamped Wachovia with more bad adjustable-rate mortgages, sending it crashing downward in the third quarter of 2008 when it posted another $4.8 billion loss. As the credit crisis deepened, to avoid collapse Wachovia hastily arranged a deal with Citigroup (at the federal government's behest) to sell its banking segment. However, Wells Fargo trumped that deal with a $15 billion offer, putting Wells Fargo among the upper tier of US banks with supposed assets pegged at $1.37 trillion in December of 2008.

In contrast to First Union's representations of the banking landscape, Wachovia promoted a vision of soft capitalism, constructed around a bourgeois aesthetic calculated to appeal to upper-middle-class clients by appreciating the small, quiet truths of nature as life lessons and financial lessons – "What can the elusive red-legged kittiwake teach us about unbiased wealth management?" These ads recast the risk of marketing wealth management instruments into therapeutic landscapes, while also masking the aggressive practices that enabled Wachovia to grow larger. Another ad asks "What can a canoe teach us about corporate and investment banking?" as a white middle-aged couple in formal evening attire quietly paddle through the morning fog towards their country retreat, attuned to nature as an aesthetic object to be appreciated rather than transformed. Peaceful, graceful, and transcendent, it provides a space for the bourgeoisie to escape the hurried life associated with urbanity and capitalism.

While each ad asks viewers to ponder a utilitarian question, the aesthetic gaze masks acquisitiveness. Each commercial aims at a "lesson" that Wachovia has learned from careful observation of the world about us. Thus canoes teach us that "You cover more distance when you work in tandem," suggesting that corporate/customer relationships are best when mutually beneficial. Sharing the profits of capital is apparently not an adversarial relation. What can canoes, greenhouses, and red-legged kittiwakes teach us about Capital? That the face of capital is the face of civility, concern, kindness, and sharing, while its practices – downsizing, redlining, foreclosures, political lobbying – are driven by market interests.

The "idea" economy

Bauman (2000) writes convincingly of a shift from heavy capitalism – solid and imposing, built out of steel, but geographically fixed and immobile – to a light capitalism founded upon the fluidity and flow of fiber-optic networks, and the flexibility of new legal forms like licensing agreements. In *The Rise of the Network Society*, Castells (1996) sees this light capitalism as both informational and global, driven by the diffusion of information technology, specifically microelectronics, computers, and telecommunications networks. What once were considered "intangible assets" now become strategic resources in the struggle over markets. "Intellectual property" becomes the watchword of the day as companies jockey for position to strategically mine the "legal monopoly" afforded by ownership of registered patents, trademarks, copyrights, and licenses. In an information economy, objectified knowledge emerges as the most valuable commodity. Turning ideas into corporate assets is appealing because they are mobile and transferable. Corporate advertising eagerly highlights this aspect of participation in an idea-innovation economy – information packets pulse through the ether, dispersing innovation and all that follows from it across the globe. Innovative ideas and systems of organizing information are shown enhancing efficient systems of finance, transportation, industrial production, and service distribution. Corporate narratives, logos, and taglines (slogans) became overwhelmingly focused on the role of innovation and the development of new ideas, on the management of information and the production of revenue-generating knowledge.

Corporate slogans were sprinkled with linguistic signifiers of knowledge, vision, creativity, and imagination. Visually, beams of light became the most common signifier of the flow of ideas. Companies in sectors as diverse as automobiles, computers, finance, consulting, airlines, energy, and electronics associated themselves with the application of knowledge. Corporate slogans expressed the centrality of knowledge in corporate self-constructions while also connoting the dynamic, forward-looking "vision" of Capital.

"The 'spirit of informationalism' is the culture of 'creative destruction' accelerated to the speed of the optoelectronic circuits that process its signals" (Castells 1996:199). In the landscape imagery of corporate advertising this translated into moving at the speed of light. Firms like WorldCom, Qwest, GTE, and Nortel stressed the birth of a new world order where the speed of conduits erased primitive forms of accumulation and all corresponding limits on the imagination. No boundaries, no limits, and no politics – these are the landscapes imagined by technologies that permit a thousand ideas to bloom. Emblematic of such visions was Accenture, the former consulting wing of Arthur Andersen. As a new corporate entity Accenture needed a brand identity, so it brought forth a new logo composed of light rays beamed from its name onto the areas of service that it provided; its graphics design adopted a "greater than" sign to accent the "t" in its name to indicate how they take your small ideas and turn them into currency – "Accenture – Innovation delivered."

Table 2.1 Corporate slogans

ABB	Ingenuity at work
Apple	Think different
Barclays	Ideas. They will strike
Boeing	Forever new frontiers
Canon	Know how. Here's the future, let's get to work
Cargill	Nourishing ideas nourishing people
CNF Transportation	Where ideas carry weight
Compaq	Inspiration technology
Computer Associates	Software that can think
Conoco	Think big. Move fast
Council for Biotechnology	Good ideas are growing
Dow	What good thinking can do
Enron	Ask why
Ford	Better ideas driven by you
GE	Imagination at work
GTE	Moving ideas
Hartford	Always thinking ahead
HP	Invent
IBM	Let's build a smarter planet
Micron	Think beyond the box
Motorola	The heart of smart
NEC	Powered by innovation
Nortel	How the world shares ideas
Schwab	Information. Access. Control
Siemens	Global networks of innovation
Wachovia	Uncommon wisdom

The Infolightenment

For ideology, which once was a road to action, has come to a dead end. (Bell 1966:393)

In the postindustrial world there would be no place for ideology. Instead, pragmatism, professionalism, and technocratic logic would prevail. Though discredited by the history of ensuing decades, a variant of Bell's "end of ideology" thesis has reprised in corporate visions of neo-liberal globalization. The supposed merit of the information age is that "information replaces ideology; access replaces praxis." Oracle's 1998 "Revolution" ad expressed this end-of-ideology stance. Juxtaposing disconnected images of civil violence against landscapes of peaceful prosperity, Oracle reiterated a central premise of post-industrial capital – the speed at which information circulates is negatively correlated with conflict. Blocked channels of communication and patterns of distorted communication impede communities of reason. The Enlightenment dream of emancipatory reason is assumed when information flows freely through unobtrusive electronic circuits. According to this vision, restrictions on information access will be abolished by communication technologies that will free humankind from our pre-history of political/ ideological conflicts. Structural constraints, resource struggles, anomic cultural conditions, ethnic hatreds rooted in history lose their material determinism in the weightless world of electronic data. Across Oracle's global landscape, a grand historical transition is taking place from violent material struggles for freedom, justice, and equality to managing prosperity via the appropriate software package.

A revolution is in our destiny. This revolution however will not be fought with guns or soldiers. It will not be a war of words or of countries.

Generic images of terror and civil war, state violence and oppression stream past – *à la* Vietnam, a bicycle taxi and an Asian couple on a motorbike flee a bombing scene; Asian rebels in black garb and red bandanas armed with automatic weapons battle in street warfare; a mother and child run to escape the violence; Euro-police stand guard in riot gear. Though stripped of specific historical referents, these images still retain vague historical allusions to civil wars associated with national liberation fronts in Laos, Cambodia, and Vietnam. Referencing the general kinds of nationalist conflict that seemed endemic throughout the "undeveloped" third world during the second half of the twentieth century, the Oracle ad directs us to view this scene as the Past, which it then positions opposite to its vision of a post-State world based on freely available access to knowledge. A Hobbesian past need not be revisited because equal access to information resources will inaugurate a global post-scarcity society (Macpherson 1962). Oracle imagines a future in which new technologies relieve us of the necessity of politics and war – this is the revolution of humankind as a whole, the one we have been waiting for, the revolution that is achieved not at anyone's expense, but for everyone's benefit.

Of course, in these texts, matters of States, competition, violence, and a new world order are merely abstractions given meaning and affect by the narrator's words, tone of voice, and the musical background. An uplifting female operatic voice signals the world-historical transition with a change of tone in mid-commercial, as the narrator continues:

For this revolution will be about knowledge and access, about progress and opportunity. It will use information networks to make computing simpler, more

efficient and vastly more affordable. Where do we come in? We make the soft-
ware that manages information – that will enable anyone, anywhere to sit at the
seat of knowledge.
    Oracle – enabling the information age.

Marking the transition from a history of violence to an idealist vision
of revolution, an orange-robed monk appears keyed to the word
"knowledge." In television advertising the orange-robed monk became
a *preferred* signifier of universal knowledge in the information age.
The ad's tone shifts from desperation to hope and utopian possibility.
Characteristic of corporate representations of globalization, Oracle's ad
weaves together a tapestry of scenes that liquidates geographical space
– all locations are uniquely discrete, but all are serially adjacent to one
another – the material distance between India's temples and the middle-
class home of suburban America evaporates. Each scene has been
selected to represent a concept in the spoken narrative – so black ado-
lescents playing ball in front of a graffiti-marked wall signify "access,"
while Chinese children rolling hoops through a plaza surrounded by
temples signify "simpler" computing, and an upward-tilting escalator
completely abstracted from place signifies "progress."

The ad ends symbolically with a light-emanating red chair in a
temple's open doorway – this is the universal "seat of knowledge" dem-
ocratically open to "anyone, anywhere." In this idealist Infolightenment
narrative, the passage from domination to a world in which the categories of master and slave are abolished in favor of the Hegelian dream of
mutual recognition is an accomplishment "managed" and "enabled"
by an enlightened global capital, Oracle. Traditional Eastern religious
signifiers (the temple, the red chair, and the Buddhist monk) have been
appropriated to signify the transcendence of Alienated Mind made
possible by Oracle software.

This utopian sophistry conceives a problematic equivalence between
knowledge attained via reflection and meditation and that attained
through an Internet connection. Indeed, Oracle collapses information
and knowledge together as if they are identical. Yet the velocity and
volume of information flows made possible by networks (the Internet)
might just as easily be a force that fragments knowledge, substituting an
emphasis on surfaces over depth.

Political power struggles conveniently disappear in corporate ren-
derings of the new economy. Efficiency replaces politics; affordability
replaces distributive justice; information flows replace state practices;
the network replaces the citizen. The State has no place in the Oracle
narrative, where politics itself is an impediment to a techno utopian
future. This vision is a far cry from Hardt and Negri's analysis.

Postmodern warfare thus has many of the characteristics of what econo-
mists call post-Fordist production: it is based on both mobility and flexibility; it integrates intelligence, information, and immaterial labor; it
raises power up by extending militarization to the limits of outer space,
across the surfaces of the earth, and to the depths of the oceans. (2004:40)

In the reality of the post-9/11 era, the State has returned with a venge-
ance. States face the dilemma of opening borders to transnational trade
and financial flows while closing them to unwanted immigrants and
unwanted information. As information networks crisscross national
borders, political insecurity builds and the demand for boundaries
escalates (Jha 2006).

Flex capital

Flexible accumulation doubles as a synonym for post-Fordism and
there are flexible workgroups, flexible manufacturing systems, flexible
work schedules, and flexible market responses. The burst of innovation spurred by the high-technology boom in the late twentieth century
and the parallel explosion of communications and media resulted in a
volatile market environment. Technology competition keyed a circuit
of almost instantaneous obsolescence in all things digitally electronic.
The master commodity here was the computer chip. As firms raced to
produce faster chips, each generation of proprietary chips was eclipsed
at a rate that approximated Moore's Law – the prediction by Intel's
co-founder Gordon Moore that the number of transistors on each chip
would double every two years, and with that doubling would come
exponential increases in computing power. A proprietary chip, under
the conditions of intellectual property law, remained the exclusive
domain of the company that introduced it for a limited time. When that
protection ends, the proprietary chip becomes a commodity and profit
margins erode dramatically as competitors copy the design. Proprietary
chips drove higher stock prices while commodity chips drove commodity prices down and ushered in wider patterns of consumer adoption.
The integrated circuit of production technologies and licensing agreements drove a dialectic of adoption and obsolescence. The promise of
budding consumer markets drove stock prices higher while the actuali-
zation of consumer adoption could never sustain growth rates for long.
From the marketing side the explosion of sign values attached to short-
lived digital commodities created a clutter that posed a major hurdle for
advertisers.

From both the chip side and the sign-value side the contradictions converged. From the chip side, rates of profit declined at an increasing velocity. From the sign side, the attempt to turbocharge the value of competitive goods gave these goods the briefest of advantages – and over time, as the circulation process raced along, the pursuit of exchange value underscored the ephemeral character of sign value. Indeed, a general law can be stated here: the greater the velocity of sign values, the greater the tendencies towards clutter and the likelihood of entropy in the value realization process. From both the material side and the sign side, such markets reveal a tendency towards the decomposition of value.

These processes promoted structural instabilities in markets. Corporations had to be ready at a moment's notice to retool and redesign their production practices, and any indication of a slippage in brand value prompted a redesign of its image. Corporations like Benetton, Nike, and Mattel were the first to be called "hollowed corporations" because the core corporation designs, markets, and distributes its commodities while outsourcing actual production to third world subcontractors. Without a costly technological (industrial) infrastructure to maintain, these corporations could adjust quickly to changing markets. Sennett describes this emergent form.

> Flexible specialization suits high technology; thanks to the computer, industrial machines are easy to reprogram and configure. The speed of modern communications has also favored flexible specialization, by making global market data instantly available to a company. Moreover, this form of production requires quick decision-making, and so suits the small work group; in a large bureaucratic pyramid, by contrast, decision-making can slow down as paper rises to the top for approval from headquarters. The most strongly flavored ingredient in this new productive process is the willingness to let the shifting demands of the outside world determine the inside structure of institutions. All these elements of responsiveness make for an acceptance of decisive, disruptive change. (1999:52)

Markets became reconceptualized. The mass market based on standardized products gave way to an array of segmented niche markets emphasizing lifestyle and aestheticized product differences. Because batch production processes became feasible, niches further differentiated into even more tightly targeted niche audiences. To dynamically respond, corporations delayered or flattened out, and developed sophisticated communication systems that monitored consumer demand and coordinated new forms of distribution. The organizational shifts needed to efficiently compete in this new marketplace required "the capacity to make a flexible response to uncertain market conditions caused by commodity saturation" (Waters 1995:81).

Such transformations have been romanticized with language suggesting that the emergent work environment composed of multi-tasking, non-hierarchical relations, flexible work hours, and a breakdown of organizational boundaries promoted autonomy, freedom, and satisfaction in the workplace. But this business discourse also disguises less benign outcomes of the same corporate practices – multi-tasking may be the outcome of consolidating different positions when downsizing occurs. Continuous workplace re-engineering may yield innovative strategies to contain costs, but it can also lead to reorganization after reorganization, recurrent downsizing, demoralization, and deskilling as job descriptions become routinely redefined. A flexible workday suggests that workers control their time, but in non-union environments it also means sending workers home early or expecting them to be on call 24/7. In the name of productivity corporations often pass along costs of responding to uncertain or changing markets to their workers. More often than not, flexible production means outsourcing manufacturing to find the cheapest labor costs or taking advantage of monopsony buying power in global supply chains.

Nevertheless, flexibility and its synonyms became desired brand signifieds. Corporate advertisers branded corporations as flexible, able to respond dynamically to a liquid environment, to rapidly adapt to market forces, and to customize products for even the smallest of niche markets – You. Flexibility also offered to reshape the landscapes of Capital in the ways that products or services were offered to other corporations to make them in turn more adaptable.

Flexibility as panoptic integration

Global competition and the evolution of global supply chains have made just-in-time sourcing of materials, labor, finished goods, currency, and capital an essential feature of any major corporation. In this context firms must navigate the relatively uncharted and always shifting territory of the market, or manage the uncertainty of demand, or locate and obtain resources at a competitive advantage. This necessitates an agile and nimble corporate form. Without the right analytical tools, costly mistakes will be made in an ever changing and unforgiving market environment. Microsoft's 2003 campaign used the catchphrase "Software for the agile business" to describe its new software that enabled users to connect with suppliers, retailers, or customers. Here flexibility signifies total network integration of supply chains via databases. These ads used a split screen to demonstrate the power of Microsoft's software to control actual material results in real time. On one side decisions are made and entered into a computer; on the other side commodities rapidly move through the production/distribution chain.

In one Microsoft commercial a manager casually paces an office high in a corporate tower, eating Chinese take-out, while his assistant types his commands into the computer: "Buy 300 hydraulic assemblies for the Washington factory by Friday." On an adjacent screen, robotic arms, cranes, and conveyor belts immediately begin moving containers. As fast as the manager can speak a directive, his colleague declares it "done." The sum of the screens defines a fully integrated technological system in which the simulation model on one screen perfectly maps the territory on the other. The movement of objects through automated transportation networks without hesitation or pause replaces actual systems of production. The absence of human labor outside the office is conspicuous, as if the whole apparatus now runs without labor. Microsoft claims its software allows businesses to participate in the complex shifting architecture of the Internet with confidence. It can identify, purchase, and move commodities through supply chains with precision and cost efficiency.

Another Microsoft ad opens with customers in a warehouse-style retail store queued in line to purchase the latest hot technology gadget. Boxes are automatically scanned when they reach the register and an inventory alert appears on a computer screen. By the time the manager checks the alert, the information has already been communicated to a truck driver transporting the necessary replacement stock. Taken out of the decision-making loop, the manager's authority is reduced to bearing witness to the software's reliability. In split screen, as the manager heads to the loading dock, a freight truck barrels across the plains. The manager meets a stock boy on the docks who starts to tell him they are sold out of the item. No worries. "It's like you think it and it happens." Without maintaining costly inventories, computer-integrated just-in-time deliveries ensure that no sale is lost. Agility means synchronizing consumer demand with a transportation infrastructure and schedule. Microsoft ads present the businessman's utopia – a totally integrated technological system of consumption. Supply and demand are fully integrated to allow businesses to profitably participate in the network economy. The relation between desire, command, and action is reduced to the speed of a mouse click and electronic information flow. These Microsoft ads demonstrate how network performance depends on "its *connectedness*, on its structural ability to facilitate noise-free communication between its components; its *consistency*, that is the extent to which there is sharing of interests between the network's goals and the goals of its components" (Castells 1996:171).

A 1999 CNF Transportation ad (itself a corporate combination of

Emery Worldwide, Conway Trucking, and Menlo Logistics) split the screen into multiple panels. Framed by an upbeat Asian soundtrack, images of transportation technology and commodity flows mix with computer screens and monitoring devices. Dynamic images of movement radiate out in all directions to signify a global transportation network built around a highly rationalized and coordinated logistics system. Flexibility means perfectly coordinating these flows via a model of real time. Simultaneity is a highly valued trait, heavily signified in technology and software advertising. It occurs when simulation and materiality are perfectly matched: the model perfectly overlays the various flows in it. Flexibility thus depends on a highly rationalized model that accounts for and controls all the variables that enter the production/distribution process. Hence, a recurring signifier in these commercials is the control panel constructed out of multiple screens.

These scenes of control panels appeared in Conoco, CDW, UPS, and Norfolk Southern ads. Sometimes the simulation appears superimposed on the operators suggesting the "seamless unity of terminal and operator." Other scenes suggest global coordination of electronic flows – the "informated gaze" that both monitors and controls (Bogard 1996). Though the maps locate a nodal point of control at the geographic center of the United States, the control rooms can be anywhere.

"Flexibility" has been made to connote a higher degree of freedom, less hierarchical control, greater voice from all corporate levels in decision-making processes, and even an egalitarian power shift in company–employee relations akin to the "consensus building" teamwork models associated with Toyotism (Castells 1996:169). Corporate ads imagine this social image of flexibility as a function of increased technological surveillance and sophisticated tracking systems: knowing where everything is at every moment. In these narratives, flexibility via integrated systems of rationalization appears contingent on the institutionalized discipline embedded in corporate technologies. Organizational flexibility depends on precise individuated information obtained through a myriad of sources – from electronic badges, cell phones, server connections, to cookies. Benign tracking is applied to all movements of employees, commodities, capital, and information.

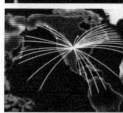

Dreams of total integration

Themes of innovation and integration dominate corporate advertising about an information economy. New computer-driven technologies and advances in production and distribution techniques became the hallmarks of competition. Competition via innovation also prompted anxious vigilance about being technologically outflanked by competitors. Hence, corporate espionage and increased R&D budgets go hand in hand. Signifiers of innovation dot corporate ads during this time, to promote the general image of firms as forward-looking in their ability to anticipate and respond to previously untapped revenue streams.

Innovation anxieties on the one side prompt new problems of systems integration when innovations occur too quickly for organizations to adapt. In the supercharged discourse of innovation posed by the high-tech blitz, integration became a focal signifier for a nascent corporate service sector – managing technological systems (IBM, Cisco, Oracle), transportation needs (CNF, UPS, FedEx), or business-to-business (B2B) interactions. By the late 1990s few corporate organizations lacked an IT department. Transferring bureaucratic systems into electronic information networks, the goal of universal integration drove system complexity, making firms more vulnerable to system-wide breakdowns. Employee incompetence, faulty information, information overload, server crashes, software bugs, data loss, hackers, worms, and viruses became the gremlins of a network society. The goal of total integration became expensive – many firms wondered if the cost–benefit calculus would ever pay off as they struggled to set up systems devoted to round after round of technological innovation and integration.

A 2003 IBM campaign humorously addressed the problem of global complexity and technological integration by fantasizing a science fiction gadget presented to an executive as a total-management solution. The "thingamajig" functions as the ultimate integrative technology – the "UBA, Universal business adapter" – to connect "Call centers. Unix servers. Linux servers. Internet. Supply chain. Payroll System. HR. Email." All of this and it is fast, easy, and affordable. The joke of course is that no such device exists, but IBM does make "integration software."

The informational economy runs 24/7 and it runs from end to end. Down time is dead time to capital. Since the late 1990s, advertising shifted from locating threats as internal network problems (unreliability and incompatibility) to identifying them as forces outside the network (hackers, identity thieves, viruses, spyware). Though few ads acknowledge terrorists in the world today, some express fears associated with the invisible enemies mentioned above. To survive, a company must seamlessly attach itself to an electronic network which mediates its connection to all other networks – suppliers, transportation, financial capital, media exposure, and customers – while at the same time insulating itself from disruption. In the television landscapes, problems invite market solutions (commodity services) rather than government protection. Hence, a 2006 AT&T commercial introduced a female CEO who confidently narrates the security the AT&T network provides to her globally sited business: "We're in seventeen countries now and I can say *secure* in every one of them. Dynamic networking from AT&T identifies security threats before they are problems." Another 2006 AT&T commercial promised to tailor and "deliver" a coordinated suite of services that permit businesses to perform in a spatially dispersed manner across the globe. In building a global business "Our workday never ends. I'm not saying our people don't go home or have lives. But ending our workday here doesn't stop our best thinking from moving forward someplace else." A narrator adds, "Dynamic networking from AT&T enables collaboration around the world and the clock" so that companies can stay "always ahead of market demands, schedules and the competition."

A sprawling labyrinth of circuitry over which infinite bits of information packets flow becomes depicted not simply as a means of communication, or as a means of doing business, or as a means of conducting a democratic *polis*, but also as the core of a global moral order. While many commercials focus on specific sectors or functions of the network enterprise, a few ads pull back the discursive lens and provide a macro-level representation of the network. Here, in a virtual utopia, highly coordinated, seamlessly integrated informational flows cover the globe, profoundly enhancing every aspect of life they touch. Companies like Cisco, HP, IBM, Microsoft, AT&T and Verizon position themselves not just as providers of technology and services but as corporations that have truly refashioned economic, political, cultural, and social relations at the level of the quotidian.

A 2003 Cisco commercial opens with imagery of the wires, switches, routers, hubs, connectors, and cabling that form the network "backbone" of globalization: "Meanwhile on planet Earth 6.3 billion human beings are discovering something powerful." The ad takes viewers on a tour of "seemingly random events" across the population of planet Earth to show how formerly parochial ways become "all tied together by the systems of one company. Cisco Systems." The tour evinces an aura of universal humanism woven into a tapestry of multicultural and multiracial faces and communities, including scenes and sounds of heart patients being monitored virtually; dispersed textile markets being integrated by handheld devices; children laughing, playing, and making new friends across the planet via their computers; virtual lovers meeting; and even Russian hackers being arrested to affirm the eradication of threats to civility. Cisco imagines a moral landscape of a global civil society – a civil society that is integrated via "the power of the network."

Cisco now advertises its Intelligent Information Network, which is touted as a seamless integrated network designed to increase operation surveillance and eliminate system inefficiencies. Such representations are one-sided accounts that neglect layers and layers of conflict and disorder and resistance. It is undoubtedly the case that "Intelligent Information Networks" such as Cisco's aim to resolve security threats to its systems through more efficient monitoring and surveillance. A majority of transnational corporations doing business on a global scale have organized themselves through global information networks "to counter the often extraordinarily turbulent environment within which they operate." Though their ads seek to softly represent this hegemony as a unified and universal moral community, networks of power also contribute to networks of resistance (Urry 2003:57, 10). Networked capital is presented as clean capital: circuits and hubs; information workers in business suits; multiracial and diverse; abstracted light beams bringing information into offices, homes, and villages and facilitating consensual exchange – but speedy, integrated, and even intelligent networks cannot magically generate new exchange values without exploiting labor, and they cannot erase the power differentials that lie at the heart of a global system of markets.

From grand narrative to inscription practices

Embedded in corporate advertising discourse is a teleological vision, a way of seeing that joins the present with the future, connecting individual well-being and neo-Enlightenment narratives of social progress via scientific reason. In corporate versions of this story, an integrated technoscience infrastructure anchored by transnational corporations serves as the foundation of the social order.

Like networked capital and semiconductor capital, laboratory capital is envisioned as unpolluted capital – a controlled system that relies on continuous flows of data and knowledge. Scientists and technicians in clean suits, multiracial and gender-balanced, have replaced manual laborers and mechanics. In this society, symbolic labor is privileged.

Smarter streets. Smarter classrooms.
We need smarter people. Really smart. Smarter hospitals. Smarter energy grids.
Connect them all together, and what do you got?
Happier people.

That's what I'm working on. That's what I'm working on.
I'm an IBMer. (IBM 2009)

IBM's 2009 "Smarter planet" campaign presents the realization of the Enlightenment dream – "on a smarter planet we can capture, analyze and use data in new ways to. . ." predict and thus control subsystems of transportation, water use, and hospital resources. IBM representationally exaggerates an integrated system of technoscience dedicated to the pure circulation of data and information in the interest of efficiently solving the most intractable of problems, but this merely makes it representative of a corporate technoscience devoted to the greater public good.

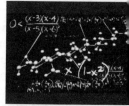

IBM reduces all activity to mathematical formulae – traffic, DNA strands, radio waves, bodily processes, urban grids, surveillance, energy transmission, etc. These images point to a grand mathematical utopia based on circulation rather than place. Here, technoscience repairs and sanitizes the disruptions produced by Capital and other unruly social processes.

Substitute Glaxo, GE, Dow, or DuPont's "To do list for the planet" and the message is the same: corporate science is committed to applying the scientific method to build a more humanitarian world. On the other hand, advertising also makes it seem as if the efficacy of knowledge resides in the relationship between commodity producers and commodities. Consequently, "knowledge will be produced in order to be sold, it is and will be consumed in order to be valorized in a new production: in both cases the goal is exchange" (Lyotard 1984:4–5). Knowledge for its own sake ceases to exist – its exchange value always premised now on its use value.

Corporate advertising locates the engines of value formation in the actions of savvy elites and information-rich investors who know where to look to find value, rather than in material labors. But the highest concentrations of value now appear to emanate from innovations sparked by developments in technoscience, the product of symbolic labors manifested in formulae, codes, programs, and models – immaterial labor performing symbolic labors. A primary signifier in corporate

scenes of science is the mobile markerboard made of transparent acrylic – a high-tech see-through blackboard on wheels. Abstract thinking is thus given material form in a sign world. Transparent panes make visible both the means and the products of knowledge production: algebraic equations, chemical inscriptions, and genomics models, as well as systems modeling and the coding of data into technical solutions. In some ads, the boards appear as if programmable, allowing scientists and engineers to watch simulated models and real-time graphs unfold. The transparent acrylic surfaces are essential signifiers of the power of technoscience because: (a) they make visible the other inscriptive processes that come to stand for the authority and promise of science, and (b) they mask the power relations of science.

The grand narrative guiding interpretation of these transparent illuminations of scientific discovery is tacitly embedded in the signifiers themselves. Enlightenment narratives of science are tightly compressed into signifiers of the inscription practices that bolster the authority of scientific knowledge. The narrative authority in these ads comes from the imagery of good souls doing good works by embracing the powers of the scientific method. The justification for capital is thus based on a slight twist on the old utilitarian ethic – capital unleashes the power of science, and directs its product not for profit, but simply to do good, to relieve suffering and contribute to "happier people," and that of course is the greatest good.

3

Landscapes of Fictitious Capital

From fictitious to hyperreal Capital

Advertising's landscapes of Capital frequently feature imaginary utopian moments that mask what might be called landscapes of fictitious capital. But these utopian moments are also premised upon the same landscapes of fictitious capital they aim to mask. Karl Marx introduced the concept of "fictitious capital" in volume III of *Capital*, where he addressed the neces-

sary role of a credit system in the expansion of a capitalist economy.

> Hence, the credit system accelerates the material development of the productive forces and the establishment of the world-market. It is the historical mission of the capitalist system of production to raise these material foundations of the new mode of production to a certain degree of perfection. At the same time credit accelerates the violent eruptions of this contradiction – crises – and thereby the elements of disintegration of the old mode of production. (Marx 1967:441)

Marx's conceptualization permits us to see a line of historical continuity from simple credit to the institutionalization of stock markets to the emergence of derivatives – particularly credit default swaps and collateralized debt obligations. This enables an examination of the utopian landscapes of Capital from a different vantage point, demonstrating that the same images of utopia both premise, and mask, the contradictions of leveraged capital.

Marx argued the credit system accelerates both "material development" and "the violent eruptions of this contradiction – crises." Simply, when growth can no longer keep up with the speculative investment that seeks to stimulate it, a crisis results. The metaphor of a "bubble" expresses the skewed relationship between fictitious capital (capital based on future earnings) and accumulated capital (existing liquid assets). Future earnings are always to some degree speculative, but a lopsided proportion of fictitious capital relative to underlying assets extends the consequences of a failed investment. When continuous growth became dependent upon leveraging more and more fictitious capital with almost no underpinning in real assets (e.g., the derivatives and swaps swirling around the subprime housing mortgages) and the inflated bubble of home prices burst, the disappearance of so-called "capitalized assets" occurred with extraordinary rapidity.

We are now experiencing the contradictions of what Robert Brenner (2003) calls the "long downturn" – a period that began around 1973 when net rates of profit began to slide. Over-capacity and over-production in manufacturing pressured prices down, and unceasing price competition eroded profit margins. From the early 1970s till 1995, productivity gains remained relatively flat in the manufacturing sector. This prompted firms to downsize, outsource, and merge in order to counter these forces. Three other developments are relevant to our story.

First, the nearly hyperbolic growth of the sign economy and branding seeks to leverage the over-production of parity goods by attaching a differentiated sign or brand to that good to boost its margins. Such strategies are, however, highly competitive and soon lose their overall effectiveness as economic levers (though there will always be individual winners) – themselves subject to the tendency for *rates* of profit to diminish. A political economy of sign value evolved in response to the historical contradictions of capital over the course of the twentieth century. When we view the landscapes as expressions of a political economy of sign value we interpret the ads and their landscapes as partial efforts to offset the tendency for the rate of profit to decline.

We share Baudrillard's view that growth of the sign economy corresponds over the long term to the declining profitability of material production (the manufacture of things). A system of commodity signs develops because in competitive markets standardized products cannot be distinguished and none can command a premium without attaching a unique sign value. Sign values can be viewed as an effort to counter the tendency for the rate of profit to decline in any particular sphere, themselves subject to the same tendency. But the much more severe consequence of a sign economy is that oversaturated fields of value imperil the very credibility of the category of value itself – what Baudrillard calls an "epidemic of value."

Second, the push to utilize information and communication technologies to boost productivity rates is premised on an ideal of a frictionless alchemy of value. The advertising landscapes we have studied glorified this window of technology-mediated productivity gains as the future horizon.

Third, efforts to counter the long downturn in recent decades have relied on the expansion of financial instruments to offset the absence of growth in the production of goods. As a result, financial profits as a percent of total profits in the US economy increased from roughly 20 percent in 1973 to 40 percent by 2005, and at the same time total debt as a percentage of the economy skyrocketed over the same period. Despite the hoopla about the new economy and the salvation to be gained via continuously increasing rates of productivity made possible by innovative technologies, the underlying economy during this period remained relatively stagnant. Though the economy became dependent on the proliferation of financial products to preserve and enlarge money capital, the story of the derivatives crisis and the subprime mortgage crisis also reveals that the frenzied financial innovations that drove investment returns in the short term could not entirely transcend, or even bypass, the limits of underlying productive capacity in the US economy.

The period of time covered by our study – from 1995 to 2010 – corresponds measure for measure to Brenner's title of "The Boom and the Bubble" (2003). The period from 1996 to 2000 seemed to depart from the long downturn in both the perception of increased rates of productivity (perhaps attributable to new computer, information and communication technologies) and a booming stock market that outperformed historical averages. At the market top in 2000, the price–earnings ratio for S&P 500 corporate stocks reached 44 as compared to the historical average of 13.2, a reflection of "irrational exuberance" about the magic of "the new economy" (Shiller 2005; Brenner 2000). Much of this excitement concentrated on supposedly high-growth markets represented by tech stocks such as dotcoms, but that asset bubble came down to earth in 2001. As stock equity prices tumbled, another asset bubble was already cooking in the form of housing prices. In the wake of the bursting technology bubble, the Federal Reserve lowered interest rates to stimulate growth. Lower mortgage rates fueled the speculation process and housing prices continued to rocket upwards. Homeowners found it tempting to take out second mortgages, based on inflated models of appreciation, to purchase a range of other commodity goods. With wages stagnant and savings rates at an all-time low (−0.5 percent), household debt reached 120 percent of disposable income (Brenner 2006:321–2). Without this, aggregate consumer demand would have dropped dramatically. To keep this growth machine running, and keep fantasies of an "ownership" economy going, companies dug deeper to exploit the subprime mortgage market. When joined to the scale of the securitization process described below, the conditions for the abrupt economic crisis of 2008 were in place.

As Gillian Tett (2009) tells the story of the global financial crisis in *Fool's Gold*, the development of ever more convoluted financial instruments – starting with collateralized debt obligations (CDOs) and moving on to the array of synthetic derivatives that flooded the market in the last decade – began initially as an innovative way of managing risk before flowering into a mechanism for "turbo-charging" bank profits that had been relatively flat for some time. CDOs are complex instruments that pool risk, carve it up, and repackage slices of different levels of risk (tranches) so that investors can select the degree of risk and the corresponding rate of return they want – the greater the risk, the greater the return. What happened in the bank sector reiterates the general tendencies of capital during this time period – the profitability of packaging debt obligations into new financial instruments soared and then dropped back to earth as competing banks raced to grab a share of this new market. Intense competition created a premium for newer and more daring ways of packaging risk and so banks such as JP Morgan, Bank of America, Citigroup and Merrill Lynch raced to find lucrative advantages in these markets. Competition prompted pressure to commoditize the CDO – but this meant repackaging debt obligations in such volume that few investors could perform the due diligence necessary to understand the underlying risk. Such volume may have offset briefly the shrinking rate of profit on such instruments, but soon the banks that failed to stay at the front of the pack in terms of profit rates found themselves vulnerable to acquisition and takeover because their rates of profit corresponded to the multiples (the projected future price–earnings ratio) used to value their stock prices. With everything geared towards the metrics of stock prices, the pressure continued to find new avenues of growth. Traditional investment banking based on the growth of industry was simply too slow.

By 2002, the CDOs had become so popular that "insatiable investors quickly began demanding even better ways to juice up returns" so banks developed what Tett calls the "CDO squared," or a CDO of CDOs (Tett 2009:93–4). And motivated by the frenzied pursuit of higher yields, the CDO-cubed followed quickly. The CDO-squared "is backed by a pool of collateralized debt obligation (CDO) tranches," allowing "the banks to resell the credit risk that they have taken in CDOs" (Investopedia 2009). The CDO-cubed, in turn, was pegged to the CDO-squared and its tranches – slices of pooled risk.

CDO-squareds and CDO-cubeds can be repackaged countless times to create derivatives that are quite different from the original underlying debt security. These are also referred to as CDO^n, to show the unknown depth of some of these securities. (Investopedia 2009)

With each new instrument the original underlying assets became farther removed from the marketed product and the risk of an unraveling grew. With each new instrument the underlying asset became more and more abstract. As competition heated up, major financial institutions began to back up (collateralize) the debt obligations with subprime mortgages (loans to borrowers whose credit history is weak, where default rates are likely to be higher).

Financial instruments like the CDO-cubed demonstrate how finance capital and semiotics mirror one another in structure. Just as the fuzzy referent lies at the heart of the simulacrum, so has the slipping referent become an essential ingredient in the recent securitization[1] of Capital that fueled a subsequent global financial crisis. The CDO^n is testimony to the fact that the disappearing referent is not merely a product of the spectacle. A commerce-driven sign system generates its own signs and substitutes them for their external predecessors; likewise, the "new financial capital" substituted its own models for the "real" material world of actors exchanging assets and cash: "The debt was being sliced and diced so many times that the risk could be calculated only with complex computer models" (Tett 2009:99–103). The result is "hyper-real" capital, which stands at some distance from any underlying assets, let alone the materiality of everyday life.

After absorbing First Union, Wachovia hired Interbrand to develop a hyperreal logo and associative image that supposedly represents a promise to "deliver flawless, consistent, timely and convenient service to every one of our customers" (Wachovia News Room 2002). Ironically, Wachovia, a casualty of the subprime crisis, was then taken over by Wells Fargo.

What is the representational equivalent of hyper-real capital? Advertising plays a prominent role in constructing a socially meaningful face for "hyper-real" capital. The advertising landscapes of Capital give meaning to "hyperreal" capital – the "brand-scapes of capital" (Goldman and Papson 2006). In the public domain, Capital becomes a series of signs substituted for the operational relations that actually constitute the nitty-gritty of everyday life in corporate business sectors. Advertising piles one form of hyper-real capital on another – let us call it hyperreal capital

squared or compound hyperrealism. The forces producing hyperreal capital converge from different directions. The hyperreal commodities we discuss above emerge out of innovations that seek to leverage basic commodity assets. These financial instruments based on complex computer models move beyond specific referents to such a degree that the signs, which stand for them, begin to have a life of their own. Advertising provides a vehicle for fashioning hyperreal commodities – constructing signs that stand for the commodity or brand being offered, and then substituting the sign for the commodity. When it comes to advertising for hyperreal capital, the advertising signs perform a double movement – they stand for the brand, while also accomplishing a representational erasure of the underlying financial instruments.

Whereas derivatives are efforts to leverage additional layers of value out of limited assets, the sign value is an effort to add a layer of exchange value over another product and thus amplify its value. The difficulty in every one of these areas is that the competition to secure extra profitability via derivatives, hedge funds, or sign values races along faster and faster – so that each offset is exhausted more quickly, each offset itself succumbs to declining rates of profit.

During earlier stages of capitalist development, instruments of fictitious capital were not detached from the forces of material production, but rather provided a crucial investment moment in the circulation of capital. But in recent decades fictitious capital has taken on an "immaterial" dimension in a capitalist economy that hinges more and more on speculation. In this sense, the corporate ads that we have studied convey, oddly enough, an account of global flows of capital, labor, and information that corresponds to the thesis of an "immaterial" economy (Hardt and Negri 2001). As capital investment sometimes ceases to have a necessarily immediate relationship with material production, it becomes an end in itself, chasing its tail through the circuitry of financial instruments where the referent is no longer necessarily the world of infrastructure, labor, production, or commodities, but rather a bond, or a security, or a securitized debt package.

"Immaterial" though it may be, hyperreal capital is nonetheless real – certainly real in its material and social impact; retirement funds, health care, scholarships and mortgages all were affected by both the boom and the bubble of hyperreal capital. Fictitious capital is also a real, and necessary, element of the capitalist system. Without credit, without the imaginary pool of capital created via the forward-looking stock market, there would not be adequate investment to fuel the system. Capitalism can never be static; its essential logic is pinned to growth as if growth (and not simply growth but an increase in the rate of growth as well) can be infinite. For this to happen requires more and more "juice." So creative destruction has morphed into "disaster capitalism" in order to find new opportunities for economic growth (Klein 2007).

Hyperreal capital also develops as a means of trying to bypass earlier limits to capital. Hyperreal capital is an image of capital constructed to support a profit boom by boosting the appearance of value. The aim is to shorten the circuit of capital circulation, thus speeding it up, and with it the profit-making process. Hyperreal capital seeks to *extend* the law of value to cover all spaces (both material and imaginary), but the most recent "innovations" of the commodity form also seek the grail of *exceeding* the law of value – this is the seduction of super-sized profits generated purely through the mechanisms of exchange, minus the presence of labor.

Merrill Lynch and the crisis of Capital

As the debt crisis unfolded, a few major US banks had significant overexposure to default risk. A 2008 report by the Comptroller of the Currency showed 96 percent of derivatives activity concentrated in five of the largest commercial banks. The "notational value of derivatives held by US commercial banks increased $24.5 trillion in the fourth quarter, or 14%, to $200.4 trillion." Almost half of the derivatives contracts in the US banking industry belonged to JP Morgan Chase: against $1.75 trillion in assets the notational value on their derivatives contracts was $87.36 trillion. JP Morgan Chase's "percentage of total credit exposure to risk based capital" measured 382 percent. Goldman-Sachs held fewer contracts but their percentage of credit exposure was 1,056 percent, while, even prior to its takeover of Merrill Lynch's inventory of toxic assets, Bank of America had a 179 percent exposure risk (Office of the Comptroller 2008).

After four successive quarterly reporting periods during which Merrill Lynch recorded massive losses and write-downs to their capital stock, totaling $19.2 billion, the company launched a TV ad during the summer of 2008. The ad symbolically addressed the financial credit crisis sweeping through global markets by telling the story of a severe thunderstorm that batters a barn and the animals that live within.

The thunderstorm approaches, the skies darken, and howling winds send birds off in flight. As the winds build, the barn doors violently swing open and shut. Sheep mill about, scared and restless. Rains pelt down and a lightning bolt strikes the weather vane, frightening a horse. The shutters slam back and forth, the chickens nervously flit about and the barn dog barks, trying to restore order amongst the other animals. The camera pans to a barn owl, sitting calmly on a beam before the camera cuts to a scene of the barn from outside and the sky framing it seems to be clearing, the clouds pass away and rays of sunshine come through. The collie pushes open the barn doors and comes out into the sunshine. The ad ends with a shot of Merrill Lynch's bull insignia on the weather vane.

> *Narrator: In the midst of the storm, it's only natural to wonder where the future will lead.*
>
> *To people who worry about the winds of change today, we'd like to remind you that no adversity lasts forever. And we'll be there with the strength and resources you can count on. Because at Merrill Lynch we're bullish on the future.*
>
> *Written: Merrill Lynch – a tradition of trust.*

Weeks later, still hemorrhaging its capital resources at an alarming rate, Merrill Lynch looked unlikely to survive unless it agreed immediately to being taken over by Bank of America for $44 billion. It did not have the resources to fulfill its obligations. A system-wide financial meltdown seemed imminent at that moment in mid-September 2008.

> That same week, Lehman Brothers failed, and American International Group was prevented from failing only by extraordinary government action. Later that month, Wachovia faced intense liquidity pressures that threatened its viability and resulted in its acquisition by Wells Fargo. In mid-October, an aggressive international response was required to avert a global banking meltdown. In November, the possible destabilization of Citigroup was prevented by government action. In short, the period was one of extraordinary risk for the financial system and the global economy, as well as for Bank of America and Merrill Lynch. (Ben Bernanke of the Federal Reserve testifying to Congress in June 2009 about Bank of America's acquisition of Merrill Lynch)

The much-touted fluidity and flexibility of less regulated financial instruments now came back to bite investors. The sheer complexity of variables structured into the credit default swaps in conjunction with the "volatility of the underlying market factors" made it impossible to accurately assess credit exposure

Punctuating the Merrill Lynch ad is this image of their sign logo as a weather vane atop the barn after the storm. The financial storm is over, skies are clear and the Merrill Lynch signifier remains "bullish." And yet, we cannot help but notice that the arrow is pointing south, its own sign indicating that Merrill Lynch was still tanking?

– "because the credit exposure is a function of movements in market rates, banks do not know, and can only estimate, how much the value of the derivative contract might be at various points of time in the future" (Office of the Comptroller 2008). This is such an extraordinary observation, it bears comment – routine market volatility undermines the conception of value as solid, objective, or durable. As the referents for value become a dizzying blur, shared conceptions of valuation become a thing of the past. So Lehman Brothers came to an abrupt end when they released a statement saying they had several billion dollars less than they had claimed days before. That prompted a panic, a run on the mega-banks holding huge investments in securities backed directly or indirectly by subprime mortgages – because no one could say with any degree of authority how to value the strange brew of securities. Certainly Bank of America failed to get a handle on how to value Merrill Lynch's exposure, as their proposed investment in Merrill Lynch continued to lose another $15 billion in capital valuation between the merger agreement and its closing date. The Merrill Lynch ad sought to reestablish a climate of trust and to soothe the fretful anxieties of animals (investors), but contra Merrill Lynch's tagline about a "tradition of trust," investors had lost faith and wanted out. The skittishness of the barn animals had to do with the fact that they could not assess the value of the stocks in which they were invested.

Though Bank of America had already received $25 billion from the US Treasury, Bank of America's CEO approached Secretary of the Treasury Henry Paulson and Ben Bernanke and threatened to withdraw from the agreement to purchase Merrill Lynch because of the severity of Merrill Lynch losses since the agreement. Paulson and Bernanke, fearful of what might then happen to an extremely fragile financial system, forcefully persuaded Bank of America to follow through and subsequently arranged another substantial package from the Troubled Asset Relief Program, an "additional $20 billion equity investment" to Bank of America along with "a loss-protection arrangement, or ring fence, for a pool of assets valued at about $118 billion" (Bernanke 2009).

The matter of trusting Merrill Lynch became even messier when it later became known that bonuses of $3.6 billion had been secretly paid to Merrill Lynch executives who oversaw the losses of $25 billion in 2008. It thus seems appropriate that the Merrill Lynch advertisement – shown in the midst of the most significant crisis to rock capitalist systems since the Great Depression, and against the backdrop of its own overexposure to the securitization of residential mortgages that was a factor in unraveling the financial system – refused to accept, or even acknowledge, responsibility as a party to the global crisis. Why depict complex global financial systems as a barn in a thunderstorm – a pre-capitalist set of rustic metaphors – when the crisis was a function of postmodern concoctions of value? In this parable of an animal farm, Merrill Lynch conceives of the financial system as a weather system organized around an equilibrium model. Turning to nature as a metaphor invokes a simplistic account of capitalism as a cyclical system with peaks and valleys. But it also invokes an inexorable determinism that eliminates any need to examine the agency of actors or the institutions that they direct. Storms happen and then they pass.

Throughout the corporate ads that we have studied, a consistent theme in depicting the landscapes of corporate globalization has been the disappearance of government – in its stead, the ads show a well-ordered world where businesses, technology, and markets regulate and direct everyday life. The staggering losses of banking capital threatened the financial system of global capitalism. Paulson and Bernanke fought to preserve fictitious capital because they feared the liquidity of capital would dry up, stop moving, and, if it did, a terrible economic depression would follow. Looking back now, we can say that hyperreal capital (subprime mortgage-backed securities) nearly destroyed fictitious capital (capital credit markets). Had governments not stepped in to aggressively prop up capital reserves at the largest financial institutions it is likely that the global financial system would have stalled in its tracks by an abrupt loss of credit flows. During this moment of crisis, ads like that by Merrill Lynch fundamentally mystified the contours of corporate globalization – the rustic barn metaphor and folksy parable of the storm do their best to divert attention from the extraordinary concentration of financial capital, and with it the concentration of financial contradictions, within the global system.

Spectacular tales of phantom Capital

Enron and WorldCom were among the fastest-growing corporations of the 1990s, based on stock capitalizations. Each firm engaged in particularly assertive corporate advertising, grandiosely casting themselves as a new breed of companies for a new kind of economy. Enron made itself into "a poster child for innovation and free-market competition" (Tett 2009:83), veering in the direction of becoming a post-Fordist energy company. Taking advantage of deregulated energy markets, Enron vaulted to the upper echelon of corporate growth rates by trading energy resources, rather than actually generating energy. At its peak, Enron sold over 3,000 "futures and derivatives contracts on everything from fiber-optic cable capacity to the weather." Enron spent aggressively on political lobbying and used its political connections to gain access to a deregulated energy market: "Its relentless pressure for deregulation reflected a wish to escape competition by opening up new pastures." In the early 1990s Enron sought and gained a "rule change that explicitly excluded energy derivative contracts and interest-rate 'swaps' from government supervision, opening the way for the company to speculate freely in energy futures" (Blackburn 2002:28). Deregulation created market uncertainty and Enron was well positioned to play market spreads in energy pricing. Enron turned into a financial company whose innovations had to do with its approach to organizing markets, and its use of "financial engineering" tools – once again CDOs and asset-backed securities (ABS) – to boost and accelerate profit margins (Blackburn 2002). Enron was among the first to broker energy futures and then water futures, but competitors quickly followed and began to squeeze Enron's profits. As Enron encountered declining rates of profit in its core businesses, it turned to concocting Special Purpose Vehicles (shell companies) to buy assets from itself, so that it could book sales and revenues while hiding its debt. This accounting sleight-of-hand permitted Enron to maintain the appearance of robust cash flow while keeping its debt off its own books. This was crucial because as a finance company Enron depended on having an AAA bond rating to keep its interest payments at a minimum (Feldstein 2002).

Enron launched its "Ask why" campaign in 2000 to solidify its name recognition and brand equity, and to hype the aura surrounding its growth stock. The campaign stressed "thinking outside the box" – outside of conventional wisdom and accepted practices – in the name of innovative market practices. Its campaign ads ended with a placard stating Enron had been voted "Most Innovative Company in America" by *Fortune Magazine*. Constructed as a global montage, the images assembled in the campaign's introductory ad were sutured together to reinforce the message, "If you are not afraid to ask why, you can change whatever it is you want."

Two ads from that campaign advanced focused ideological arguments for market innovations. One ad titled "Change" flatly declares: "Enron online will change the markets for many, many commodities. It is creating an open transparent marketplace that replaces the dark lined system that existed." An ideological buzzword, "transparency" signified unrestricted access to pricing information pertaining to markets – this rhetoric of free markets presumes that the free flow of knowledge makes for the most efficient markets. Enron may have benefitted from the appearance of transparency, but transparency itself was not their stock in trade. Enron's online trading units used a variety of schemes to manipulate energy prices. A few examples are pertinent. Their "Fat Boy" strategy created artificially high demand loads while, with their "Richochet" strategy, "sometimes called megawatt laundering, Enron bought price-capped electricity in California and sold it to an out-of-state buyer. Later Enron bought the same amount from the other company at a slightly higher price and shipped it back to California, where it could be resold for an even higher price." Or their "Get Shorty" scheme sold "fictitious emergency backup power it didn't have at a high price in the 'day-ahead' California energy market. Enron traders would then collect the money, cancel the contracts and cover the commitment by purchasing lower services in the 'hour-ahead' market and profit from the difference" (*Houston Chronicle* 2004).

Another ad reflected the formation of Enron Broadband Services in 1999 to trade Internet bandwidth capacity as a commodity. The ad, shown a year later, claims "Enron has created the market to buy and sell bandwidth like a commodity." Set against the visual frame of a montage of global cities from across the planet, the following conversation is heard.

> *Man's voice: From 7.00 p.m. to 7.00 a.m. we're paying for bandwidth that we're not using. Why?*
> *Chorus: Why?*
> *Woman's voice: We're paying for something we are not using?*
> *2nd Woman's voice: Why do we accept things the way they are?*
> *3rd Woman's voice: If we have a problem other people do too. There's our market.*
> *Man's voice: Why can't we sell the bandwidth to other companies. Make it a commodity like . . . uh . . . pork belly?*

Initially this ad seems a direct and practical instance of the benefits of innovation in a deregulated market place – greater efficiency and more effective controls over costs. A non-rational economic condition is observed – businesses paying for something they are not using – and a solution is offered, creating a market. Instead of invoking the need for government when there is a "problem," Enron invokes the need for a new market. Enron sees a situation of incomplete commodification as a limit on the rationality of resource utilization and suggests a new globally integrated commodities market that would structure trading in bandwidth around futures contracts (this is the reference to pork bellies). Turning bandwidth into derivatives contracts suited Enron's particular interests because it would allow a hedging of risk, playing spreads in pricing, and speculating on future pricing.

However, executives of this Enron division were later put on trial for "overhyping" their supposed technology to facilitate trading in bandwidth, allowing it to fluidly pass from buyer to seller. A year-2000 Enron press release in question at trial stated that Enron's "Broadband Operating System allowed application developers to dynamically provision bandwidth on demand for the end-to-end quality of service necessary to deliver broadband content." But prosecutors argued that Enron had never developed the necessary technical *models* of network demand on which to base such a market. There could be no efficient market in bandwidth futures without such a model.

Following its acquisition of MCI in 1998, WorldCom's advertising agency produced a grandiose ad that situated the newly assembled telecom giant as the culminating moment of modern history, a narrative that equates the transcontinental railroad as a world-historic event with the fiber-optic networks of data, voice and television transmission that will integrate the next and higher stage of global capitalism. With its stake in the future of a cyber-economy, WorldCom translates the material referent of fiber-optic networks and the broadband capacity of speedy global data-transmission into a new landscape that justified their power as an institution. The ad heralds the merger of these firms as the global capitalism analogue to the railroad infrastructure that unified the markets of the industrial age of national capitalism.

The WorldCom story represents in concentrated form the boom and bubble cycle that we have discussed. Begun in 1983 as LDDS (Long Distance Discount Service), WorldCom rode an aggressive acquisition strategy to stratospheric growth during the 1990s, absorbing 65 companies over a 19-year span. So many acquisitions in so little time created difficulties in integrating organizational cultures and organizational structures. Instead of economies of scale creating new efficiencies, disorganization and internal rivalries made the patchwork WorldCom an inefficient behemoth.

The 1996 Telecommunications Act deregulating the telephone markets further opened the door to a frenzy of consolidations. Despite the fact that it was significantly smaller than MCI, WorldCom could take over the larger firm because the price–earnings multiple for its stock price was 115 compared to a forward multiple of 22 for MCI's stock. WorldCom issued 900 million new shares (effectively doubling the number of stock shares in the company) to purchase MCI's shares. WorldCom's rapid rise, based on using its overinflated stock price as a means of acquiring rivals, also turned out to be the product of accounting maneuvers – some legal and some illegal (reporting operating expenses as capital expenses).

The simple mathematical fact is that anytime a company with a high multiple buys one with a lower multiple, a kind of magic comes into play.

> Earnings per share of the new, merged company in the first year of its life
> come out higher than those of the acquiring company in the previous year,
> even though neither company does any more business than before. There
> is an apparent growth in earnings that is entirely an optical illusion. (John
> Brooks cited in Spiro 1997)

It was precisely this optical illusion that WorldCom sought, because,
with each new acquisition, accounting sleights-of-hand "allowed the
company to report higher per-share profits, even when its core business
was barely growing, or losing ground" (Eichenwald 2002). This explains
why, barely a year after the MCI merger, WorldCom sought another
even-larger merger, this time to acquire Sprint for $120 billion in stock.
The Justice Department blocked this merger from going through because
of concerns that it would give WorldCom too much control over "backbone" networks and would "cause significant harm to competition in
many of the nation's most important telecommunications markets" (US
Department of Justice 2000). This decision spelled the beginning of the
end for WorldCom – without another "optical illusion," the accounting
tricks began to show through and the bubble burst.

The wireless telecommunications sector exemplified the euphoria
associated with the new economy. Telecommunications equipment
makers were among the most lucrative – Nortel, Lucent, Corning, JDS
Uniphase. Between 1997 and 2001, the telecommunications industry
took on over $1.8 trillion in new debt. Expenditures on telecommu-
nications equipment and services throughout the world totaled more
than $4 trillion during that time (Schiller 2003). "The bankers in turn
promoted the sale of shares and bonds to investors eager to believe the
promises of unending gains" (Belson 2005).

Industry leaders, particularly those at WorldCom, claimed the
Internet was doubling in size every three months. "WorldCom was also
among the most vocal cheerleaders for the Internet and the billions
of dollars it was supposed to spawn for businesses" (Belson 2005).
WorldCom's chief officers spoke of industry growth "exploding at
exponential rates." Business news media and stock analysts uncriti-
cally accepted and reproduced this "hype" as fact. Here we can see the
intensified speedup of capital processes that we discuss throughout this
book. The myth about an industry doubling in size every three months
fed overinvestment and an industry-wide buildout of equipment and
infrastructure that was too much too fast, oversaturating the market and
generating massive overcapacity. Unintegrated network capacity grew
more rapidly than network traffic (actual business).

The TV ad heralding the MCI–WorldCom merger hailed the wider
investment community that surrounded this gleeful market mania.

The ad offers a concentrated visual symbolization of the same narrative that executives like Bernie Ebbers of WorldCom were telling the investment bankers. The narrative opens with the transition from a preindustrial society to a full market economy with the building of the transcontinental railway. An army of preindustrial laborers swings their hammers, laying the track that united the continent. Corresponding to "the merger of the largest railroads" as a turning point in history – a transition from one stage of development to another – that transformed the landscape of the United States, so now the merger of MCI and WorldCom unifies "the largest networks on earth" and the landscape of globalization is now "officially open for business."

> *It was the merger of the largest railroads in America, and it touched everyone.*
> *For when the last spike was driven into the last tie,*
> *America was officially open for business.*
> *"East and west have come together" [intones a background voice]*
> *And now, it's happening again. A new and critical link has been formed.*
> *Two of the largest networks on earth have just become one,*
> *With capacity so vast it can carry all the data traffic of all the other carriers combined.*
> *To more places around the world than any other network.*
> *Introducing MCI/WorldCom*
> *Now the world is officially open for business.*

In these screen shots taken from the MCI/WorldCom ad we see the respective modes of production (railroad v. cyber-networks); tools of production (embodied labor v. satellite transmissions); and history (the golden spike connecting the rails and the information stream connecting the world).

A laborer's sledgehammer drives the famous "golden" spike that united the North American continent by railroad, igniting a golden beam of energy that visually hurls us into an era of global, as opposed to national, integration. The information age of fiber-optic networks has replaced the iron, coal, and steel based industrial age. The fixity of historical modes of geography is now transcended as beams of information take any path we wish. Laser beams of light are refracted, bent, relayed, transmitted, streamed, and pulsed – forming the

Only MCI WorldCom owns its entire network from origin to destination in many locations worldwide.

Whereas Walter Benjamin's angel of history faces backwards, if we consider WorldCom's girl as an angel, she has her back turned away from history, away from the forces of technology that are annihilating time and space. She does not contemplate the past, but gazes into an empty, lonely future that suggests liberation.

representational backbone of a global society without labor. Immediately we are transported to an utterly abstract, ultramodern rendering of the information infrastructure – a space uncluttered by human beings – confirming that space has rendered place superfluous and taken us to the end of history.

Once the golden spike has released its energies, everything is transformed. Whereas the landscape of the first industrial age is depicted as an age of labor, the fiber-optic age shows virtually no sign of human labor. Labor has been absorbed into the technology itself. As fantastic as the narrative appears, it also reveals the underlying dream of Capital, the steady replacement of labor by technology. The landscapes of the fiber-optic era reveal the death of the social precisely because Capital's new technology ostensibly makes labor unnecessary. "Capital," wrote Marx, "is dead labor."

The golden spike's release of light energy carries viewers through a fiber-optic corridor to the skyscrapers of the global city, where the light beams turn the buildings into spectacular image-bearing screens. The only face seen in the contemporary half of this narrative is the face of Bernie Ebbers (WorldCom CEO) screened across the side of a skyscraper. The ensuing scene traces the river of golden light as it crosses the planet, portraying a young girl who seems to just barely float over the lip of the Grand Canyon. Geologically, the strata of the Grand Canyon represent the physical manifestation of historical time, so the ethereal apparition of a young girl floating on the edge of the Grand Canyon evokes a postmodern landscape where the material restrictions of time, space, and social structure have become immaterial; time and space have been surpassed. Through the base of the canyon, the river has turned into MCI/WorldCom's light-beam. Technology has now replaced Nature – turning its rivers into technologized flows of information that cut through time and space. If the young girl appears ghost-like, we might also say that the human spirit has been turned into a "ghost within the machine." The technology of global data trafficking not only seems to have liberated us from labor, nature, time, place, and history, it has also made the body dispensable.

This vision of the information age and MCI/WorldCom's role as a telecommunications visionary concludes with a peculiarly postmodern rendition of the future global city – where the streaming pulses of light turn into a metaphor for the information superhighway. The high-speed beams of light are accompanied by sounds of speed to signify the rapid movement of data. Is this utopia amid the ruins, a liberated society minus the agency of human beings? Built around the material relics of our history, the technology of a global communications network eclipses traditional institutions and particular localities, leaving behind the ruins (or memorials) of past institutions (see image 3.08). The fiber-optic network (the light beam) operated by MCI/WorldCom forms the pulsing flow of a future city (society) otherwise decayed and in ruins, a graveyard of signifiers of the stately modern era (the rotunda) and Greco-Roman columns, ruins of the classic era. A continuous information stream pulses through this landscape, apparently carrying the vitality and hope of the human spirit, which, though visually banished from this scenario, has been building to a crescendo in the singing voices on the background sound track.

Visually this is the post-historical era, a puzzling scene of a post-apocalyptic space, where time and history have worn out. This scene suggests an imagined geography of a cyber-economy. A concentrated symbolic effort has been made by the advertiser to reiterate its narrative of technological evolution and paradigm shift. Heavy capitalism has been replaced by light capitalism – the latter characterized by continuous flows, from which follows socio-spatial separation and disengagement. The immobile, archaic ruins of the prior stages of Western history stand in marked contrast to the pulsing fluidity of a globalized blur of information streams. This mimics Castells' (1996) argument that, in a Digital Information Age, "society, now aided by the necessary digital technology, is rapidly reorganizing itself around networks, a kind of infinitely adaptable organism that has no center – unlike traditional governments – and no geographic boundaries." MCI/WorldCom's landscapes attempt to capture these kinds of relations – round-the-clock flows of capital and information make traditional communities and governments an anachronism. Indeed, the technology of global data trafficking traveling at the speed of light not only seems to have liberated us from time, place, and history, it also seems to make society itself dispensable.

4

Representing the Social Relations of Production in the Network Economy

Thus the social relations within which individuals produce, the social relations of production, change, are transformed, with the change and development of the material means of production, the productive forces. The relations of production in their totality constitute what are called the social relations, society, and specifically, a society at a definite stage of historical development, a society with a peculiar and distinctive character. (Marx 1975:207)

Market forces, commodity relations, and the formal–legal relations of property ownership and contracts define rights of access to productive resources as well as governing how surplus is appropriated and by whom. And the wider relations of production encompass those who are not directly in the labor force – children, retirees, and those who help reproduce the conditions of everyday life (e.g., by performing unpaid housework). The social relations of production in a capitalist society are complex, contradictory, conflictual, and unequal – shaped by technology, division of labor, and organizational practice, and stratified by class, race, gender, age, and ethnicity. It might seem odd then to envision the social relations of production through the lens of advertising; after all, ads are all about superficiality. They celebrate the sponsoring corporation, place a halo around its representation, gloss social relations, and repress as much as possible that which is negative, conflictual, complex, or unequal about the corporate political economy. Ads compose spatial landscapes of production relations, while also sketching quick portraits of subject types who occupy these spaces. Some ads personify Capital in the idealized figures of a highly mobile business elite, while others offer tightly condensed apocryphal stories of success and failure. No less than the landscapes they occupy, representations of contemporary business and technology elites reflect characteristics associated with the new information economy: flexible accumulation, deterritorialization, space–time compression, electronic markets, and incessant technical innovation.

Corporate ads may celebrate the surfaces of global capitalism, legitimating neo-liberal market capitalism by leaving out the consequences of capitalist institutions on non-elites, especially those who own nothing and those who must bend to unpredictable labor markets. So the same ads that highlight the distinctions of status, honor, and privilege that go together with accomplishment also seek to downplay gross inequalities that might threaten the legitimacy of the system. While political-economic inequalities rarely register in these ads, there is no corresponding repression of the cultural contradictions that Richard Sennett (1999) traces out in *The Corrosion of Character*. When individuals actually internalize the requirements of flexibility, risk, and job mobility, ideals regarding close familial relations may be compromised. Hence we may see the celebration of flexibility and mobility in ads, while also encountering "landscapes of fear" and "abandonment" (Gold and Revill 2003; Salerno 2003). Advertising frequently offers to resolve the fear of loss (e.g., separation from loved ones) with symbolically mediated commodities or services.

How does the "capitalist realism" of corporate ads portray the social relations of production *circa* the millennium? Or is this "capitalist realism" something closer to the postmodern simulacrum that Jean Baudrillard theorizes? Do corporate visualizations of production derive from actual historical referents or are these representations the original – are we looking at a substitution of signs of the real for the real? With this in mind, what role do markets and commodities play in people's lives as represented on the small screen? How does technology redefine the categories of producers in these representations? What groups rise in importance? Who disappears? How are the managers of capital, the information workers, the entrepreneurs, the individual investors, the manual laborers, the farmers, and the poor represented? How are their images gendered and racialized? What happens to the frames of social class? How are spatial representations of production relations linked to axes of control and agency?

Social relations in a universal market

Money may seem to be the motive force of capitalism, but its importance derives from the deeper workings of the capitalist system. Beneath the surface of the cash nexus lies the structuring logic of commodity relations. Marx's analysis began with labor as a commodity (wage labor), in which the real laboring activity of individuals was transformed into abstract labor to make it possible to freely substitute one person's labor time for another's. Labor measured in standardized units could be compared across time and place, making possible a universal currency that could turn all non-equivalents interchangeable. Wage labor extended the commodity relationship into consumption relations since one now had to purchase one's needs through the wage. Capitalist development pushed commodity relations into more and more areas of life; after nearly two centuries, the universal market has left few relationships untransformed into commodities.

While advertisers have an obvious self-interest in repressing the conflicts that surround class relations, they cannot ignore the cultural uneasiness prompted by the extension of the commodity form and "callous cash payment" into the whole of social life. Marx described the consequences of turning everything into commodities and markets.

> It has pitilessly torn asunder the motley feudal ties that bound man to his "natural superiors," and has left remaining no other nexus between man and man than naked self-interest, than callous "cash payment." It has drowned the most heavenly ecstasies of religious fervour, of chivalrous enthusiasm, of philistine sentimentalism, in the icy water of egotistical calculation. It has resolved personal worth into exchange value. (Marx and Engels 1978:475)

The extension of commodity relations undermined traditional values, encouraged extreme individuation, and reduced decision making to cold commodity calculation. When market forces dictate values, there tends to be greater cultural volatility as "all that is solid melts into air, all that is holy is profaned." For this reason, ads seek to arrest the process of change when it comes to the supposedly deep values held by Anglo-Americans regarding that which is "holy" – family and community. Though the combination of labor markets and universal consumption has "reduced the family relation to a mere money relation," advertisers reassert the "sentimental veil." Corporate advertising routinely swathes the imagery of commodity consumption in emotionally meaningful scenes of parent–child bonding, seeking to veil the impersonality of market forces with a tapestry composed of signifiers of warmth, community, social comfort, and caring.

Depending on how ads frame the handshake, it may signify the agreement to consummate an exchange relation, but it can also evoke a folksiness that removes the structural constraints of market forces from view. Even as capital reduces all relations to exchange value, the handshake symbolically reverses all this, transforming the formal contractual relationship back into the appearance of a personalized agreement. This adds a human touch to the cold hard logic of Capital, associating the corporation with connotations of neighborliness, community, and friendship. The handshake signifies a unification of the dual myths of Patriarchal Individualism and Jeffersonian *Gemeinschaft*, summoning forth imaginings of a precapitalist space in which a multiplicity of bonds determined the character of people's dealings with one another. Though these corporate handshakes are abstracted gestures that occur in placeless spaces, the handshake representation remains unshakably a marker of consensual, uncoerced, and fair exchange amongst equals. Social relations appear guided by norms of mutuality rather than the calculus of contracts.

While advertising spectacularizes the power of commodities to enhance social relations, the real nitty-gritty of producing value is omitted, abstracted, or aestheticized. Advertising spins narrative webs of commodity fetishism and technological fetishism, and viewers get used to seeing objects of value materialize out of thin air; neither does advertising dwell on the amount of labor necessary to acquire the cash equivalent to participate in the exchange. Advertising stands in a necessarily ambivalent relationship to commodification. As advertising seeps into every nook and cranny of our social lives, it becomes curiously sensitive to popular criticism of "over-commercialization" or "crass commercialism." Hence at the same time that ads seek to turn what is valuable to us into new sources of commodity value, more than a few campaigns seek to distance themselves from the excesses of commodity fetishism by conjuring up nostalgic markers of life in a non-commodified world. Advertising blankets the cash nexus with narratives and signifiers that situate the meaning of commodities within non-commodified relations. Hence, value is located in claims to authenticity based on the assumption that commodities have no soul, but rather masquerade as authentic in search of an easy buck.

A common advertising strategy relegates matters of price to the tacit dimension, thus allowing ads to sidestep the messy and conflicted terrain of privileging exchange value over use. Whereas consumer-goods ads sometimes adopt playful approaches to mock the premise of commodity fetishism in order to distance themselves from the practice, corporate ads do more than sell particular goods and services – they also promote the institutions that organize the exchange, circulation, distribution, and production of the commodities themselves. Corporate ads therefore adopt a more sincere tone of voice that is less cynical about the commodification of place, sentiment, and social relations. Capital positions commodification as an inevitable process driven by technological advances, neatly reversing the relationship between commodification and technology. In corporate advertising, commodification coincides with an antiseptic, tidy, civil society in which intelligent corporate stewardship of technology and capital turns alienation on its head – distilling out the cold, impersonal calculus of market logic. The ads show a process of globalization that is contingent upon the free movement of capital in all its forms.

Amongst companies involved in the flow of money or its equivalents, there emerged, *circa* the millennium, an inclination to soften their push to turn the entire world into a stage for callous cash exchanges. Banks and credit card franchises routinely remind viewers that, though their business revolves around pushing the commodity framework everywhere (e.g., Visa), they remain committed to a moral hierarchy that recognizes our nearest and dearest relations can never be reduced to commodity form. Citibank ("Live Richly"), Chase ("The right relationship is everything"), and Bank of America, three of the largest banks in the Western world, all stress the importance of that which cannot be commodified – love and caring amongst family members or the experience of true friendship. Similarly, MasterCard's long-running "Some things money can't buy" campaign highlighted the prices of commodities that we purchase as a prelude to stressing how the relationships and experiences we value most are "priceless." Rhetorically, Bank of America ads pushed the envelope further, touting the nobility of altruistically contributing to the greater good rather than merely seeking to maximize self-interest, while also criticizing those who wear the blinders of the commodity form and thus lack vision: "People who know the price of everything [but] the value of nothing."

Re-visioning class formations

While evidence points to a widening income gap and burgeoning disparities in the distribution of wealth spurred on by the globalized "free"-market economy, television representations of inequality and difference have moved in the opposite direction. Social critics point to a new binary in which the concentration of wealth disproportionately ascends to the smallest fraction of the population. World news can scarcely avoid photographic reminders of the dire forms that extreme poverty takes – drought-stricken Ethiopia, Palestinian refugee camps, and victims of civil war in the Sudan.

Though inequalities deepened across the global landscape, the concept of class – much less, class conflict – is scarcely visible in the landscapes of ads. Over recent decades, industrial labor and the production of goods have steadily disappeared from ads. Today material production has been reduced to fleeting signifiers of self-moving, apparently autonomous, technologies. Social class as a function of occupational location appears infrequently in ads, usually as a means of hailing potential consumers – the most obvious instance involves selling tough trucks to rugged working-class men. Glimpses of the working class are at best transitory in corporate ads – a passing shot of a hardhat, or Chinese stevedores unloading a ship, or shots of construction workers chosen to evoke the historical authenticity and durability of a corporate insurer.

When the occasional allusion to craftsmanship is made, the reference is to preindustrial capital, or, intriguingly, to postindustrial capital, where computer-driven machinery is shown imagining a smooth precision compatible with a craftsman-like view of quality, sometimes without the presence of human beings being required at all. As with commodity advertising, the site of material production is largely absent. When signifiers of production do appear, they take the form of high-speed automated robotics. When workers appear, they most likely gaze at control panels and other simulations of the act of production. If we see either factories or workshops, workers have been turned back into adjuncts to computer-controlled tools – this is not the first time in the history of industrialization that workers have been depicted as machine tenders, but this time the role is glamorized by the presence of glinting, streamlined high-tech tools. Though the work shown is probably still tediously repetitive, the references are so brief and the settings so heroized, that the possibility of alienated activity seems remote. Value seems to be produced by technological magic without labor.

A 2005 Bank of America ad references the new global proletariat while also burying their significance beneath a discourse about perfecting customer service. The ad features an African-American corporate banker at Bank of America who is charged with seeking perfection – zero tolerance for errors – in check processing. As surprising as it might be to see an African American featured as a corporate banker, more surprising is a brief scene that visually captures the new global working class, employed not as industrial workers but as check processors. Like their boss they are people of color, apparently Hispanic, Asian, and African. But there the similarity ends. We might guess them to be largely immigrants, and we can see they are female by a two-to-one ratio. The remainder of the ad visually swamps this scene with image after image of the equipment and software that make high-speed processing of checks possible. This ad permits us to disentangle a set of self-contradictory representations: acknowledging this stratum of low-paid, unskilled office workers, this ad contains a kernel of truth; this is an instance of how computer-age proletarian work has evolved, no longer on the industrial floor, but doing repetitive data entry and paper

processing tasks. The ad also acknowledges how the disposability of these workers can be calculated in relation to the visual centrality and importance of automated machinery that now drives the circulation of money.

> Scenes from the Bank of America ad draw attention to proletarianization and computer automation of check processing. The spokesperson lauds the 40 million checks processed each day: ". . .to us this is like an assembly line."

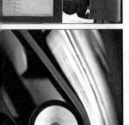

Class does not entirely disappear, but it ceases to exist as a category of production. Instead, class continues to be meaningful in the sphere of consumption and aesthetics. Ads for upscale hotels like Doubletree, Westin, and Starwood that cater to business elites signify social class as an aesthetic disposition expressed through the pure gaze, which "implies a break with the ordinary attitude towards the world which, as such, is a social break" (Bourdieu 1984:31). Elite status turns into a series of consumptive choices made by people who possess a self-reflexive appreciation of their own refined sensibilities. Questions of class position are not transposed to the sphere of consumption alone, but also to the sphere of investment. This in itself is unsurprising. What has changed is the new relationship between investing and social class as defined by ads. Ads redefine investing not as an elite domain but as a sphere accessible to everyone regardless of race, gender, creed, and even class. An American Stock Exchange ad (2002) went as far as to declare across their ticker tape, "We're equal-opportunity capitalists." As implausible as it may seem, ads redefine investing as beyond class, as part of a post-class social landscape.

During the boom phase of the late 1990s, everyone was pictured as having access to the means of acquiring wealth via their investments. Typical was an Ameritrade ad set in an English-as-second-language class for immigrants. This melting pot of people from Africa, South Asia, the Philippines, Eastern Europe, and Latin America may not understand much English, but they quickly assimilate the economic culture as they show their teacher the joys of *Ameritrade* and the ability to trade stocks on your computer. This tribute to the proprietary excellence of *Ameritrade* is capped when a Russian émigré exclaims, "And they said capitalism would never work," while the word "believe" settles across the screen. The stock market

boom set in motion a frenzied competition to reach the great unwashed (as far as stock trading went), and reduced sales commissions enticed many who had never traded stocks before and were eager to get rich quick along with everyone else. This vision of trading stocks abolishes all hard-and-fast stratification boundaries – here is the long-awaited utopian capitalism where the possibilities of achieving prosperity are available to all, where there appear to be no structural losers. Of course, such a conception requires that we push aside questions about where profits come from. This view of a universal stock market requires either the open admission that some other group is getting shafted elsewhere, or the pretense that investment only produces win-win situations. No one will acknowledge the former as a possibility, but the latter rationale grew pervasive. A 1998 Travelers campaign gave voice to the narrative rationalizations of middle-class investors about how their investments benefit themselves along with distant others in the developing world. One ad pictured a single young woman seated amid her sedate middle-class furnishings, thinking to herself about how her investment will go to:

> *South America to build a gas pipeline over the mountains, so people in Chile can have clean air and hot showers. And the pipeline is gonna help the economy, and that's gonna help my dollar so when it finally comes back to me it might be more like $4. And I might be more like looking at the real estate section.*

The investment process seems tranquil and serene, almost dreamlike in the video editing, without a hint of coercion or unequal exchange. In fact, visually the process takes place without any exchanges whatsoever, although as her musings move to the economy and her return on investment, the landscape of Chile turns into an aesthetically pleasing, abstract waveform pattern, its imagery of eternally recurring flows a metaphor for consensual intercourse in the marketplace.

An emergent social character in the investing landscape appeared as a confident and self-assured independent investor with entrepreneurial spirit. The ads depict a new breed, ideologically presented as "mavericks" and "pioneers," defined by a shift in attitudes and paradigms – they are looking neither to government to solve their problems nor to corporate giants in which to entrust their futures. They are sanguine that computing technologies applied to trading stocks create a democratized playing field that puts them in the driver's seat. Arranging soundbite montages to form serial soliloquies, Suretrade strung together the following ideological portraits across three commercials. The speakers have been carefully chosen to represent a relatively young middle-class demographic segment, diversified by ethnicity.

1st woman: We're not relying on the government.
1st man: We're not relying on the company.
2nd man: We're not relying on a big, fat inheritance.
3rd man: We trade online.
2nd woman: We're betting on ourselves.
1st woman with a laptop on the couch: We don't need a financial babysitter.
1st man: We're declaring our independence.
4th man: We're realistic, but hopeful.
2nd man: We'll find our own way.
2nd woman: We work harder for ourselves than anyone else will. We're pioneers.
1st man: We're not caught up in the hype of technology, we're just using it.
2nd woman: Corporations are slower than we are.
5th man: We are a million individuals.
3rd woman shown with daughter and pet rabbit: We're modern capitalist mavericks.
3rd man: We're shattering the old broker universe.

Like the skilled information workers to whom we shortly turn, these characters tend to represent a new generation that appears confident, self-contained, and unconstrained. Their apparent social and economic success represents a function of their own choices, the gifts neither of inheritance nor of entitlement. These self-portraits are shot in individuals' homes, spaces where they exercise autonomy, where they smugly declare themselves capable of self-motivation without the whip of authority to spur them on. They are made to represent a new social class of modern capitalist mavericks who refuse to bow to convention or to the hierarchical system ruled by Brahmin broker elites. As do-it-yourselfers, they play out a populist imaginary for an era of networked technology, in which those who make themselves savvy in the use of new technologies can claim to be more agile and swift than the behemoth corporations.

Mirroring what Richard Florida (2002) calls *The Rise of the Creative Class*, ads for financial devices, investing, software, computers, and telecommunications all hail the "creative subject." This expressive subject feels restricted and unfree within the confines of bureaucratic organizations, aspires to own her own business, work from home, or invest with sufficient success that she can pursue her goals independent of the rat race if necessary. American Express ads for their small-business card feature subjects who possess "vivid imaginations" – they are restaurateurs, chocolatiers, landscape designers, dress designers, veterinarians, architects, wine merchants, bakers, and sculptors. Microsoft ads similarly position its name as synonymous with a new stage of human development that aims at customizable freedom – no dream is impossible and no person or place is insignificant. The new Capital (say,

Microsoft) exists to serve the self-expression of the sacrosanct freestanding human subject: "At Microsoft we stand in awe of you and your potential. It's what inspires us to create software that helps you reach it." Financial services and software ads promise tools and instruments to transform creativity into economically lucrative ways of life.

Movers and shakers

These shots, captured from a 2006 ad celebrating the future created by the merger of Verizon and MCI, as well as from ads for Scudder, AT&T, NYSE, Smith Barney, and SBC, summarize the fundamental representations of an imagined political economy of work in the coming decades. Work is situated in front of computer screens; it is performed alone or in small groups in open-architecture environments; it is mobile, performed on the move and wirelessly; and it is presided over by a young multiracial elite. These scenes assemble elements of the real into hyperreal tableaus that are more glorious than anything that most of us will experience in our quotidian moments. This hyperreal is an imaginary with roots in a technologically real set of possibilities that covers the self-contradictory capitalist relationality of a real that is left absent.

Hegel once observed that a master is not a master without a slave to recognize him as such, yet in TV ads fragmented glimpses of figures marked as occupying dominant positions are usually framed in isolation. It is enough that viewers recognize them. It is not surprising that images of the world poor are mostly absent from the landscapes of corporate advertising. When the poor do appear, it is to demonstrate that human dignity has not been forgotten by corporations such as Philip Morris, American Express, or Occidental Petroleum that care about people and empathize with profound human suffering. The poor, as we shall see, retain this semiotic functionality in how capitalist firms represent themselves.

Television images of corporate executives include glancing shots of them directing fiefdoms, issuing directives, demonstrating resolve, applying new technologies, jetting around the world, and reaping luxurious rewards. By ghettoizing the "functionaries of

capital" to a world of corporate towers, jet planes, *haute* architecture,
and exotic resort hotel settings, these representations refuse to divulge
that a global underclass might be swelling or that the middle class might
be eroding as a result of how capital has expanded.

Corporate executives (capitalist elites) appear in television advertising unidentified as class subjects, so that questions regarding their
social and economic rank and clout can be kept undefined. Only
one campaign (UPS 2002) ever specified or differentiated functional
responsibilities within a corporate hierarchy. When real CEOs appear,
as in NASDAQ ads, they are positioned as dynamic dreamers who
recount with passionate excitement their pioneering status at the center
of the nascent capitalist universe for the twenty-first century. Along with
professing infinite faith in the entrepreneurial path that enabled them
to translate visions into reality and thus realize wealth and success, they
reiterate a litany of motivational maxims (e.g., "Success is not an entitlement, it has to be earned") that articulate a future of global capitalism
composed by companies that have just "scratched the surface of what's
really possible." High-tech advertising *circa* 2000 envisioned a world of
CEOs atop an open-architecture world, while computers both operated
and monitored factories.

Establishing the visionary character of corporate leaders who possess
a "passion" for realizing their visions, the NASDAQ campaign played to
a mythology of a revolutionary post-bureaucratic economy – successful
companies depend on leaders who innovate, inspire, and have a cou-
rageous "entrepreneurial spirit." In such representations, the CEOs
are the companies; they have engineered productive facilities devoid
of workers. The leading edge of contemporary capitalism thus seems
constituted by companies defined by forward-thinking visionaries,
automated technologies, and distinctive brands. The NASDAQ ads
knit together a philosophy of corporate organization and motivation
that drives the leaders of Dell, Starbucks, Microsoft, Cisco, Staples,
and Intel. Similarly, Carly Fiorini, the first female CEO of a Fortune
100 company, took the stage in HP ads to narrate her philosophy of re-
dedicating HP to the "radical simplicity" of entrepreneurial invention
and innovation – the symbolic garage of its founders. When Michael
Dell, founder and CEO of Dell Computer, appeared on behalf of his
company, he struck a commanding pose surveying the outside world
through his window from the peak of his company's grand architectural
housing. If this influential corporate leader has gained wealth or fame or
power, it is because he contributes to a greater good:

*I like to think of myself as an Innovator who started a company – Dell Computer
– around an idea that everybody should be doing business directly with one*

another. One to one – with no barriers. To me that's the power of the Internet.
We'd like to show you how to empower your business in ways you'd never
imagine. I'm Michael Dell and it's our reason for being.

Dell's self-presentation as an innovator seeking to harness the power of
an idea that empowers others rather than seeking to enrich himself suggests a new kind of world-historical elite, dedicated not to preserving its
own power but to revolutionizing the social relations of production to
make everyone an owner and a winner.

Another familiar signifier of dynamic capital is constructed from
tightly edited scenes of leather shoes striding across floors, up stairs,
through corridors, and sometimes even around the globe. Crosscut
into financial narratives, these signifiers of dynamic movement connote
power, determination, and direction. Executives are often shot from a
low angle, a cinematic device that lends the figure a dominating presence
in the frame. At other times executives are placed on high, suggesting
superiority, vision, knowledge, and success. Scenes of executives striding in formation, flanked by aides and subordinates, connote a sense of
decisive purpose put towards achieving goals like mergers, takeovers,
and lucrative contracts. The wingtip shoe is so clearly marked as a signifier of power that Morgan Stanley Dean Witter used the device of the
shoeshine stand to play up the idea that Capital no longer discriminates
against women as it includes a woman's high heel in the "new old boy's
club."[1]

Situated in positions of power, a corporate elite is visually portrayed
as active, informed, dynamic, mobile, determined, focused, and surrounded by technological sophistication. Information flows through
them via cell phones and electronic information tools integrated into the
scenes. Uniformed in pinstripes, wingtips, and the other accoutrements
of power, these scenes suggest that markets may be volatile but Capital
is composed and disciplined in its pursuit of profitability. Campaigns
for investment firms especially stress a world moving at warp speed
while their elite investment bankers calmly survey it for "opportunities"
that will pay off.

These representations resemble what Thomas Friedman (1999)
termed the "Electronic Herd" in *The Lexus and the Olive Tree.* His
metaphor embraces the volatility of markets in conjunction with the
diffusion of electronic circuits of finance across the landscape of capital.
Competing to maximize rates of return on investments, the herd obses-
sively scours the planet for opportunities. Their manic need to invest is
matched by panic selling to cut losses as quickly as possible. Friedman
explains that in a global economy no corporation or nation-state can risk
losing the favor of the herd, because, when combined with the ability to

transfer funds and monies electronically, this herd mentality can halve a stock valuation within minutes, or throw a country's currency into crisis with a speed hitherto unknown.

The electronic herd pictures an economic elite dashing about in a global free-market economy fueled by technological innovation and the liquidity of capital forms (currency, stocks, commodities). The figures that compose this group are shown fluidly traversing the world of non-places and occupying office suites in corporate towers surrounded by personal communication technologies. Yet, even in these idealized abstractions, uncertainties and anxieties leak through. Narratives of success are sprinkled with hints of impending crisis, or stories of those who made the wrong choices – the wrong office equipment, the wrong software, the wrong package delivery service. The exhilaration associated with accelerated social, economic, and technological change mixes with an undercurrent of apprehension because there are more losers than winners in casino capitalism.

True grit: the persistence of bourgeois maxims in the age of globalization

Even with the changing landscapes of global capitalism – Internet networks, high-risk strategies, the decline of old-fashioned virtues such as debt aversion in favor of stressing the necessity of consumerism – the rhetoric of motivation heard in corporate ads still sounds like nineteenth-century fictional success stories, such as Horatio Alger stories with their emphasis on individual pluck and determination. The further corporations drift towards concentration and consolidation, the more they seem to fall back on the work ethic and its associated ideological maneuvers. A 2004 Smith Barney campaign hails this old-fashioned ethic of motivation as the basis of business success. Speaking in a serial monologue, multiple executives delineate the key values of their work ethic.

> *1st man: What's the secret of success?*
> *2nd man: You start with an insight. A vision.*
> *1st woman: An indicator.*
> *2nd woman: There is no secret.*
> *3rd man: No secret.*
> *4th man: It's 1% inspiration*
> *5th man: Followed by midnight oil*
> *1st woman: Lots of elbow grease*
> *6th man: Determination*
> *2nd woman: Sheer stubborn*
> *2nd man: Relentlessness*

2nd woman: Determination.
7th man: Where there's a will
1st woman: There's always a way.
8th man: Provided, of course, you know what you're doing.
2nd woman: I don't know anyone
6th man: Who's better trained than we are.
1st man: You want results?
2nd woman: Come prepared.
4th man: Stay late.
4th man: Smith Barney.
6th man: This is who we are.
2nd woman: This is how we earn it.

A key difference between this enunciation and that performed by their bourgeois precursors is that it's no longer the
sole domain of Anglo males – the old-fashioned work ethic is
now an equal opportunity ethic that draws race, gender, and
ethnicity under the same umbrella. The ad opens by superimposing a white male over the financial landscape to suggest
power, knowledge, and determination, followed by quick-
cutting close-ups of Smith Barney people on the move, each
of whom speaks with confidence and conviction about what is required
for success – theirs is the language of motivational clichés, old-school
homilies about the values and practices of preparation, elbow grease,
stubborn determination, and will.

Zygmunt Bauman (2000) contrasts the historical stages of heavy and
liquid capitalism. Heavy capitalism designated that stage of industrialization during which capital depended on a massive, fixed infrastructure
with industries like iron and steel in the lead. Material solidity was the
hallmark of this era and its values seemed correspondingly stable, chained
in time and place. The movement towards liquid modernity entailed a
shift to electronic flows of information and a preference for fluidity.
Contemporary corporate ideologues generally praise all that is mobile,
flexible, and agile, yet these very attributes of light capitalism and liquid
modernity yield cultural values of inconstancy and weightlessness. Aware
that fixations on celebrity and the cult of personality return ephemerality
and a loss of depth, New York Life pledges its corporate fidelity to the
abiding values of integrity and humanity. "What stands the test of time?"
asks their narrator. The answer lies in *values* that insure security in a
rapidly changing world. "Integrity is our foundation," declares another
ad that anchors the firm in the historical imagery of heavy metaphors –
muscular labor constructing monumental buildings of stone and steel.

Amid headlines about corporate fraud, accounting irregularities,
embezzlement, unemployment, price fixing, cost-cutting at the expense

of quality, and warranties that are nothing but fine print, invoking a nostalgic *mythos* of a shimmering past shores up a value system driven by the imperatives of an incessantly shifting marketplace. But this true grit floats like a signifier, summoned from an image bank of our past and fashioned into a pastiche that calls itself by the names of past virtues (hard work, integrity, pride in work and in one's word), as if conjuring up their images will insulate us from a fickle culture of images.

The modern nomad: seeking equanimity in a world of non-places

Bauman conceptualizes contemporary elites and non-elites by their relationships to space and time, with mobility as the primary indicator of class. An estimated 25 million persons work in foreign countries for global corporations. Trade agreements like NAFTA have eased restrictions on corporate and business executives, professionals, and highly skilled workers as they move from one country to another (Anderson and Cavanagh 2000:25). Capital's privileged classes tend to be globally mobile, unbound to place; they match the fluidity and liquidity of capital and traverse national borders with ease. Equipped with technologies of mobility – laptops, cell phones, platinum credit cards, and wireless connections to the global information system – the globe-spanning nomadic elite inhabits what Marc Augé describes as the "non-places" of supermodernity.

> Clearly the word "non-place" designates two complementary but distinct realities: spaces formed in relation to certain ends (transport, transit, commerce, leisure), and the relations that individuals have with these spaces . . . For non-places mediate a whole mass of relations, with the self and with others, which are only indirectly connected with their purposes. As anthropological places create the organically social, so non-places create solitary contractuality. (1995:94)

A 1999 Allianz ad entitled "The Promise" captured both the privilege and the anxiety of elite status. As a father prepares to leave for a business trip, his daughter plaintively pleads, "Promise to call me?" His odyssey takes him through the glamorous but empty contractual spaces of airports, hotels, rental cars, and electronic communication circuits. A global actor, assured and confident, he travels through spaces drained of time and place. The son of Capital, he is likewise liquid and flows across landscapes. Allianz insurance underwrites the circuits of capital connecting these non-places, the insurance to cover uncertainties in the ungrounded spaces of supermodernity.

The global insurance company fuses liquid global capital with concern and dependability, muting the logic of Capital through a familial analogy. Father is to daughter as Allianz is to its clients. Like a father who thinks about his daughter during his travels, Allianz always considers its insurees: "a promise is a promise. Wherever you are and whatever you do, Allianz with its global partners is the power beside you." And just as a father fulfills his promise to his daughter, Allianz will fulfill its promise.

Mobility. Covered by Allianz.
Risk. Covered by Allianz.
Performance. Covered by Allianz.
Technology. Covered by Allianz.
Life. Covered by Allianz.

A recurring social tableau depicts separation from family members and the psychological response of longing. Separately father and daughter gaze upward in their spatially abstracted solitude. Using slow motion, superimpositions, dissolves, and soft focus with the soothing lyric, "no matter where you go I will be with you," the ad pledges to keep alive organic relationships in a world of supermodernity that has been stripped of a mothering female presence. The moment of identity is the father/daughter relation; their pleasure and affect are connected to each other's voice. Satisfying as this paleosymbolic drama might be, the prospect of singular identity is unlikely to be found in the emptiness of non-places, "only solitude, and similitude" (Augé 1995:103).

Even the winners must confront the fragility of a world in which the social is falling apart. Modern business nomads who circumnavigate the globe may long for the warmth of place, but they settle for signifiers of affection: a photograph, a hair barrette, a faxed note, and a memento. Advertising representations capture the social and psychological contradictions of a fast-paced economy: euphoria and worry, change and uncertainty, possibility and risk, mobility and longing. The volatility and instability of a fluctuating market economy produce anxiety, and in advertising anxiety can be a powerful psychological force linking corporate brands to anxiety-alleviating strategies – investment for the future, protection of one's family, competing against invisible enemies.

Infrastructures of anxiety management

Advertising reiterates the prevailing business-channel wisdom that technological innovation generates a productivity advantage. But the ads also project consternation that technological change will precipitate obsolescence, or that inappropriate technological choices can spell competitive doom. The logic of Capital has long necessitated creative destruction; now this process has accelerated, folded along creases of time–space compression. Corporate ads celebrate the animating force of capital with images of triumph and accomplishment, while also revealing anxious undercurrents of uncertainty and nervous apprehension associated with the instability and rapid turnover of corporate structures, unremitting competitive pressures, market volatility, and the unforeseen consequences of technology choices. As Hobbes noted long ago, the marketplace that is a "war of all against all" induces perpetual fear as well as perpetual motion. Capital is in a perpetual state of motion and so are its functionaries, trying to keep up with competitors, innovation, and market volatility. Hence, technology firms like IBM, Microsoft, and Oracle market their services in a therapeutic voice, offering cool confident consultants or software that never gets rattled to restore a sense of serenity. In a business world that demands an incessant capacity for flexibility and adjustment, Microsoft Enterprise software makes the perfect employee because it does not have those pesky human emotions that would make it vulnerable – "the software is not flustered by this sudden turn of events, because the software does not fear change."

In a global economy, growth and survival are contingent on having an integrated technological infrastructure. Inexorable demands for efficiency and cost-savings amid an ever-shifting landscape of technological and organizational change contribute to chronic anxiety. The seemingly continuous overhaul of information technology in the business world puts additional pressure on executives who must select the appropriate technology. Not surprisingly, anxiety and failure ads frequently highlight executives who chose the wrong brand of technology. As the pace of computational change in the information economy accelerates the obsolescence of each "knowledge generation," knowing who to trust becomes key. Software and hardware ads depict corporate executives pressured to promise too much growth too quickly until their organizations threaten to snap. IBM's 2001 campaign crafted vignettes highlighting lurking techno-anxieties that haunt corporate leaders as they grow to their level of incompetence, followed with the tagline, "And that's when it hits you. You are so ready for IBM."

IBM addressed fears of downsizing following mergers and acquisitions in a 2001 ad entitled "The Axe." The title, tone, and dialogue suggest that a CEO will fire his chief information officer, who has already meekly accepted his fate. This anticipation reflects the volatile instability of the economy and the corporate labor market. However, his real disquietude begins when he learns that he is not fired but has been assigned the newly merged job, and with it a task that goes beyond his technical experience – "the hairiest integration project ever. With servers, storage, databases, it needs the right guy." All is not lost however, since with IBM one can outsource the expertise and the solutions in the form of "business infrastructure" services.

Apprehension about information technology deficits becomes compounded in other ads that address bewilderment about identifying the appropriate landscape at all. Another 2003 IBM ad pictures a young female executive restlessly pacing a psychiatrist's office as she recounts her dream: "I'm floating in water." Scenes depict her dream, seated with other executives at a conference table floating at sea. Her voice rising in alarm – "Can't you see we're adrift, we're lost" – she tries without success to turn their attention to the predicament. Hearing this, the psychiatrist interprets, "Ahhh, liquidity issues," to which she vehemently responds, "No, water, we're at sea! We're rudderless, we need help." In her dream account, her fellow employees ignore her distressed warnings because their petty status preoccupations ("this is Bob's meeting, Beth") preclude a culture of rapid response. What does her dream mean? Her psychiatrist reiterates the obvious: "That you're lost, adrift and need help . . . Call IBM Business Consulting."

Landscapes of fear are visually conceptualized in different ways, but most speak to anxieties of illegibility. A 2004 Siebel ad shows a boss interrogating his underperforming sales staff about lead conversion rates. They hesitate with their answers while visualizing their worst punishment fears, like being lowered into a vat of molten metal. But with Siebel's "more productive call center . . . say goodbye to that awkward, uninformed feeling." Magically, the mood changes and each salesperson answers again, this time knowledgeable and confident about new sales leads and increased conversion rates. As expectations concerning growth and productivity inflate, so do the terrors associated with meeting those expectations. Software makers particularly seize on graphic visual metaphors, such as being adrift at sea, to capture worries associated with the uncertainty of performing in a post-Fordist informational economy in which change is so pervasive that virtues of personal flexibility are simultaneously exercises in disorientation. Where mergers, corporate downsizing, and re-engineering are the coin of the day, and where career paths erode and destabilize, there exists a climate of vulnerability. Despite the therapeutic image of the psychiatric couch, the IBM ads suggest that the only therapeutic solution is a short-term commodity fix, and strangely, given a therapeutic culture that counsels repairing the self from within, the only way to solve the problems presented here comes with pleasing an external authority whose standards appear illegible (Sennett 1999).

Information technology workers

Rooted in the microchip, computer software, and telecommunications industries, the information technology revolution has spread out into enterprises across the economic landscape. Information networks and flows grew exponentially as corporate institutions adopted electronic networks – this began with financial institutions, and by 1990 "network applications occasioned a spectacular increase in capital expenditures that showed no signs of letting up" (Schiller 1999:16). With this expansion, demand increased for skilled information technology workers whose labors involve the "study, design, development, implementation, support or management of computer-based information systems, particularly software applications and computer hardware" (Information Technology Association of America 1997:9).

The telecommunications sector became a key driver of Internet expansion in the early 1990s. Telecoms invested heavily in the installation of routers and switches with the aim of providing integrated communication systems. Already deregulated in the 1980s, the telecommunications sector continued to be restructured by a focus on systems integration whereby corporations outsourced the management of their business computer networks to firms such as MCI and then WorldCom. "Digital capitalism" freed up corporations "to physically transcend territorial boundaries and, more important, to take economic advantage of the sudden absence of geopolitical constraints on its development." And, perhaps just as significantly, "the corporate political economy" began "diffusing more generally across the social field" (Schiller 1999:205).

By the decade's end, WorldCom would define itself around the *face* of its information technology employees. WorldCom's *Generation D* campaign positioned infotech workers as confident "in-the-know" employees who solve network problems.

Call them generation D.
The generation that was born digital and raised on the net, speaking a language of zeros and ones.
Now they're at WORLDCOM, developing web centers, the wireless Internet.
And for them it's a joyride.
Want to feel comfortable with new technologies? Work with people who are comfortable.
WorldCom. Generation D.

WorldCom pictured Generation D as youthful employees who navigate the architecturally open workspaces of a corporate campus on scooters, past clusters of fellow employees casually gathered in conversation. A young woman perched cross-legged atop a bookshelf with her laptop signifies a new kind of workplace – a relaxed and unregulated atmosphere where employees informally lounge about drinking coffee (or herbal tea), all digitally connected to their work via wireless laptops and handheld PDAs. There are no suits – no office dress code – in this office, because these are grown-up Gap kids.

They are not simply comfortable, but effortlessly at ease with themselves, with each other and their ultramodern, communal office spaces. Since they are not hung up on appearances, individuation takes the form of the unconventional. These unconventional moments define the landscape of the new corporate workspace by an absence of visible authority. The scooter represents the employee's mode of expression as he flows through the workspace, and thus iconically defines a playful model of behavioral motivation in the workplace. Akamai, another technology company that operates a global network of servers to distribute Web content, foregrounded the scooter as marking the new breed of worker in the network-structured workspace. Why pose a hipster information worker next to his desk that features, side by side, a state-of-the-art computer and a no less state-of-the-art high-tech titanium bicycle (cousin to the scooter)? Each signifier suggests an emblem of identity, and this identity is indicative of the company's personality. The scooter signifies an unalienated attitude to work, the intentional choice of free-thinking, value-producing individuals who choose to work for the kind of company that respects creativity by providing the casual informality of fluid, unregimented workspaces.

Firms in the networking and telecommunications sectors self-consciously view themselves as the cutting edge of the new capitalism, hailing the creative class of information technology workers.

They're young. And some just think that way. The people in companies who were born digital, or reborn. As comfortable with data as the last generation was with the telephone, as long as they have the right set of tools, and the right company behind them.

This advertising extends the social category of generation beyond age as merely an ascriptive category. Stressing their enthusiasm and caffeinated leisure, WorldCom turns a glossy translation of self-consciously quasi-hipster ambivalence into a picture of a nascent corporate stratum defined by its attitude to technology. Blending tech skills and corporate vision with a casual tolerance for risk, Generation D thrives on techno-social change. Work is play – it's a "joyride."

To be born digital is to be at ease with oneself and a network environment, to exhibit a certain habitus, ways of seeing and doing that are so deeply internalized that they trump race, gender, and social class. Even though representations of Generation D include overabundant signifiers of multicultural gender and race, these borrow from a bourgeois aesthetic device, off-center portraiture, to connote creativity and intelligence. Their culturally shared technological identity appears to shove aside social class as a classificatory device. Class connotes structure and hindrance; generational culture suggests choices, movement, and progress.

As a narrative device the serial montage has been widely adopted by information technology firms – particularly those competing in the networking sector (Cisco, Akamai, WorldCom, Verizon). Serial montages of this type accentuate a unified diversity of subject types. Each subject can be conceived as a serial node in the communication network, their shared connection constructed via the editing of their voices and their appearances within the framework of a corporate worldview. Spaces are open and without limits, contriving an Internet-simulated world without visible authority structures or hierarchy. In these landscapes suited to the expression of personality, work appears to be driven by desire rather than necessity, unbound by the parameters of either time or space.

Campaigns pushed the centrality of this technology-savvy stratum beyond the nation-state to a global scale connected not by place but by totem identity. Their totem identities testify to their allegiance to the corporate brands that stake out the territory of the resource landscape and thus make possible this new way of working. WorldCom's Generation D campaign defined its "in-the-know" employees as cool and confident, the vanguard of the future, committed to a corporation that supports innovation. The digital competency evoked by this global technocratic stratum promised freedom from techno-anxiety. Crafted by sequencing brightly colorful portraits to melodic, upbeat corporate techno background music, each subject within this global stratum directly addressed the camera in a tone infused with bold technological confidence. Stop-action photography created the impression of a global culture speeding across the background, while the portraiture composing the foreground stayed securely fixed. Hierarchy and authority seem non-existent; social connection is constituted on the lateral axis. Composed by differences of dress, gender, ethnicity, and location, this emergent subculture nonetheless speaks a common language: "Digital," or English with an accent, mixed with a few technical acronyms. This global stratum appears emancipated from the confinements of place-bound culture, even as it defines diversity by signifiers drawn from the spectacle of cultural geography. Disentangling the constraints imposed by antiquated expectations about the unity of place and culture occurs when a woman of Asian descent, wearing signifiers of an Asian culture, drawls "I'm from Oklahoma"; the disjuncture between cultural signifiers is sufficiently incongruous that the ensuing speaker raises an eyebrow. When an ostensibly liberated global society permits people to move freely across spaces, adopting a confident disposition towards digital technology shapes identity. Another frame flashes past as the name "WorldCom" and the address www.votedemocraticsociety.com appear on a wall as graffiti.

No such website existed. The irony that the address of democratic society could be put into .com domain must not be allowed to go unnoticed though, and let's not forget that WorldCom's financial collapse was rooted in old-fashioned fraud driven by the arrogance of power. Though these ads highlight flows – of ideas, of information, of services, of commodities – they repress the reverse flow and accumulation of capital and the undemocratic ways that accumulation pools.

Two faces of rhizomatic labor

In the giddy euphoria that surrounded the explosive growth of the Internet economy, the information technology worker seemed to have limitless opportunities. Companies aggressively competed for superstar programmers, and many assumed that salaries throughout high tech would follow suit. However, with the shake-out of the dotcom sector, the collapse of tech markets, and the increasingly rationalized integration of networks, this class may be turning into a new working class composed of cube farm info workers who experience mind-numbing computer work under constant oversight, the unvarying demands of bureaucratic deadlines, and the always looming re-engineering of jobs. As the entrepreneurs of the tech boom transformed their firms into ultra-competitive high-tech giants, their rank and file have been inexorably deskilled into lesser-paid tech specialists. It is by now a commonplace that software programming and call center jobs have migrated from the United States and Europe to India. The global search for cheap labor and subsequent downsizing extends well beyond manual labor as the search for cost savings moves up the infotech work ladder.

In contrast to celebrations of this technologically savvy stratum, Peoplesoft (1999) sketched a darker representation that stressed the incipient centrality of knowledge workers in the new economy. Rather than romanticize an airbrushed portrait of Generation D, Peoplesoft spoke in apprehensive tones about the absence of loyalty amid ceaseless waves of change. Peoplesoft's campaign skipped the fashionably multicolored plumage of the new tech workers, dwelling instead on the

Akamai fashioned colorful technological *qua* cultural landscapes populated by independent and apparently unconventional personalities. Their ads closely conjured up a rhizomatic landscape fashioned to permit the expressivity of those who perform the mental labor that will spark the new information economy. The ad intersperses flashing glimpses of high-tech workspaces with multicultural portraits of the digital artists who are the leading edge of painting, restaurants, and music. They appear supremely at ease with themselves, and, by inference, with their work. Spaces are open and unbounded and authority structures are invisible, where knowledge workers and cultural agents are free to express themselves via uniquely constructed pastiches of ethnicity combined with punk disregard for all past traditions of self-presentation. Theirs is an environment that is open and without walls or limits, simulating Internet spaces unfettered by hierarchical power relations.

Realpolitik of global capitalism as an uncertain and unstable landscape. The Peoplesoft ads opted for a didactic style, presenting chilling lessons in black-and-white about the perils of failing to be vigilant in the fast-changing currents of market forces. In the new corporate survival of the fittest, "Success today is network knowledge, intellectual capital. Inspire your people with the tools to collaborate. Nurture this and survive. Curtail it and become extinct." These are the new relations of production in the post-downsizing era, in which flexibility demands an ever-evolving panoply of shifting partnerships and alliances based on innovation and collaboration. Peoplesoft ads darkly counseled about the necessity of adjusting to the new social relations of production in an e-business economy:

> *This is your future – The next generation.*
> *They won't settle for life in cubicles.*
> *They will demand access to information to innovate, collaborate.*
> *Their branches will rupture your walls.*
> *Their only boss will be the best idea and it can come from anywhere.*
> *Will they want to work for you or the competition?*

"Their branches will rupture your walls." Networking collaborators cannot co-exist with old-school corporate organizations and boundaries. It almost seems as if this line was extracted from Deleuze and Guattari (1987) discussing the rhizome as the antithesis of the "arborescent" model of social organization "rooted" in hierarchical structures and linear thinking. Whereas the celebratory adulation of the hipster infotech stratum fashions a liberatory version of a rhizomatic landscape designed to permit the expressivity of those who perform the mental labor that will spark the new information economy, the ominous Peoplesoft landscape depicts the necessity of rhizomatic labor relations as a function of the rigid determinism enforced by a capitalist economic competition that has already "cut down to the bone." Here we see the other side of capitalist social relations – not as opportunities for personal growth as such, but as the conditions made necessary by the shifting contradictions of Capital. Hence it is not surprising that this new class of worker is given no face at all, no personification, in the Peoplesoft campaign – they are what they are, a necessary human capital component in the value production chain.

Towards the wireless office

Laptop computers, the Internet, and wireless communication technologies have opened up the possibility of new spatial arrangements for doing office work. In the capitalist workplace this presents clear tensions between the possibilities afforded by workforce flexibility and the fears of what might happen if employees are not continuously monitored for output. The same forces that unleash employees also countenance keystroke counts. Whereas the rhizomatic stratum might be encouraged to work at their own creative pace, less trust is afforded to those who are considered more readily replaceable.

A Haworth Office Furniture ad defined "The ins and outs of 21st-century business" with an instructive ideological summary of the changing parameters of corporate office work technologies in the new economy. Structured as a series of semiotic binaries – what is "out" and what is "in" – the ad contrasts archaic hierarchical forms based on access to closed offices ("out") with open, collaborative, and hence necessarily more egalitarian team spaces ("in"). The inefficiency of paper waste delivered to bureaucratically separated desk spaces has been supplanted by cool, digital efficiencies of e-mail as a means of working in a distributed manner. Airplane travel linking geographic spaces is negated in favor of electronic video conferencing: "Walls are out. Wheels are in." The flexibility of open architectures replaces the static formula of cubicles and divisions amongst employees.

The hell of being cubicle-bound is a recurrent theme among those who offer wireless solutions. Depictions of wireless freedom began in the mid-1990s with Sharp and MCI and have become a staple advertising trope in recent years amongst computer and telecommunications companies. Intel illustrates its injunction to "unwire" by showing people dragging their desks and chairs anywhere and everywhere – from football fields to loading docks to the edge of a 3-meter diving platform. Work becomes spatially unbound. A jogging financial manager in an Office.com ad for distributed computing services envisions a new pricing model and proceeds to work through the mathematical proof for the pricing model on the side of a dirty truck with his finger before rushing to a conveniently located Office.com outlet to send his idea back to the office. Office.com called itself "The new way to work."

In "Wireless Solutions for a Portable Planet," an Aether ad tracks a small start-up company consisting of four twenty-somethings riding around in their convertible, as they compete for a contract with a large – and smug – corporation. The semiotic contrast is easy to follow: wireless, youthful, mobile start-up in a red convertible versus a bureaucratic, fixed, and colorless corporate Goliath; and the winner is equally obvious as portability prevails. But the same technological forces that promote flexibility, mobility, and freedom can also be used to discipline, monitor, enforce, and control. A 2000 Nextel ad addresses this latter issue with a story about two corporate suits in Hong Kong. One man exults about being in Hong Kong where there is "no leash . . . no way for the office to keep tabs on you." At that moment his companion receives a phone call. When the wannabe slacker asks "What is that?" his companion declares "Nextel worldwide – works everywhere we do." The first man retorts, "Well that just means you're gonna have to work everywhere, Bob!" To which the second man replies, "Actually it means you do, I just got promoted, you work for me." As he snickers, we can almost feel the prison door slamming shut, but only for those who aren't savvy enough to embrace the most efficient communications technology – those who use it first, get promoted. First, the privilege of corporate work sets you free, then the technology catches up and there is nowhere to hide. Ironically, all ads that promote the panoptic potential of new technologies structure their narratives around humor.

Parables of career and technology in the new economy

The parable form permits advertisers to translate changes in the landscapes of technology and corporate organization into individual outcomes. By the late 1990s some ads hailed female executives, addressing questions of both success and barriers on the corporate ladder. A 1999 Micron Electronics ad promoting its computer technology takes place in a corporate cube farm, where an angry young female employee gains control of the scene and demolishes the workplace status quo.

Her ability to smash down old tyrants, antiquated hierarchies and inefficiencies stemming from obsolete technology ostensibly stems from a revolution in computing technology that makes conventional practices anachronistic.

Amid the hum of office noises in an office complex partitioned into cubicles as far as the camera will let us see, it is business as usual as male executives move along the corridor, briefcases in hand. The camera cuts to the blonde woman inside a cubicle as she slams her hands down on her desk and screams, "I will not do this!" Her face is a study in frustration and anger, as she asserts her refusal to work under these conditions, and her refusal freezes all action in the office space! "I will not be a cog in a machine," she exclaims as she seizes a golf club from the frozen grip of her white male middle-aged boss who had been strolling through the office, club in hand, when she arrested time. She marches deliberately across the room and swings viciously at a conventional computer monitor, smashing it as she continues delivering her manifesto: "I will not accept the obsolete!" Making the boss's golf club her assault weapon of choice symbolically captures, and reverses, the privilege of the old boy's club that runs the corporate show.

"Keep your corporate ladder," she defiantly growls as she takes another savage swing at a ceiling panel, shattering it irreparably. Using the master's tool to smash the notorious "glass ceiling" that keeps women from getting their just due in salaries or positions certainly makes a vivid metaphor. Spitting out her fury, she approaches her immobilized boss, and snarls directly into his face, "Keep your empty mission statements. I will never play by the old rules again!" The boss's head then cracks like a plaster mask and crumbles into pieces, an image that figuratively suggests a crumbling of his authority due to her defiance. This ad heralds nothing less than a reordering of capitalist relations of production because of changes in the forces of production (technology): "New Rules. New Tools." The reference to "empty mission statements" takes a swipe at faddish corporate public relations lip-service regarding product excellence and respect for employee work satisfaction. But this is hardly an anti-mission statement – despite its angry tone, it resonates with much of the rhetoric about corporate culture. Though the Micron Electronics ad represents an attack on a generic corporate workplace, "empty" mission statements typically weave together buzzwords that echo this call for "new rules," e.g., open architecture, working outside the box, and non-hierarchical culture.

An allegory about power in the corporate workplace, this ad implies a revolution from below, here waged by a woman denied leading-edge technology and her rightful place in the hierarchy of responsibility, discretion, power, and rewards. It offers a cautionary tale of what happens when the rhizomatic wannabe is treated as human capital (a factor of production) and denied the opportunity to fully express herself in her work. This story of empowerment gone awry may remind corporate executives that disregarding new technologies and their organizational implications can generate crises of morale, productivity, and even control. We are not sure whether one can build a new house with the Master's tools, but, in this story, the Master's tool can be turned to tearing down the walls, ceilings, and power structures of his building, while the new tools apparently belong to "everywoman."

Most post-2000 commercials tend to falsely presume that gender and race have been seamlessly integrated into the corporate hierarchy. The multiracial cast of males and females as executives, managers, financial consultants, investors, and spokespersons suggests an evolving corporate landscape that inclusively operates on meritocratic principles to produce both gender and racial parity.

Going up: networked mobility in the flat hierarchy

In 1998 AT&T told a story about the career fast track in an era of distributed organizations as a means of selling a narrative about how the speed and agility that businesses must achieve to stay competitive in a global economy depend on using communications technology that integrates organizational systems. A junior executive enters an elevator occupied by a bike messenger. At the next elevator stop, a female manager enters saying, "Matt, got your e-mail. Vancouver. Genius." Meanwhile the organizational technology narrative begins to unfold as onscreen the label "Linking Company Offices" appears over an organizational flow chart and pop-up images of managers in the Seattle and Portland offices to illustrate the process of moving an idea through a distributed, and synchronized, division of labor.

At the next floor another manager cheerily informs Matt about the progress his idea is making through the organization: "Hey Matt, idea's a hit in the Northwest. Expect love letters. I've got Purchasing checking suppliers." We see in visual counterpoint the diagrammatic connections stretching across the network via a computer software application that links supply-chain nodes. It seems that everyone in this organization knows instantaneously of innovative ideas and their movement. The celebration continues as colleagues greet him on successive elevator stops, with comments that track the process of vetting his idea: e.g., "Legal's putting it through the mill." Confirmation that Matt's career is on the ascent comes when a senior executive greets Matt with a casually bemused smile, "Looking a little golden this morning son." And sure enough, before exiting the elevator on the ground floor, an administrative assistant stops him, "you're wanted up top. Client briefing. Your Vancouver idea." As the elevator carries him towards his new status, Matt exchanges glances with the bike messenger, who acknowledges the junior exec's success with an approving nod.

Why measure a corporate technology by the approval of a bike messenger wearing a goatee and tinted shades? The bike messenger carries the authority of subcultural coolness and confidence. In the post-Fordist urban political economy, the bike courier offered a flexible means of circulating and delivering small batches of information as corporations downsized, outsourced, and spatially decentralized. And yet, like other elements of a post-Fordist universe, the courier is disposable, replaceable, and expendable. The significance of his look of approval rests on his symbolic presence as the antithesis of corporate culture – in the folklore of postmodern urban spaces, the bike courier has been constructed as a non-conformist risk-taking renegade who symbolizes freedom and refuses to be tamed by the rules of wage labor. Unbound by chains of corporate regimens, the hipster's nod of approval affirms that unconventional and innovative thinking will be recognized and adopted where it justifies itself.

This story of individual mobility in the new economy highlights the business rationality of networked decision making. An innovative idea can be turned into a marketable service in mere moments because AT&T technology electronically streamlines organizational decision making by linking all elements of a business efficiently with suppliers and customers. Across the landscapes of the new, networked capitalism, the best ideas win out because the ultimate arbiter is speed to market. The final scene shows the elevator ascending upward through the elevator shaft into the bright light of corporate salvation as the voiceover asks, "Want to take your business to the next level?"

As a narrative device, the elevator might seem better suited to an era of vertically integrated bureaucratic organizations, but here it conceptually frames a story about a geographically dispersed global corporation reshaping itself via the adoption of network communication systems to span geography and division of labor. As a spatial metaphor, the elevator suggests vertical movement through the built environment. But there is more to this elevator than directionality. This story takes place in a vintage elevator decorated by art deco aesthetics that signal a golden age of modern business. Its bas-relief bronze motifs signify the aesthetic of Metropolis, reminders of an era of material substance. Digital innovation does not appear to imperil the bourgeois heritage of business, nor does it require the negation of classic infrastructure. Visually highlighting and juxtaposing the elevator's mechanical functionality against the digital flows of information makes the elevator ride a convenient measure of the rapidity with which ideas move through the organization, while the elevator buttons chart a familiar indexical metric of individual mobility in which the fiftieth floor is the ultimate indicator of success. Images of organizational flow charts and screens of software functionality, intercut into the elevator narrative illustrate how network connectivity works in a distributed work environment. The commodity premise here is the linked organization – the coordination of functions and decision making when employees are geographically dispersed throughout large global firms. This implies a business organization with fewer bureaucratic levels of decision making to go through. Demonstrating the virtues of a "flat" organization, the ad still locates an authority and reward structure at the top. And if instantaneity of communications yields transparency of decision making, it does so by keeping authority visually muted yet panoptic.

Manufacturing labor in postmodern discourse

Factories appear few and far between as sites of production in corporate ads, especially when compared with other sites of value production – scenes of corporate headquarters or corporate research labs. The only consistency of factory representation occurs in corporate automaker ads in which nearly identical scenes of capital-intensive production facilities mark advertising for GM, Saturn, Ford, Mercedes, Acura, Honda, Hyundai, and Toyota. Such advertising features automated computer systems controlling precision technologies, while autoworkers appear in cameo, auxiliary roles. Spotless factories gleam and shine like the cars they produce, the site for graceful ballets of meticulously choreographed movements. Production is turned into an aesthetic, a fireworks display of sparks described as art. The occasional workers display the exactitude of technicians and the sensitivity of artists. As might be predicted, these ads are more about the manufacture of desire than the manufacture of industrial goods.

Manufacturing labor continues to disappear from the landscape of work in advertising that glamorizes the consequences of a globalized political economy marked by deindustrialization, offshoring, and outsourcing. The vast manufacturing districts of the western Pacific Rim do not appear in corporate advertising – in thousands of ads we found few visual references to factories in China and South Asia – except to denote the efficiency of just-in-time production (FedEx) or to depict an investment firm's (Morgan Stanley's) claim to understand the big picture of globalization.

Spectacular manufacture: Sparks represent the spectacle of manufacturing. The magic of spark showers, like fireworks, dances in red and yellow arcs to indicate the productivity of high-tech manufacturing equipment. Sparks most often appear as a marker of precision production when robotic arms are shown transforming raw materials into objects of value. Scenes of automated manufacturing, assembly, and distribution facilities represent both a boast about corporate productivity and efficiency, and a reminder that adoption of self-moving technologies also means that labor forces have been outsourced, downsized, or eliminated. Outside of automobile production, scenes of automation confuse assembly, packaging, and distribution centers with manufacturing facilities. In the current post-Fordist historical moment, such apparent industrial scenes speak to an important transformation in the configuration of production with the outsourcing of manufacturing to lower-wage offshore labor markets.

The infrequency of traditional factory imagery corresponds to the steady loss of North American and European manufacturing jobs over recent decades. During the 1970s and 1980s, when the ranks of US farmers diminished sharply, the farmer remained a TV icon for all the virtues of American workers. Representations of manufacturing labor sometimes become indistinguishable from those of rural labor – heavy labor and rugged individualism converge on the advertising landscape. Nostalgic representations of farmers and ranchers have not completely departed the scene, it's just that, *circa* 2000, their unadorned salt-of-the-earth work ethic was reintroduced to demonstrate how advanced technologies can sustain an otherwise declining way of life by making it more efficient. Microsoft tells the story of a ranch-oriented, rural Wyoming town where enlightened citizens are adopting advanced communications technologies to preserve a bucolic and romanticized country way of living. Farm communities have suffered enormously in recent years, hit hard by an epidemic of bankruptcies, the loss of jobs in rural industries, the erosion of tax bases, dismal schools, and the hemorrhaging of the best and brightest to sites of greater opportunity.

Male voiceover: This is Lusk, Wyoming. Cows outnumber people here 100 to 1. The thing that isn't apparent about Lusk is it's wired. Lusk has strung fiber-optic cable for the future of high speed Internet. The schools have 320 computers for 500 kids. Home businesses and PCs are common. Why? They're practical people. They want to talk to the outside world using technology. They want to save their ranches with technology. They want to talk to the kids who've left and keep more kids from leaving by having the technology. They want to save their small town and keep it exactly the way it is, and they're using everything they can think of to do that. Technology is a tool. Software is a tool. These are the dreams it's made for, and that's why we make it.

The Microsoft narrative puts an interesting twist on a Marxian model of social change. Forget the contradictions between the social relations of production and the mode of production – we now live in the era of re-engineering. Not just companies can be re-engineered, now communities can be too. Want to hold on to a form of social and cultural life that is no longer consonant with the macro political-economic forces of globalization? Then invest in the very technologies that make it expedient to go global. Microsoft imagines that new computer and communications technologies leveraged to take advantage of emergent political-economic contradictions can restore a practical vision of a prosperous Jeffersonian democracy.

The presence of labor unions has also diminished throughout the corporate advertising landscape. GM and Saturn stressed "partnership" with the United Auto Workers to highlight their general profile of corporate citizenship and as makers of quality products. Toyota campaigns show foreign capital creating new jobs in the US (200,000) without disrupting the nostalgic imagery of American landscapes. Toyota celebrates its manufacturing investments in the US with ads that include close-up shots of solemn autoworkers (non-union) devoted to tasks in the assembly of small trucks. These ads give no indication that capital-intensive vehicle assembly plants have diminished the workforce, deskilled the labor, and paid the remaining workers less than their historical predecessors. What began with blue-collar jobs has continued with the outsourcing of jobs from professional sectors – software development, telemarketing, accounting and financial services. The labor forces imagined in Cisco and Boeing campaigns actually reflect those firms' interests in trends towards global workforces connected through networks.

As a productive force, labor has lost its Promethean connotations, supplanted by smiley-faced service symbols (Wal-Mart), computer-controlled robotics, or numbed apparitions that impassively function according to script. The face of labor as heroic – the image of larger-than-life labor capable of conquering nature (and enshrined in the imagery of socialist realism) – has retreated from the site of production to a rural, de-industrialized landscape where the hard-working masculine demographic of traditional heavy labor (hardhats, construction workers, railroad workers, mechanics, welders, and men who tow or demolish) still roams.

Wal-Mart uses the smiley face to signal their commitment to consumers by slashing prices lower. The smiley face actually represents the unseen face of managerial practices (or, as one author puts it, "the ever less visible hand of the manager") that enable Wal-Mart to exercise control over manufacturers. Wal-Mart's logistics infrastructure imposes a relentless pressure upon manufacturers that forces them to continually shave their costs – for example, by chasing cheaper labor across the planet (Hoopes 2006; Petrovic & Hamilton 2006).

With their space of labor outdoors, close-up shots of calloused hands, muscled shoulders, and unsmiling, unblinking, weathered faces speak to the purpose, pride, integrity, and toughness of a form of labor driven to the margins by the transition to light capitalism. Ironically, the chains of heavy labor appear to be what makes them free subjects.

Another face of industrial labor today is positioned as a caricature to signify an inefficient mode of production compared to the instantaneous electronic circuitry that speeds processes of value construction online. The gray model of industrial organization once associated with depictions of the Soviet Union now comes to stand as a generic representation of an industrial process that yoked employees to a rigidly bureaucratic, antiquated, and outmoded system of rules, gears, and assembly lines. Computer-driven robots have replaced mechanically robotic behaviors.

Outsourcing the labor search

A central tenet of flexible accumulation is the need to adjust labor supply to the circumstances at hand. Reducing fixed labor costs and the long-term commitment of health care benefits has led to abandoned manufacturing plants in the US as well as the movement towards using temporary labor for light manufacturing and office work. Since the inception of capitalism, labor has been a commodity, but with the dotcom frenzy of the late 1990s came the invention of the online employment agency that sought a niche in the logic of corporate concentration and globalization – they delocalized labor markets, and offered to outsource the organization, coordination, and management of the hiring process so that client firms could outsource their labor requirements as well as downsizing their own in-house personnel and human resources staffs.

Companies that advertise in this space may hail employers or potential employees. The pitch varies accordingly. When addressing employers, the stress is more likely on recruitment issues – on managing an orderly and efficient process that identifies the appropriate skills while assuring a dependable and reliable supply of labor when needed. While this is generally a deadly serious matter for employers, the ads frequently lean towards a humorous tone of voice. Accountemps promotes its expertise in "specialized financial staffing" by making fun of a whining male executive who gets outflanked by a savvy female executive who knows who to call to get the job done. EDS advertises its experience in IT outsourcing by illustrating the perils of grabbing homeless people off the street to fill temporary IT staffing needs. When Hotjobs.com wants to impress upon employers the scientific precision of their panoptic sorting process in "pinpointing" the most appropriate job candidates, they opt to buffer the Taylorism of their pitch by sewing together a stylized pastiche of archived training film footage:

> *Female voiceover: Look potential in the eye. Searching for job candidates that measure up? Let us assist. The hot jobs database let's you gather and inspect only the best candidates. Our easy to use technology allows you to pinpoint the people with precisely the training you need, and enables you to manage the entire hiring process.*

When it comes to supplying manual labor, however, the visual tone becomes more sunny and sincere. Labor Ready is a multinational source of unskilled labor. Reflecting its claim that "Not all temps type" its ad orchestrated a montage of energetic working images that include janitorial services, catering, loading and unloading, unskilled construction, waste hauling and disposal, maid service, landscaping, window washing, and agricultural field labor:

> *Male voiceover: No matter what your business, if you need to move it, clean it, cater it, build it up or tear it down, you can use Labor Ready temporary labor. Just call 1-800-24-LABOR or order on line at laborready.com and you'll get all the help you need. You can find good help these days. Labor Ready. Dependable Temporary Labor.*

This is the public relations picture of a political economy of temp labor: "We help companies turn on-demand labor into a strategic advantage. No matter what the job, no matter how many extra hands you need, our team can show you how deploying the right workers can cut costs, increase efficiency, expand revenue opportunities, and make your life easier." The appeal to potential job candidates is about finding a future that is not alienated, by finding a meaningful job worthy of you! As labor markets become corporatized and globalized, these ads depict the negotiation of labor markets as hostile and perilous spaces that few can navigate without the aid of a branded online site to clear a path. Online employment agencies – Monster.com, Hotjobs.com, Thingamajob, and K-Force – promise more lucrative and satisfying jobs, by stressing the existing landscape of boring and alienating jobs. Competition among online employment agencies to differentiate their brand identities fed a contest to stylistically vary their representations of alienation. Hotjobs.com reprises the vision of industrial work as equivalent to imprisonment in a Soviet-era gulag work camp. The soul-crushing environment of factory work and conveyor belts is narrated by a melancholic song about dreams ("Rainbows are visions, but only illusions"), which ends with the vague hope that someday there will be a better life. To differentiate its image, Thingamajob ads claim to critique bureaucratic rationalization and commodification in corporate labor markets, with visual representations that offer a bleak vision from dystopian science fiction aesthetics.

> *Female voiceover: You are not a number.*
> *You are not a nameless résumé on a faceless website.*
> *You are not corporate cannon fodder.*
> *You are not a cog in a machine.*
> *Your destiny will not be determined by a keystroke.*
> *You are not a disposable commodity.*
> *You are a human being.*
> *Need a better job?*
> *Connect with a counselor at Thingamajob.com.*
> *Life 2.0 begins here.*

Shaved heads tattooed with barcodes signify the objectification of workers in scenes that create a grimly regimented vision of being a nameless, faceless cog. In this caricature of postindustrial jobs, movements are regulated – strictly controlled, over-disciplined, and standardized – and the forbidding spaces in which the "undifferentiated mass of automaton-workers" mechanically moves have been stripped of color and emotional vibrancy (Castoriadis 1997:116). As the manifesto builds to the declaration that "You are a human being," one shaved head (yours) breaks ranks. The Monster.com, Hotjobs.com, and Thingamajob.com ads depict existing work environments as deformations rather than as opportunities to realize one's personality through one's work. The online job searches don't promise to change the landscape of work, but do promise that their computer skills will make you one of the fortunate few who occupy a sunny job.

Corporate narratives of poverty

The vast disparity in wealth structured by globalization vanishes with nary a trace in advertising. As might be expected, television ads contain few references to the world's poor. Advertising keeps the material conditions of poverty out of sight, while adamantly refusing to acknowledge either structured relationships of inequality or modes of exploitation. Ads insulate elites from non-elites, keeping the global middle class in safe havens. Elites travel through the spaces of non-places, spaces generally depicted as desirable because they are devoid of social contact. When refracted through the lens of advertising, elites and poor may be even more segregated than in everyday life.

Advertising represents the global poor not as active subjects, but as tragic figures assisted by the compassion of Capital, usually in the form of charity. They have no voice. They are spoken for. Abstracted from conditions of poverty, the poor in developing countries are sometimes presented as the beneficiaries of corporate largesse and scientific – medical and agricultural – research. No form of resistance is visible or necessary, because, like everywhere else in these landscapes, matters of power and domination have been put to rest. Neither market forces nor concentrated corporate power appear to contribute to poverty in any systematic way. Rather, poverty and misfortune seem to follow familiar cultural geographic contours of race and continent. There is a curious absence of neo-liberal evangelism in these ads – no moralizing about how market forces will save the poor from corrupt regimes or starvation. These landscapes of globalization bear no signs of structural adjustment austerity programs and the harm they inflict on local populations in an effort to stabilize currencies and attract foreign capital. There are no hints of maquiladora zones, no wide-angle shots of ever-expanding urban slums, no global circuits of prostitution, no civil strife, no environmental destruction. Instead corporate brands (e.g., Philip Morris, American Express) represent themselves as the conscience of the world, devoted where necessary to enhancing the lives of the poor whose circumstances remain unexplained: simply their fate. Truly this is a simulacrum, for it has no original. The referent is imaginary.

Inhabitants of the third and fourth worlds – those places on the planet that are systematically underdeveloped, thanks to the legacy of colonialism, imperialism, and now globalization – do occasionally appear in corporate ads. Bringing a smile to Africans was the subject of a 1998 Crest ad that stressed educating the poor in developing nations about dental hygiene. Shot in Zimbabwe, the ad offers testimony about the efficacy of this humanitarian strategy. Rotting teeth have long been an easily identifiable signifier of poverty, and while a big bright smile might not erase poverty, it does seem to erase one of poverty's painful and ugly markers. The Crest ad is unusual in that it identifies the geographical and social location of its subjects, unlike the more generically abstracted images of third world peoples, where silhouetted images of women carrying baskets on their heads signify a new global prosperity.

Charities introduce images of undernourished, poorly clothed children who have names – like "Michelle." The naming process emotionalizes her, encouraging viewers to connect to her plight and make donations so that her poverty might be ameliorated. In charity ads, children don't smile, play, or run. Their saddened faces and tattered clothing draw attention to a body language of helplessness. Often depicted clinging to an adult or some dull inanimate object, they have no energy. Colorless, lifeless slums in the backgrounds remain unidentified – they simply permit us to locate the world's poor "overseas" in grim zones of semi-urban poverty apparently unconnected to markets, or politics, or wars that might have generated such squalor. A majority of third world people shown in television ads are children. This fits nicely with allusions to future transcendence. But corporate imagery differs from the gaunt representations that one sees in ads for charities seeking to stave off malnutrition, disease, and death among starving and mutilated children.

Childhood poverty in the developed world receives a different representation. In a series of images linking childhood with future potential, Cargill took the poverty out of being poor by espousing an ideology of universal humanism. Cargill succinctly reiterates a variant on the rights of man: here are the rights of children – every child is born not so much equal as special. This offers a noble vision – nourish "every [hungry] child on this planet" and imagine what accomplishments individuals contributing to the greater good will make. The goal of commodification is envisioned as a means to a greater end – feeding the children of the world and watching flowers grow:

> *Female voiceover: Every person on this planet, no matter how big or small – is filled with potential. Every mind, whether it exists in wealth or poverty has the ability to think great thoughts. Every idea, no matter who it comes from, is full of possibilities. Cargill believes this potential must be nourished, because the better we are fed the more we hunger to achieve.*

Keyed to the word "poverty," a child appears next to an abandoned British factory (deindustrialization), but the image remains uncontextualized – or rather, contextualized by the sweeping emotions of choral music and uplifting narration. With this narrative aesthetic, Cargill celebrates universal humanism and its ideological assumptions of abstract individualism. Though categories of social class, nationality, gender, and ethnicity are visually evoked, they dissolve against the

overarching abstractions of "every person" and "every mind." Cargill celebrates universal humanism by situating every child as a singular subject in its particular locale of global cultural geography. Cargill visually imagines itself as a corporation committed to feeding the children of the world, as if their empire of trade steers a progressive path towards achieving a healthy world. Not to be outdone, ADM's 2003 ad campaign superimposed faces of universal humanism over abundant fields of crops to hail ADM's role in feeding the world by using futuristic agricultural technologies. The limits of local ecologies will no longer matter when "In tomorrow's global food economy every crop will grow where it grows best."

Like Cargill & ADM, the Council for Biotechnology Information aired ads in 2001 that positioned their works as insuring progress against poverty. Airy and optimistic soundtracks narrate a montage that alternates between poor and privileged, between the global South and North. Biotechnology researchers explain how "golden rice" containing beta-carotene "can prevent blindness in millions of the world's children." While positioning biotechnology research as a route to first world cures for cancer, the ad also claims that genetic modification "is providing solutions that are improving lives today and could improve our world tomorrow" in agriculture. The Biotechnology montage closes with a Vietnamese woman holding her child, posed for the camera in a farm field. Behind her are fellow field workers, who remain anonymous, their faces hidden under the broad-brimmed hats they wear. They are all gently stooped over at their labor. But theirs remains abstract labor – it is the pose of labor rather than the labor itself. This depiction plays on our longstanding stereotypes of Asian peasants bent over in rice fields. Stoop labor meets glamor photography. Indeed, the photographic codes seem to veil questions of either coerced labor or the grinding poverty associated with this kind of field labor.

Amidst this display of labor, the frame of the Asian mother and daughter portrait acquires an aura of quiet dignity and purpose that may even be interpreted as exuding a confidence that the future belongs to them. She appears as a poster-figure of the world poor who will achieve future transcendence within a globalized economy of capitalist technologies. Positioned in the montage immediately following scenes of a white middle-class, American girl who has survived cancer and has happily resumed playing softball, poverty is no more visible in the Asian agricultural fields than in middle-class suburbs. Each scene is framed as an equivalent instance of how biotechnology research has produced discoveries "that are improving lives today" (suburbia) "and could improve our world, tomorrow" (the fields of the developing world).

How do images of third world peoples fit into any conception of capitalist relations of production? We have seen that poverty is represented as a function of providence – an act of nature, or misfortune, or corrupt leadership. Though it hardly seems possible in an era defined by globalization, third world peoples appear even less involved in systems of production than do those in the first world in these corporate ads. Political-economic forces are never shown in relation to social problems such as lack of basic needs – food, shelter, and medical care – but they are also repressed in relation to production. The reasons are obvious – there would be steep legitimation costs to pay if sweatshops, child labor, migrant field labor, shantytowns, and slums appeared in proportion to their frequency in the system of commodity chains that shapes global capitalism.

There are momentary exceptions. We have mentioned the FedEx representation of global just-in-time manufacturing in which disciplined squads of South Asian workers show up at otherwise quiet factories when they are needed to fill a European order. Fleeting images of third world youth, minus poverty, appear in montages for tech giants like Cisco, SAP, GE, IBM, and Microsoft. These ads see third world youth not simply as future consumers but as part of a future trained and educated global labor force. Recently, oil giants like the combined ChevronTexaco have quietly acknowledged that previous approaches to energy extraction may have mismanaged the environment and exploited third world peoples. But now, "Working together, we're developing energy faster. Developing people faster. And accelerating prosperity for all of us." Consistent with other corporate ads, Otherness is displayed with poised dignity – in fact these ads narrate the visual transcendence of poverty in the developing world, thanks to technology, investment, and "partnership."

Contradictions of the code

Summarizing the representational patterns in TV ads, we cannot avoid the self-contradictory character of this discourse. The same ads that deny the conditions of class also fantasize about the pleasures of privilege; the same ads that paint a utopian moment of retirement unconstrained by either scarcity or the performance principle also acknowledge that capitalist work relations are essentially a constraint on human potentialities; the same ads that betoken freedom and flexibility in new wireless electronic technologies also treat it as a necessary leash.

Taken collectively, these ads make it difficult to conceive of social relations outside of markets. And yet, conflictual market relations disappear from view. Generalized markets seem to float in the ether, without need for laws or authorities to enforce rules. In fact, one can scarcely imagine any market in the world that is as purely self-regulating as the electronic markets represented in these ads. While the ads glory in the supremacy of open markets, they are not so forthcoming about the rest of capitalism. Capitalism mostly lingers in the shadows, an absent presence that shapes everything, but miraculously leaves no imprint of its grip.

Corporations utilize advertising discourses to legitimize their practices by naturalizing and universalizing the social relations produced by capitalist economic formations. These discourses about markets and technologies, coupled with an absence of national boundaries or state institutions, leave the impression that, in an ostensibly post-Fordist network economy, corporations provide the conceptual infrastructure that holds together, and gives order to, the networks of production, distribution, consumption, and reproduction that constitute civil society.

Of course, consumer possibilities rather than production relations are the primary focus of advertising. The material production of commodities in factories, in workshops, or on assembly lines has all but vanished. When manufacturing scenes appear, computer-directed technologies seem to autonomously churn out finished goods on their own. Compared with twenty years ago, there has been a decisive shift from scenes of farmers, manual labor, blue-collar labor, and even generic white-collar labor, to scenes of small work groups clustered at computer monitors, in open-architecture environments, and without the presence of external authority. Commodities mostly appear in transit, highlighting the importance of supply chains and the transportation, communications, and distribution networks speeding packages and packets this way and that across the universe. Labor generally shows up only in finished products, such that living labor has no cultural power other than the romance of individual faces isolated onscreen, or in the magic of the branded totems that now carry the fetish traces of the ghosts of labor.

Adopting the landscape metaphor for our project has compelled us to reconsider whether or not these representations reflect changes "out there" in some political-economic reality? Do they disguise, distort, or falsify fundamental changes in the relations of production? Does Louis Althusser's (1971:155) formulation concerning the relationship between ideology and the media apparatus still hold? "What is represented in ideology is . . . not the system of real relations which govern the existence of individuals, but the imaginary relation of these individuals to the real relations in which they live." Marxian theory thinks of ideology as distorting real relations of production such that it conceals relations of domination. For Marx, the critique of ideology was simultaneously a critique of exploitation embedded in the actual practices of "equivalence exchange." But the representations that we have examined wander back and forth between referencing something akin to the real and constructing imaginary landscapes, not simply imaginary subject relations. Our research emphatically affirms Baudrillard's thesis, as restated by Smith (2003:3), that "in the topos of simulacra, any distinction between the represented image and reality vanishes as the historical contexts in which images were reproduced are effaced by their (re)production and circulation." But the conclusion drawn from this, that "finally all determinate processes are overthrown and recuperated by the indeterminacy of the late-capitalist code," is an ahistorical argument that cannot be empirically verified. It may be – at least in the sphere of capitalist advertising – that the "code" is not quite so unified, but is itself characterized by unevenness and contradiction.

Do corporate advertising landscapes constitute a simulacrum of an epoch in which representations radically eclipse the principle of referentiality? After poring through several thousand advertising texts, we are unable to cleanly disentangle what Baudrillard delineates as the "successive phases of the image" in the present representational moment. Baudrillard's (1994:11) "successive phases of the image," from representation to its negation in simulation are:

> It is the reflection of a basic reality.
> It masks and perverts a basic reality.
> It masks the absence of a basic reality.
> It bears no relation to any reality whatever: it is its own pure simulacrum.

Our reading of corporate ads suggests these "successive phases of the image" are not mutually exclusive. Elements of each phase of the image can be found mashed together in the current historical moment – sometimes within the same advertising text. Baudrillard's phases are less historical stages than ideal types that help us grasp the relationship between modes of representation and modes of production. Just as there has never been a moment in which the representation has been based on an exact equivalence of "the sign and the real," conversely there is no "pure simulacrum." Rather, a dialectical history of representation can be found recapitulated and negated in the present historical moment.

Whereas consumer-goods ads have become enmeshed in a meta-communicative winking about artifice that encourages some degree of reflexivity about what constitutes the "real" in ad-land, corporate ads adopt a range of metacommunication strategies that are more *sincere* in tone. Hence, whereas consumer ads can be read as locating the "real" neither in the text itself, nor in some external reality, but in the matrix of desire that constitutes the individual subject, corporate ads still seek to locate the "real" in an external reality, albeit a referential world that has been effectively refashioned by the over-mediated codes that now stand between us and the fuzzy referents of science, markets, and the social relations of production. Once again we are reminded that there may be a reason for the recurring use of fuzzy, blurry signification strategies – they refer to a world out there that we mostly "know" via the media frames themselves. As such, the "real" world of production drifts away from our capacity to conceptually map it with precision.

5

Landscapes of Speed: Blurred Visions of Capital

How do advertising representations of speed relate to a global system of producing time and space? Intertwined narrative frames that recur throughout TV ads consistently link speed to values of consumer freedom and market freedom. Portrayed as reducing friction and abolishing constraint, speed is also linked to values of productivity, efficiency and control in ads directed at investors. Speed often takes on a populist spirit – leveling hierarchy and putting an end to unfair
privilege. Instant information flows are cast as key to future profits as if approaching absolute speed can abolish all limits to capital growth. In these ways, speed is sometimes cast as a means to a glorious end – heaven on earth.

What we see on TV is, of course, not speed in and of itself but a simulation of speed – it is spectacular speed. Because depictions of speed on television are mostly visual, speed does not eliminate landscapes, but depends on the presence of visually signified landscapes for its own signification. Still, representations of speed often hollow out spatial landscapes. Places become spaces to be passed through. And speed, though it is sometimes paired with nostalgia, tends to be incompatible with any deep sense of history or memory. After all, if everything is always a perceptual blur of speed, a blur of things rushing past, it is difficult to grab hold of the referentials that go whizzing past. Representational speed negates the referentiality necessary for history and memory to be constructed.

Bound to questions of speed and its representation are questions about deterritorialization and time–space compression. So too, abstraction is inherently weighted towards representations of deterritorialization. How are matters of "place," "community," and "collective

memory" represented when older conceptions of time and space are
under pressure? What does it mean to conceptualize our moment in
history as taking place outside time and space?

Speed becomes equated with the visual semiotic codes used to signify
it. And, as viewers, we have learned to distinguish between multiple significations of speed – productive speed, speed of convenience, pleasure
speed, out-of-control speed, and frisson speed. We examine how ads
represent – sometimes as a signifier, sometimes as a narrative frame – the
speed of Capital. We have been interested in how ads picture material
spaces in relation to time and distance. We examine the relationship of
speed to flexible accumulation and practices associated with it – just-in-
time production, supply chain management, organizational flexibility,
system integration, and efforts to conduct markets in real time.

Breaking speed-barriers is not a new obsession. Speed of movement
not only signals our capacity for overcoming the fixity of geographical
distance (space), it also suggests the possibility for increased openness,
flexibility, efficiency, and productivity. Because the amount of labor
required to produce a commodity could be readily measured in units of
time, capital has historically measured value in terms of time inputs. It
stands to reason that our "common-sense" understandings of technologies of speed point towards a future liberation from material scarcity
and the necessity of labor. In contemporary society, where time itself
has become perceived as a scarce resource, appeals to instantaneity and
immediacy are seductive. Has speed annihilated spatial distance? Paul
Virilio (1995a) observes that a fundamental transformation occurring
today "is the invention of a perspective of real time." Virilio sees a dark
side to the hegemony of speed, contending that hyperspeed induces
a general "loss of orientation" (1995b). Sometimes referred to as
time–space compression, sometimes as deterritorialization, this process
threatens/promises to transform not only the ways in which we work
and do business, but also the ways in which we conduct and experience
our private lives.

Real time and time–space compression

Karl Marx, writing in the *Grundrisse* in 1857, anticipated how the contradictions of Capital could spur on the "annihilation of space by time."
He wrote, "While capital . . . must strive to tear down every barrier . . .
to exchange and conquer the whole earth for its markets, it strives on
the other side to annihilate this space with time" (1973:538–9). The
rhythms of business life have changed – time has compressed, pace has
accelerated, and the materiality of distance has shrunk. "Time–space

compression" consists of "processes that so revolutionize the objective qualities of space and time that we are forced to alter, sometimes in quite radical ways, how we represent the world to ourselves" (Harvey 1989:240). Speedier methods of transporting material goods, information, and people have helped conquer spatial barriers while communication technologies shrink distance. As distance has been overcome, time too becomes compressed.

Electronic technologies are dedicated to speeding things up – more CPU power can mean more cycles per second, and hence more "work" and greater productivity. In a world obsessed with cutting out wasted time and going faster, experience may grow more fragmented and ephemeral. Harvey sees speed and flux destabilizing the spatial and temporal relations that underlie secure social formations (1989:238–9). Abstract spaces relentlessly peck away at, and replace, places. Though we are loath to romanticize "place," this historical process does draw out "place-bound nostalgias" (1989:218). Advertising, by contrast, frames this as unmitigated progress – "the goal is giving people back time" (AT&T).

Corporate advertising embraces the quest of real time in a variety of agendas. With general issues of competition in the marketplace, speed becomes its own justification where faster to market increases profits. The instantaneity of computerized stock trading brings the promise of lower costs and the premise of fairer trades. Real-time technologies also promise to integrate complex and far-flung divisions of labor within a globally extensive corporate world. Being able to monitor sales and inventory supplies on a minute-by-minute basis portends control of costs and integrated systems flows. But absolute time–space compression seems the most tangible in the video simulacrum where it is simulated via the magic of cameras and computers.

To investors, the speed of a trade's execution is pivotal. The trade that takes place in real time is the Holy Grail, insofar as all market information is time-sensitive. The slower the transaction of a trade request, the less advantaged one is in the marketplace. Hence, the transaction speed of brokers becomes a crucial feature of their competition. A year-2000 Datek ad took an imaginary trip through the simulated circuitry of the trading system's computerized innards, inviting viewers to experience the speed of an electronic transaction just as if you were on a roller coaster. Datek promised every trade would be executed within 60 seconds; by 2004 Ameritrade guaranteed the execution of market orders in 5 seconds or less; and by 2009 advantages of milliseconds were being exploited to arbitrage billions in profits (Duhigg 2009).

Among corporate competitors, "real time" is immediately a matter of profit imperatives. IBM's 2001 campaign situated the matter of real

time in ominous and menacing tones: either compete in real time or
become extinct. Inexorable market forces cannot be resisted or debated.

*Tick, tick, tick . . . When your assets are on the line, Real Time is the only time.
How do you win? With powerful software that can start work now.*

The insatiable appetites of market growth demand greater speed in the
circulation of capital. The forces of capital-driven markets are likened
to the laws of nature: "Time waits for no man or woman or business
. . . everything faster. Products to market, ideas to profits." In IBM's
narrative, the structural imperatives of capitalism have left room for no
other logic to influence the decisions and choices that actors must make.
IBM spells out the contradictions of capital accumulation contingent on
speed of circulation – as capital matures, intensified competition shrinks
profit margins, so that being faster to market brings with it competitive
advantage and offsets the tendency for the rate of profit to decline. But
going faster carries its own price, it pushes competition into the realm
of circulation time. However panic marketing offers a quick way out:
"powerful software" (scientific magic) can tame the imperatives of
market speed by controlling real time – the absolute present.

Telecommunications companies intent on selling bandwidth technologies situate the mastery of real time in terms of the immediate
availability of all information and knowledge, anywhere and anytime.
Firms like Qwest imagine that real time refers to the totality of instantaneous consumption options available in the here and now. In the
universe depicted by corporate advertising, all phases of the capital
circulation process became characterized in a similar way – one can
consume instantly, trade stocks instantly (e*trade and Ameritrade),
make markets instantly (NYSE), distribute goods overnight (UPS and
FedEx), and share ideas instantly (AT&T). Hence the insistent repetition of NYSE's 1999 choral refrain – "Right here. Right now. Right
here. Right now."

Such representations are tied to imagery of a global civil society
suffused by a spirit of prosperity, civility, and freedom from want or
conflict. An aggressively competitive marketplace is shown giving rise to
a civil society that seems marked precisely by the absence of competitive conflicts. In stark contrast to the speed of technology and business,
the relationships of civil society seem caught in a time warp. Baudrillard
sees in this speed a paradox of history, for history has come to a stand-
still, even though its internal mechanism whips along at hyperspeed.
Indeed for Baudrillard it is the logic of hyperspeed and accelerated
growth that has arrested history.

Corporate ads likewise imagine a curious "end of history" and an "end of ideology" (as absurd as this might seem given current global conflicts). Advertising envisions an end to history made possible by the mastery of speed in the marketplace. Given that these ads envision a post-Fordist economy, the question of speed in business has less to do with production processes than with the circulation time of exchange. The difference between Baudrillard and the advertising vision is that in the ads, hyperspeed produces not a living death, but a virtual paradise on earth. Hence we find the curious propensity for weaving together speed with slow motion in television ads to signify the advantages of speed in our lives – the opportunity to live deeply in the moment. Whereas economic time speeds up in these representations, turning laborers into a ghostly blur, consumer citizens appear to jerk back and forth between convulsive immediacy and nostalgic slow motion.

The visualization of slow motion – the elongation of time – can also signify speed across space. The spatial unification of time promises the temporal coordination of widely dispersed global markets. Like its competitors in the computer software industry, Microsoft markets real-time solutions to the problems of business integration in a global marketplace by compressing time and space into but "one degree of separation." An accident in a wine storage room visually unfolds – as bottles fall and break in slow motion, a manager on the opposite side of the world uses a handheld device to calculate the abrupt spike in prices for the wine as supply diminishes throughout the supply chain. Distance and time are no longer obstacles to the perfect information flows necessary both to inventory controls and to integrate supply and demand. Global markets across space and time become unified and synchronized. Speed, or rather the perception of speed, also disappears because it is no longer necessary to accentuate speed when there is but one singular global space – one degree of separation.

Speed of Capital

In *The Communist Manifesto*, Karl Marx and Friedrich Engels (1978) penned the famous phrase, "All that is solid melts into air," to highlight Capital's propensity (under the direction of the Bourgeoisie) for an accelerated pace of change. Later, when Marx wrote about labor time as the central determinant of exchange value, he dwelt on the fact that speed would be a crucial variable in developing capitalist political economies. Marx recognized that a labor theory of value depends on a theory of speed – or, more properly, a theory of accelerating production – to historically grasp the value composition process. Drawing on the theory that labor is the source of all value, Marx focused the labor theory of value on a critique of exploitation. Within his argument about the structural character of unequal exchange, Marx showed how capitalists recognized time, or more specifically labor time, as the crucial measure of value in its reified form – namely money. That way, Capital could make diverse forms of labor commensurate via a universal standard of measure. The category of wage labor rests precisely upon abstracting from any particular kind of labor the time expended in labor as measured in hours and minutes. Our measures of efficiency depend on this.

Marx pointed to the general speedup in production processes when addressing the contradiction between the commodity form and the dead time that occurred in the cycle of commodity production, distribution, sales, and reinvestment. Marx referred to this phase of capital in the circulation of commodities as "fallow time" or time "at rest" – his point was that such time represented "negated" capital (Marx 1973:546, 621; Harvey 1982:85). When capital takes the form of stock inventories, this is time when capital cannot be "at work." Delays in the circulation of the commodity through its cycle represent opportunity costs, for time spent in warehouses, or sitting on shelves, means that the money equivalent of that commodity cannot yet be reinvested to "earn" more return on equity. In short, time spent in circulation is time not spent in production or commodity realization.

> There is, therefore, considerable pressure to accelerate the velocity of circulation of capital, because to do so is to increase the sum of values produced and rate of profit. The barriers to realization are minimized when the "transition of capital from one phase to the next" occurs "at the speed of thought" [Marx 1973:631]. The turnover time of capital is, in itself, a fundamental measure which also indicates certain barriers to accumulation. Since an accelerating rate of turnover of capital reduces the time during which opportunities pass by unseized, a reduction in turnover time releases resources for further accumulation. (Harvey 1982:86)

Marx defined circulation time in terms of how long it takes to "realize the value embodied in the commodity through the exchange process." The speed and efficiency of the transformation of the commodity form of capital into money capital is pivotal to the reproduction/expansion of capital (Harvey 1982:62, 71).

Since Marx wrote, Capital has evolved institutional mechanisms for overcoming drags on commodity reproduction. The massification of the credit system in the early twentieth century still stands out as a dramatic intervention. The nurturing of marketing and advertising systems to stoke up additional demand for goods comprises another familiar approach. But competitors mimic each successful intervention, so that every advance in shortening cycle time contributes to a further quickening of commodity circulation, until today the structural imperative for speed and turnover has become basic to marketplace competition.

Speed has as its referent not just time but also distance. Speed refers not only to how quickly or slowly the digital pulse of a timepiece moves, but also to movement across space. For competitors like FedEx and UPS the question of speed refers to how fast they can transport goods from one geographic site to another place. FedEx and UPS have defined themselves as supply chain management specialists, each claiming the ability to move as fast as is necessary to keep up with the integrated global supply chain so that clients can maximize market opportunities while minimizing warehousing costs. For firms like Amazon.com, the question of speed refers to the absence of time spent in physical infrastructures – the effort to overcome the idle time of products sitting on a shelf that Marx referred to as a barrier to value realization. Amazon.com's business model touted its advantages as a cyber-business – the store online as opposed to the more prosaic land-locked storefronts: land and buildings have rents, taxes, and insurance costs associated with them.

In the semiconductor sector, the question of speed refers to how rapidly a microprocessor can cycle and cycle again, both reiterating and driving the general capitalist tendency (during the era of post-Fordism) towards acceleration in the rate of circulation. If Moore's Law states that chip capacity doubles every eighteen months, what should we expect with respect to the circulatory speed of capital itself? What are the limits? Teresa Brennan (1993:147, 150) observed that the space–time of short-term profit – what she calls the "consumptive mode of production" – comes into conflict with the "generational time of natural reproduction" and, in the struggle to overcome the contradictions of the profit mechanism, the market-driven "space–time of speed" eventually "takes the place of generational time." Brennan's distinction hinges on the assumption that generational time has organic (biological) limits. But does it? Not according to the mass media – which with their own axe to grind have held that generational time itself has undergone a speedup in recent decades, shrinking adolescence into a series of fashion cycles. This prompts concerns about how children are growing up too fast, losing out on the romance and innocence of childhood. Generational time itself has been turned into a commodity and is thus subject to the same internal pressures as any other commodity.

Brennan poses a contradiction between the "competing dynamics" of the speed of capital, driven by the demand to realize short-term profits, and the existence of "organic time" (the natural order) whose rate of reproduction must remain relatively constant (1993:133). Is this organic time, the pace at which generational change takes place, a question of empirical reality or metaphysics? The premise here is that both humans and nature become fundamentally alienated and deformed by the social contradictions of speed as capital "governed by the speed of acquisition and expanding scale" feverishly churns up human and natural resources (2003:160). Perhaps because we still want to believe that our most inherent sensibilities will prompt us to snap back against mounting forms of capitalist-mediated technological alienation, this argument about a fundamental schism between the accelerating cycle time of commerce and the "natural" time of organic life remains inviting. A myth of organic time beckons because it offers the prospect of achieving a form of spiritual salvation. The landscapes of speed fashioned by corporate ads seem to recognize this tension and oscillate between pictures of speed as a means of dominating our business environments and speed as a means of preserving organic forms.

Blurred labor time

A 2001 Cisco ad visits an integrated just-in-time production system for manufacturing and shipping bicycles. Located in a warehouse/production facility, the ad distorts and speeds up motion to create an impression of hyperactive productivity around the axis of a packing crate (the primary signifier for on-time inventory). The music races along, relentlessly hyperactive, edgy but energetic, framing a manufacturing and shipping process that also races along in a blur of motion. Once again, both the method of signifying speed and the ultimate signifier of speed is time-lapse photography. Though time is accelerated, space is held constant as the camera circles the men and the packing crate. Holding space constant, Cisco technology races to eclipse temporal limits, and with them the asynchronous dilemmas – inventory problems, "too late, too soon" bottlenecks – that cut into operating margins. Of course, the goal and the achievement in the advertising narrative is to get as close as possible to frictionless synchronous time.

Accelerating the video simulates the speed of an Internet-facilitated just-in-time production process. Depicting speed via video time-compression is not a new technique, but it is pivotal to the representation – film a day's worth of activity and compress it down to 15 seconds. What remains is the perceptible blur of meaningful activity, rather than the meaningful specificity of the activity itself. And yet as the ad winds down, as it seeks to drive home its message about gaining control over the inventory process, the music calms and soothes out, and the video slows to focus on a title frame that reads, "Inventory management on the Internet." This gives way to a computer screen showing part inventories and an image of the "black widow [bicycle] crank," followed by a sequence of nearly-still scenes of detail work – an older craftsman checking a bicycle wheel as it slowly rotates and a welder poised to fuse together a frame.

Why follow the imagery of a high-speed workspace with portraits of craftsman-like characters? The pace and duration of these scenes suggest the persistence of craft in production. A hint of nostalgia surfaces in this moment of apparent stillness, albeit nostalgia for the future of a computer-facilitated craftsmanship. This mythological revival of craftsmanship depends upon the semiotic opposition between the faceless blur of a workday in which, truly, workers have become just another factor of production (Braverman 1976), and the most stable image in the commercial, the older worker's face. Cisco suggests that harnessing the power of the Internet returns the face of humanity to work. While all other workers have been blurred into fleeting anonymity, his is the only face recognizable as such, the only face on which we can see the traces of motivated subjectivity. An ensuing image of a welder as a signifier of a skilled producer is also mobilized strictly for the purpose of signifying the craftworker, since he too merely feigns the act of work.

Compressing three moments of history, this Cisco ad moves from the blurred hyperspeed of post-Fordism to the uninterrupted production of the industrial assembly line to the aesthetic gaze of craftwork from a preindustrial era. Behind the male narrator's softened tone the background music shifts from a frenetic pace to slower chords, suggesting that speed can be controlled with Cisco products.

Your business depends on inventory that arrives right on time.
Too early it costs you money.
Too late it costs you customers.
You can use the Internet to make sure your inventory arrives
exactly when you need it and each customer gets their order
exactly when they want it.
Discover all that's possible on the Internet.
Cisco systems
Empowering the Internet generation

But what values does Cisco promote in depicting human labor as a time-compressed blur? And what is the relationship between a time-compressed labor process that adheres to the competitive logic of capitalist time and the almost paradisiacal craft labor time that Cisco technology makes possible? Such ads distinguish pure speed from controlled, managed and integrated speed. This advertising suggests that a competitive advantage can be gained by synchronizing the division of labor via the Internet as a technology that permits the asynchronous management and coordination of data. Though the logic of Capital pushes to continually speed up production to extract more out of labor, Cisco imagines computer-assisted inventory management will somehow cultivate un-alienated labor. Every movement of the laborer may be geared to the predetermined movement of objects, but Cisco promises that within a context of high-velocity system speed, labor speed can unify body and spirit.

Friction-free flow

Capitalist investors know that as industries mature profit margins tend to shrink due to competition. From the other side of the coin, the idealization of free markets recognizes that any form of governmental regulation creates friction, and thus reduces profit margins. Deregulation sought to eliminate the latter type of friction, but unregulated competition accelerated the competitive maturation of industries. Particularly amongst companies in the telecommunications, computing, Internet, and software sectors, ads portray the speed of competition and the means of coping with it as dependent on the intelligent deployment of new technologies to both accelerate and integrate the cycle of production. Productivity is seen as a function of the velocity of the flow of objects, goods, personnel, services, signs, and data that move through organizations and extra-organizational systems. But how fast can the flow move before systems break down? On the flip side, what are the obstacles and friction points that limit or restrict velocity?

The premise of a friction-free economy harkens back to Adam Smith's model of a market driven by an "invisible hand" that assumes all market participants share complete access to unrestricted information flows and act rationally. This is an assumption that even Thomas Hobbes would have rejected, recognizing that power not only comes from having access to all relevant information, but often accrues to those actors who can take advantages of disrupted and uneven flows of information. Indeed, the rationally maximizing market agent is one who may in fact instigate bottlenecks and delays to maximize self-interest.

In a global economy, it is no longer enough to run an organization efficiently. Efficiency must now extend beyond organizational structures into the circulatory world of supply chains. When consumers come armed with "smart" credit cards and wireless technology and are encouraged to expect that all commodities and services will be within 24 hours' reach, corporations are expected to design friction-free response mechanisms. On the other side of the supply chain, B2B providers promise just-in-time delivery of production materials. Flexible, friction-free integration of supply chains is an oft-repeated mantra in the corporate world of globalization (Friedman 2006). Advertising addresses this in two ways. Commercials often depict episodes of failed integration in which corporate employees and executives confront system breakdown. Against the backdrop of overwhelming anxiety associated with failure and the threat of job loss, corporate brands offer to provide services that can keep complex technological systems from failing. On the other hand, orchestrated by upbeat musical scores, integrated firms such as GE and Siemens depicts its systems' capacity for fluidly responding to the unpredictable nature of fast-moving competitive decision making. The imagery of integrated instantaneity permits undisturbed production to continue seamlessly.

An emphasis on blending speed with integrated supply chain management highlights ads for firms like UPS and FedEx with a special interest in depicting globalization as a coordinated corporate division of labor organized around the flow of information data and goods. Central to this vision of a logistics landscape is the capacity to surveil the rates at which data and materials flow along complex supply chains. In *War in the Age of Intelligent Machines*, Manuel DeLanda observes that "a commander must track the points at which friction may be dispersed within tactical command systems in order to preserve the efficiency and integrity of a war machine during battle." The commander's role is to disperse "the 'friction' (delays, bottlenecks, noisy data) produced by the fog of war" (1991:61, 23). In this vein, UPS depicts a CEO confidently declaring that UPS's "technology helps me see my supply chain minute by minute." Not only must the organizational apparatus run friction-free, it also must continuously monitor the entire supply chain to locate the position of any object (or the data simulation of the object) as it moves through the chain. UPS sells itself as a self-contained system that accelerates the flow of objects and data while simultaneously tracking every element. Scanning technology and tracking numbers position every object in the flow. Increasingly, this technology has been applied to human movement across borders, through airport terminals, across toll bridges (EZ Pass), and at cash registers.

Contemporary social spaces are designed to facilitate greater efficiency of transactions with customers. Wal-Mart, like the large grocery mega-markets it competes against, works to technologically streamline the purchasing/exiting function, so as not to slow up the transactions that may follow. A 1999 IBM ad played with the fine line between dystopia and utopia in depicting the supermarket of the near future. A trench-coated man walks through the aisles grabbing goods and stuffing them in his pockets. Egged on by the dramatic music and the surveillance camera watching him stuff his pockets full, we assume he is shoplifting. And as he exits the store, a security guard calls out for him to halt: "Excuse me sir. [pause] You forgot your receipt." The speed and invisibility of total scanning technologies permits the abolition of "check-out lines" – one of the time vortices of everyday life in the modern world. This is a lonely, cold, and asocial vision of consumption, but an entire shopping cart barcode scanner promises self-service (elimination of labor costs) and greater speed of transaction in one move, along with the comforting extension of panoptic security.

A 2006 Visa campaign vividly brought consumer spaces into the imagery of friction-free commerce. Its ads visualize the circulation of commodity interactions paced with choreographed precision. One Visa ad imagined a deli as a space of perfectly Taylorized flows. Perfect synchronization between producers and consumers allows consumers to stream through the delicatessen without skipping a beat. Sandwiches are made, bags are packed, and drinks served without wasted movement or time. But when one man attempts to pay with cash the finely tuned supply chain of food comes crashing to a halt – trays of food fall to the floor, juices spill, and there is, as Mary Douglas (1966) put it, "matter out of place." Fellow customers glare at the cash user with irritation because he has slowed/inconvenienced them. When the next customer swipes his Visa card, the music resumes and the rhythm of the deli returns. The voiceover explains, "The Visa check card. Because money shouldn't slow you down. Life takes faster money. Life takes Visa." The moral of the story is that money is an archaic form of exchange that has been supplanted by the more rational, the more liquid, form of electronic currency.

As a landscape of capital, Visa's staged deli rhythms stand for the managed synchronization of a universal system of integrated consumption. The advantage of electronic currency though falls primarily to the system, even though this staged representation suggests the individual consumer benefits from the enhanced convenience. The truth is that paper money impedes the speedy flow of a hypermodern system of commodity circulation.

In Visa's account of life, "the world of consumption and mass communication appears like a waking dream, a world of seduction and ceaseless movement." The subjective experience of the lack of time exerts increasing pressure on both organizational and everyday life: "In hypermodernity, there is no longer any choice or alternative other than that of constantly developing, accelerating the movement so as not to be overtaken by 'evolution': the cult of technocratic modernization has won out over the glorification of ends and ideals" (Lipovetsky 2005:36, 34). The colorful dream-like flows of people and objects in Visa's deli are a product of their opposite – systemic technocratic rationality. Visa's daily dance of commerce appears choreographed with clockwork precision only because the montage structure of the ad permits the artifice of video editing to sequence music and movement so effortlessly. In this model of hypermodernity, flows of people are matched to the flows of commodities and the flows of capital. Here consumption is no longer even an end in itself, but merely a means to the continuous reproduction of a system of circulatory flow.

In this simulated landscape of perfect circulation, people and commodities share a systemic equivalence – they are all reduced to objects in motion. Neither worker nor consumer needs to think, but merely to execute their predetermined movements. Though Visa simulates a commodity space of utopian sociability, it is precisely sociality that is missing here. There is no banter with the store clerks or other customers – not even time for a thank you. This stylized account of seamless consumption is not so far-fetched, it resembles recent trends in the fast food industry where interaction between customers and service is minimized and set to a prescribed script, like McDonald's six steps of service, relaying drive-through orders via Indian teleworkers in order to shave precious seconds and speed up the flow. The real virtue of "fast money" is that it reduces to an almost-vanishing instant the social relations that are embedded in so-called "equivalence exchange."

The casino cyborg: speed, simultaneity, and identity

Critiques of free-market capitalism often bemoan the consequences of social disintegration. The volatile instability of global markets can devalue the economic base of real lives, or in more macro-scenarios can lead to the collapse of national and regional economies. Strange (1986:9) calls this instability "casino capitalism," a phenomenon she links to five trends: innovations in how financial markets are structured; the sheer size of markets; commercial banks turned into investment banks; the emergence of Asian economies; and the shift to self-regulation by banks. The speed at which globally interconnected markets operate, combined with their nearly universal extension across the planet, results in volatility that links everyone. In *The Crisis of Global Capitalism*, investment king George Soros (1998) highlighted the potential for disequilibria in the financial system, and the inability of non-market sectors to regulate markets. John Gray echoes concerns that "national governments find themselves in environments not merely of risk but of radical uncertainty." Gray blamed neo-liberalism for weakening social and political institutions in both first and third world nations: "In the late twentieth century there is no shelter – for corporations or for governments – from the global gale of creative destruction" (Gray 1998:74–6).

Mergers and takeovers, institutionalized market volatility, and the velocity of technological change contribute to unpredictable employment histories. Sennett (1999) explored the impact of flexible capitalism across generations of workers for whom the rules of success have become increasingly illegible and job security increasingly tenuous. Technological innovation drives organizational instability and destabilizes whole sectors of the economy, both eliminating and deskilling jobs. Especially in the realm of technical knowledge, skills become quickly superseded. Negotiating the volatility and unpredictability of the economy is coupled with the anxiety of precarious uncertainty that now lurks on the edges of one's work.

Advertising acknowledges market volatility and the creative destruction that accompanies the technology arms race as shadowed risks that loom in the background. The risks take the form of investment insecurity, failure to innovate technologically, lack of flexibility and speed, or being overwhelmed by information. But with risk there is opportunity. This is the premise of an IBM ad (2000) featuring a young businessman seated on a bench surrounded by pigeons in an Italian piazza. Wearing a voice-activated computer, he excitedly buys and sells commodities and jubilantly leaps into the air with each successful exchange, sending the flock of pigeons into flight. After his last sale, his computer phone rings and he lets his significant other know the meeting went well and he is taking the next flight home. "Traveling light, rather than holding tightly to things deemed attractive for their reliability and solidity – that is, for their heavy weight, substantiality and unyielding power of resistance – is no asset of power" (Bauman 2000:13).

IBM's young entrepreneur travels light in many senses. First, his technology is light, a wearable computer with a wireless connection to the Internet via a global communication network. The computer screen is miniaturized for his eye. The computer itself is not visible. Voice-activation frees his hands to feed pigeons as he interacts with a global economy. "Wireless communication technologies diffuse the networking logic of social organization and social practice everywhere, to all contexts – on the condition of being on the mobile Net" (Castells, Fernández-Ardèvol, Qiu, and Sey 2007:258). Second, his relationship to space is light. He pays no overhead to sit on a bench in front of St. Mark's Basilica – a space weighted with connotations of sacred tradition and high culture. And yet, this young entrepreneur has no relationship to history or meanings associated with it. While this backdrop demonstrates the freedom of wireless technology, it also produces an ironic moment – the seamless penetration of capital into the realm of the sacred. Third, this outdoor space affords him emotional freedom. He screams, cheers, gesticulates, and leaps about as he buys and sells. Could he express such emotion in an office space where organizational restraints impose limits on personality and demeanor? Fourth, his relationship to the commodity market is speculative. The tonal pattern of his voice mimics the excitement of gambling at the craps table. The ad captures the psychological thrill of casino capitalism where winning the game has intrinsic emotional rewards for this player. Fifth, his relationship to family is expressed nonchalantly as if he were at a corner grocery store. It does not seem to matter that he is in Italy; such nomads do not have ties to community but to a scaled-down nuclear family.

Haraway (1991:149) says: "A cyborg is a cybernetic organism, a hybrid of machine and organism, a creature of social reality as well as a creature of fiction." IBM's cyborg is juiced on adrenalin, his buzz proportionate to the speed of the market. His animated, out-of-breath style replicates the speed of capital and the kind of competitive excitement that goes with it. He wheels and deals in the hypermarkets of commodity futures. By donning this cyborg apparatus he stays abreast of the accelerating speed of the marketplace driven by electronic information technology. Economic survival necessitates adaptation to network velocity. Consequently, human nodes must be constantly re-fitted to respond to accelerations.

IBM's cyborg offers an account of capitalism's "New Man" as spatially and emotionally liberated. But this account neglects the isolation and loneliness that also accrue to this model. Elliott and Lemert (2006:104) distinguish between diffused and thick globalization. The former refers to "high levels of extensity and intensity of global social forces, but in which the impact of such forces is highly regulated." In IBM's scenario, the entrepreneur recognizes the flows and is able to control them, but the repetitiveness, impersonality, and anonymity produces an emptiness that extends into other life spheres. The latter is characterized by the penetration of these flows beyond the economic realm into the intense privatization of lifestyle.

Quotidian speed

Advertisements frequently reference quotidian time, intermingling consumption time with spectacular time, while also jumbling the time of capital and markets with reproduction time, family time, and transit time. Corporate advertising draws on a now-standard signifier of speed – the blurring, pulsing light beams, generated by time-lapse photographic techniques of urban traffic to visually stretch out time. Flashes of light seem to stand for the time-spent-in-between the destinations of life. Dancing arcs of light speed come to define the capitalist cityscape.

Montages of mixed landscapes suggest spatially dispersed lifestyles that become subject to a harried pace, scheduled days chopped into personal time, transit time, market time, work time, and family time, each occupying separate spaces. Telecommunications companies advertise "personal networks" as tools for managing spatially scattered everyday lifeworlds, unifying socially privatized relations into well-adjusted and fulfilling family lives worth celebrating. Speed and busy schedules are turned from negatives into the glue of daily life. Having too much to do in too little time in too many places is usually a recipe for stress and anxiety, but AT&T's advertising turns the psychology of stress into imagery of everyday vitality and accomplishment.

> Networks are appropriate instruments for a capitalist economy based on innovation, globalisation, and decentralised concentration; for work, workers and firms based on flexibility and adaptability; for a culture of endless deconstruction and reconstruction; for a polity geared towards the instant processing of new values and public moods; and for a social organisation aiming at the supersession of space and the annihilation of time. (Castells 1996:470–1)

Time overwhelms space in telecommunications ads. It does not so much eclipse space as "fold" back on itself to form a new kind of space. In the ad, the iconography of the spatially dispersed family now appears in its sublated form – connected by communications devices rather than by face-to-face social locations – as a confederation of instant text messagers. The ad makers use split screens to reunify the simultaneous, though spatially separated, frames that represent everyday relationships with significant others in the mobile family. The speed of the network offers itself as a therapeutic solution to a hectic lifestyle by appearing to hold together vital social relations. AT&T claims to change "forever, the way you communicate," visually referring to a new mode of communicating – wireless and mobile, we chat and correspond in transit, making use of otherwise "wasted" time, with handheld devices redefining the way mobile users communicate. It is no accident that individuals are shown happily isolated in the most abstracted of spaces – non-places – where they seem to find comfortable social spaces.

Driven by landscapes of streaming communication, the incessant pursuit of immediate gratification may lead to a declining half-life of consumption-based gratifications. No single act of consumption is sufficient to achieve satisfaction; rather, consumption must be engaged continuously and on the go – including the consumption of communication. The immediacy of frenetic gratification forms the flip side of political-economic necessity – for the economy to function efficiently there must be ever-expanding consumption. Speed is fun, and while excessive speed may strike some as rebellious, it also takes shape in the underbelly of conformist consumption. Hyperactivity is addictive.

Representations of speed

The form of TV advertising contributes to our imagery of speed and deterritorialization. No matter what the subject matter, television advertising is predicated on abstraction, and thus tilts towards deterritorialization. This decontextualization process always – and necessarily – involves lifting meaningful action out of its time–space coordinates. These coordinates may be recontextualized through the framing process, but given the premium on brevity in television advertising, the tendency is almost always towards condensation and abbreviation.

The same logic of Capital that applied to material objects during prior historical stages of commodity production now also applies to the production of images. The rule can be stated quite simply – a tendency towards the accelerated circulation of commodities can offset the tendency towards a declining rate of profit. When the commodities in question are already-abstracted images – signs – the tendency towards deterritorialization becomes compounded because the duration of images diminishes while the velocity of turnover increases. Not just in a single advertising campaign but across the whole of advertising then, there is a tendency towards representations of a world without moorings – a world in which decontextualized signifiers sometimes float, sometimes rocket about. This is one meaning of deterritorialization.

In a rudimentary way, the historical processes of deterritorialization have been rooted in the evolution of commodity abstraction. As Marx pointed out, the money form permitted all forms of value to be converted into their general equivalent. Money, of course, was the universal currency that facilitated this process. When land became a commodity that could be bought and sold, the process of deterritorialization was already well under way. When forms of value tied to that land – e.g., iron ore, coal, trees – could be extracted and shipped elsewhere in exchange for currency, these too were steps along a path of deterritorialization.

Representations of speed in the discourses of corporate capital cannot be separated from questions regarding the speed of representation.

Representational speed is not simply a product of pictures of speed, but of the very process of turning culture into commodity signs. As competition in the sign-value economy intensifies, the circuitry of signification speeds up the velocity of free-floating semiotic particles that hurtle through the circuits of capital.

> Just as each particle follows its own trajectory, each fragment shines for a moment in the heavens of simulation, then disappears into the void along a crooked path that only rarely appears to intersect with other such paths. This is the pattern of the fractal – and hence the current pattern of our culture. (Baudrillard 1993b:6)

Speed is both a means of countering the tendency for the rate of profit to fall and a chief culprit in accelerating that process. The culture industry spreads this tendency from the economy to culture by trying to force culture into the service of commodities. The obsessive quest to expand the realm of value undermines the very condition of valuation, yet further contributes to the speed of abstraction and decontextualization that is a necessity in a political economy of sign value.

The representational structure that best fits the slice-and-dice signification strategies of fast capitalism is the montage. Built around a relentless flow of combining images, the montage limits the possibility of reflective critique despite the gross distortions inherent in its use as a signification practice. Unless we freeze the montage, isolate its frames, and unbraid the signifiers of sound and narration from image, the capacity for critique is dulled by the twin forces of representational velocity and decontextualized referent systems. As each ad goes speeding past, what remains is the blurred ideological framework of global capital. The "blur" turns out to be the perfect signifier for the current moment of global capital's hegemony. The montage permits corporate ads to tie together a collection of geo-culturally marked spaces that evoke memories of territory. Advertisers join fast-paced video editing styles with musical orchestration to reintegrate the disconnected and floating markers of territorial space under the aegis of the corporate sign. Corporate montages deterritorialize, potentially subverting for an instant the structural codes that bind us to the machinery of capital, "recod[ing] everything within the abstract logic of equivalence... 'reterritorializing' them within [the logic] of the state, family, law, commodity form" (Best and Kellner 1991:89). Corporate montages fixate on floating landscapes and bodies, abstracted, hollowed-out, and turned into second-order signifiers. The representation of deterritorialization is thus made to serve the production of myth – reterritorialized landscapes rearranged to signify the branding of corporate territories.

To signify global corporate reach, the ads flatten the world into an edited jumble of landscapes. Dashing from scene to scene to signify how the speed of technology has allowed global corporations to render distance a non-issue – "No matter where you are anywhere in the world, you're never very far from a Siemens product" – the landscape remains a necessary element in signifying the overcoming of distance. A nascent syntax of geography rapidly juxtaposes scenes of technology with marked and unmarked scenes of geography to construct a vision of a world made unified and coherent by the ubiquitous distribution of unobtrusive corporate technologies. Deterritorialization of both core and periphery becomes a necessary prelude to the overcoming of spatial distance as a function of a technologically driven civilization process.

Capital's codes of speed

To summarize, speed manifests itself along three dimensions in corporate advertising. First there is the thing being represented – the technologies of speed in communication and transportation that permit the shrinking of distance as a material concern. Second, after a century of organizing cultural spheres of meaning around the operating logic of the commodity form, processes of cultural commodification feed an accelerating circulation of meaning aimed at promoting an economy of sign values (including brand values). And third, the speed of representation within the ad itself: in the length of scenes, and in the rapidity of editing cuts from frame to frame. So advertising culture is not only accelerating internally, it also seeks to represent an external economic and social speed as our already-emergent normative future. Hence, we must consider the relationship between the intensifying digitalization of cultural space as a material force in the expansion of global capitalism and, simultaneously, as a representational force.

Common encoding strategies can be found across the collection of ads in our database. Corporate advertising routinely relies upon a cluster of signifiers to represent speed. The compression of time must be a visual concept in the world of television advertising, even though the visual codes are backed by sound effects and music. Once time is given representation, time is never again neutral; it now has an ideological dimension.

Signifiers of speed take multiple forms. Referential signifiers take an object that can be photographed or filmed to connote speed – a "speeding" bullet, or a motorcycle, or a pulsing light beam. Cinematic signifiers are film techniques used to speed up motion either within a shot or externally; the length of time shots are held; or how much the photographic technique "warps" the usual relations of time and space.

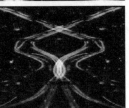

Referential signifiers generally are given perceptual velocity by cinematic techniques. For example, the speed of light cannot be signified without referring to the frozen traces left behind by blurred light paths. The blurred speeding path of streaming or pulsing light is especially appealing to advertisers because it also offers a metaphor for information flows in an information economy.

Cinematic devices create an illusion of perceptual speed by appearing to accelerate the velocity of a moving image across a visual frame. The initial image referent disappears and the blur takes its place as referent. Various techniques create a blur: time-lapse photography, swish pan camera movements, or rapidly shifting lens focal length – the zoom. Blurring is a form of abstraction in which the accelerated speed of the quotidian disguises the boredom of the everyday (see Lefebvre 1971). Ads use transportation technologies ranging from escalators to bullet trains to reinforce movement and directional speed.

In the commercials mentioned thus far, harnessing technologies of speed has become synonymous with Progress. Ultimately, for the consumer, this is the speed of delivery – of pizza, prescription drugs, information, and movies. But around the emergent Internet, what's important is the speed at which data move. Qwest advertised itself as "Moving at the speed of light" and "Riding the Light." Telecommunications giants like Qwest (1998) claimed to have "harnessed the speed of light, and the world is going to become a very different place." Visually, Qwest conceptualized this claim to "harness" light speed via its opposite – a nostalgia for naturally fixed coordinates of space and time. Set against the undisturbed silence of lapping waters and early morning sky, a fishing boat floats silently, while a shooting star crosses the sky in slow motion. "If you could travel at the speed of light, the barriers of time and distance would be erased." Qwest offered something quite spectacular and extraordinary here: the ability to arrest time: "In the time it takes a shooting star to light the sky, every book in the Library of Congress can be sent coast to coast, flawlessly."

Light beams seem the ideal signifier because fiber-optics utilizes laser beams to carry information packets. And the success of the information economy is contingent on reliable and rapid flows of information that are instantaneously available on demand. Communications, computer, and networking companies rely heavily on the light beam to visually demonstrate the superiority of a particular network. Beams of light often zip through electronic circuitry or across the metaphoric landscape of the semiconductor microchip. Qwest signs their ad by graphically "harnessing" the wave of light into their insignia.

Another preferred signifier of speed is the vortex of hyperdrive. This signifier usage is familiar from *Star Trek* when the spaceship (Starship *Enterprise*) shifted gears into hyperspace at warp speed – a momentary burst of converging light trails signified the starship's passage into and through time – a science fiction technology that imagined escaping the normal forces of nature that limit us to the speed of light. Kubrick used this technique in *2001: A Space Odyssey* to signify the passage of human-kind through its next evolutionary stage. Pop science presentations often conclude with this abstracted imagery of streaks of light bursting outwards into a distant vortex of the future.

Another convention for speed comes from modern art and design where streamlines displace the heavier referents of conventional realism. Binary code, equations, numbers, genetic encoding turn into visible, but fleeting, signifiers that fly across the ad screen on streaming fields of whitish green or blue lights before entering into the combina-torial blender of branding. Their use as signifiers harkens back to the power of pure mathematical abstraction, the power of Enlightenment solutions to life's problems. In these positivist ad dreams, a mathemati-cal equivalent underlies all forms of reality, and, once that is mastered, so too reality can be controlled. As the camera moves towards the vanishing point, this motif suggests we are entering the future at a hyperspeed driven by technological innovation. Some ads complete this cinematic movement with a burst of light, named the "dawning of a new age."

Images of jets, rockets, light beams, fiber-optic cables, and satellites make perfect sense in corporate advertising for digital technologies. But to convey the promise of high-speed bandwidth, advertisers turned to the train as a digital metaphor to make comprehensible speed as a commodity – overcoming the limits of time and geographic space. The train helped initiate time–space compression as an early modern transport system and thus became a prime signifier of the Industrial Revolution. Now advanced train technology design has become a visual metaphor for the Information Revolution. Advertisers link the train to a multiplicity of landscapes to conjure up the concept of an information economy – an economy in which the "most precious cargo" (read com-modity) to be moved is "your ideas" (GTE 1998). Against the train's former functionality as a mover of heavy goods, telecommunication company ads turn the train into a purely symbolic vehicle to signify the transition to light modernity and the movement of information across networks. Like GTE, MCI WorldCom juxtaposed the railroad and the movement of material goods to the fiber-optic beam and the transmission of information. Nearly everyone in the telecommunications sector turned to the train trope. To signify the time–space compression of an AT&T managed network, a 2002 commercial pictured a model train maneuvering from one disconnected landscape to another, before orbiting around a simulated blue globe. While the train once symbolized the national landscape, it now speeds across transnational and transcontinental scenes. Qwest visualized a stream of fused data hurtling down train tracks into a vanishing point to signify their Internet capacity; and Akamai signified its claim that "The Internet is faster because of us" by depicting speeding trains passing through a digital landscape formed by monitors.

Train travel changed perceptions of time and space in the nineteenth century. Train travel "destroy(ed) the close relationship between the traveler and the traveled space . . . The train was experienced as a projectile, and traveling on it as being shot through the landscape – thus losing control of one's senses" (Schivelbusch 1986:53–64). Vision emerged as the dominant sense when travelers watched landscapes sail past, even as "visual perception was diminished by velocity." Panoramic perception, in contrast to traditional perception, no longer belonged to the same space as the perceived objects: travelers saw objects and landscapes through the apparatus that moved oneself through the world. Machine motion became integrated into visual perception. But now that we are asked to imagine moving from machine-induced speed to light speed, how does one imagine "rid[ing] the light," or rather being a spectator to this phenomenon? It means accepting the almost imperceptible flashes of light as the experience of disorienting speed – its raw transformative energy harnessed by the mind of the corporate brand.

At the turn of the twentieth century, an intensified nervous stimulation in the city associated velocity with stress (Simmel 1950). Just as the urbanite's blasé attitude developed as a buffering response to the accelerating pace of urban life in the early twentieth century, by the end of the century audiences grew blasé about the velocity of decontextualized signifiers forced through the engines of advertising. Mimicking the technological competition to go faster, there has evolved a semiotic competition to appear faster. Signifying speed accelerates representational flows and boosts the volume of signifying debris that goes careening through fiber-optic beams.

Beams of light moving through a physical landscape connote the "annihilation of space by time" – collapsing distance by bridging it with instantaneity. Another signifier used by advertisers to signify pure speed is time-lapse photography of highway traffic at night. The technique came of age in a film, *Koyanasquatsi*, and has since become a clichéd metaphor for the speed of life in modern, and now postmodern, society. Time-lapse photography exaggerates the speed of movement in urban environments to establish the pace of modern life. Opening from a beam of light, a 2004 SBC montage depicts fast-twitch city life connected by wireless technology. The ad highlights the architecture of modern mobility: cloverleafs, freeways, revolving doors, and escalators. Coupled with blurred shots of speeding automobiles, speeded-up temporal and spatial superimpositions and overlays of action quicken the circulatory pace of the ad. Distortions of soft focus and the superimpositions of multiple time tracks in the same spaces create a ghostly impression of modernity with its spaces of anonymity. The shaded presences mark figures as momentary occupants of non-places, shuttling through the spaces in between home and work, between an ever-more nebulous here and there. "We are . . . a very active and vital member of the most mobile society on earth" – SBC's male voiceover thus hails a national desire for mobility: a cultural sensibility that claims the freedom of open spaces as our heritage, now fully realized with a wireless technology that supplies the image of new forms of connectivity and integration. The difficulty, of course, is that in a mobile society unending movement makes the matter of social connection a problem. Rather than condemn the automated circuits of movement that swirl about in a murky sea of abstraction, SBC hails the social privatization, isolation, and anonymity that are carried along in the paths of a mobile society – the secret lies in wireless technology.

Controlling anomic speed

Whether framed as the heartbeat of a vast and efficiently rationalized economic system, or as the symbolic equivalent of unrestricted movement within a market society, representations of impersonal urban speed also carry anomic overtones. Images of speed have become so abstract, their interpretation hinges on how they are framed emotionally. In the information economy, oversaturated speed occurs when information flows become overwhelming and turn into noise. A 1998 Invesco ad constructed disorienting and distorted scenes of the Stock Exchange – a turbulent, indecipherable cacophony of noise and speed – with a calculated video-editing assault on the viewer's nervous system. Jumpy camera movements, disruptive transitions, random color shifts, and lens distortions all speed up the real-time perceptual disorder and dislocation of the stock exchange floor. Decision-making is impossible when the volume and intensity of data zoom along like a bullet train. When there is pure noise, there is no way to distinguish meaning: "How do you separate knowledge from noise?" The answer offered is "Call Invesco" where experience and global perspective eliminate the stress of noisy meaninglessness.

Northern Light, a corporate search engine, used the cinematic devices of montage and blurring to demonstrate the difference between a blizzard of data and the precision of knowledge. A lone individual enters a white-walled isolation chamber. He pushes "enter" on the keyboard and a woman intones, "World Wide Web." Suddenly, accelerated information flows span the walls and ceiling of the cubicle, surrounding him in a totality of humankind's recorded information. The sound effects are again discordant, chaotic, and noisy. The Information Society bombards us with too much information too fast. The walls flicker with a myriad of informational forms: symbols from ancient peoples, mathematical formulae, computer programming, binary encodings, cells, and skeletal forms, suggesting that all knowledge is immediately available. But how does one make sense of so much meaning when there are no spaces between the units of meaning, when all the semes of meaning blend into one massive seme? Northern Light organizes the info stream into manageable categories. As the music softens, the therapeutic search engine "prioritizes, categorizes, and organizes it into neat little folders . . . artificial intelligence, semantics, intelligent agents, psychology of learning."

Network speed can also be portrayed as promoting a *Gemeinschaft* effect. A 2000 US West ad illustrated the linkages between speed and our human desires for contact in "the new west," where communicative speed equals friendship networks and a pulsing interactive leisure that turns nature and cities alike into fields of gratification. The ad opens with a nostalgic memory of the past, kids talking to each other via tin cans connected by a string across a rural landscape. The slow-moving video breaks up and the music scratches to a halt before racing forward into an exuberant hyperdrive. Rows of satellite dishes realign, setting in motion a frenetic race through spectacular scenes of consumption mixed with multiracial friendship groups of kids mugging for the camera. The US West network supplies the spirit of community that connects the diversity of otherwise privatized, separated bodies and souls. In such narratives, the speed of connectivity enhances sociability across the freedom of open spaces – "Don't Fence Me In."

Deterritorialized speed

One mythological representation played out in some ads is the science fiction conception of time–space compression and deterritorialization in virtual reality. Here, eclipsing time figuratively abolishes territorial space. Though this vision of a unitary world space is predicated on the development of computerized communications technologies, there is only minimal visual reference to speed as such in these representations because, as we have pointed out, there is no need for the illusion of speed when all relations can be conducted in a unified time–space coordinate. By annihilating space, time can appear to be synchronous and unified. Harbinger (2000) represents itself thus in a darkly futuristic, neo-Orwellian style in which virtual space connects those who conduct market exchanges. Mediating this dark space is a Matrix-like female spokesperson who appears as the face of Harbinger. Her face emerges from darkness before being multiplied 36-fold, defining the video landscape that commands this new organization of virtual space that will outmode the spatially far-flung and dispersed marketplaces composing global markets. Old-school landscapes disappear in this style of representation, and the markets of the world are converted into a giant wall of video monitors representing companies' sign presence – Dell, Deutsche Telecom, Genentech, BP, AT&T. Hardt and Negri (2001:347) observe that deterritorialization "imposes a continuous and complete circulation of signs." Corporate signs symbolically replace the companies they stand for, so that business-to-business commerce can occur in Harbinger's imagined time–space compressed virtual market.

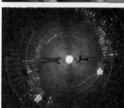

Across this hollowed-out, but completely fluid, space, the ceaseless movement of symbols and people seems random unless we assume that their robotic patterns are programmed in pursuit of profit. Like other ads that cast themselves in cyberspace, Harbinger ontologically and epistemologically redefines the world via an array of monitors – "welcome to a whole new world of e-commerce." The monitors form the background, the new landscape, and speed of movement embedded in this layer takes the form of mediated digital and video information. Meanwhile, in the foreground, figures perform their duties in a regulated and controlled fashion.

The monitors' architectural prominence suggests an encompassing capacity for a total global mediation and synthesis of reality; they form a necessary structural condition for an emergent world of 24/7 commerce. Where commerce is an uninterrupted stream, these screens do not simply evoke mediation, they become digitally constitutive – they come to define the nature of reality itself; they form its skin. The membrane of monitors lights up the space, while mediating the dispersed speech acts occurring synchronically. This video membrane is a communications device that makes possible an efficiently rationalized world market – decomposed and fragmented into an infinite array of fields that cannot be fully mastered until re-mediated through the computerized video apparatus of Capital. Here we encounter not just a series of blue flickering simulations, but the one true simulacrum – the copy that precedes the original – for the assumption here is that this is reality, but with value added!

> Today abstraction is no longer that of the map, the double, the mirror or the concept. Simulation is no longer that of a territory, a referential being or a substance. It is the generation by models of a real without origin or reality: a hyperreal. The territory no longer precedes the map, nor does it survive it. It is nevertheless the map that precedes the territory – precession of simulacra – that engenders the territory. (Baudrillard 1994:1)

In a world shrouded in darkness, Harbinger appears as an intensely focused beacon of brightness. In this representation of casino capitalism, like Las Vegas, one can no longer tell day from night. Harbinger claims to abolish the restrictions time and space otherwise impose on the possibility of uninterrupted processes of circulation and exchange of capital, by compressing the time–space relationship into a virtual cyberspace where none of the laws of gravity seem to apply anymore. This yields the commercial's most vivid image of a floating man, looking very much like an inflatable balloon in the Macy's Thanksgiving parade, who drifts into position to consummate a handshake (the universal signifier of a non-coercive market exchange) in space with another floating hand: "Here customers and suppliers connect and trade on the net. Here business is conducted globally in real time." It is worth noting the contradiction in this imagery of weightlessness to represent the supersession of time and space. Weightlessness has been a correlate of deterritorialization and the annihilation of time. This particular imagery of floating man representing freedom and possibility, however, transforms the representatives of capital more and more into puppet-like entities, unable to control their own movements, but governed instead by the extraordinary magical powers of the new sorcerer (presented here in female form). What makes this version of time–space compression possible?

Harbinger is unequivocal in its answer. The ensuing picture of giant telecommunications satellite dishes is shown precisely as the voiceover refers to the conduct of business-to-business exchange in real time.

While the monitors that form the skin of this space display the circulation of corporate signs, all references to nations have been omitted. If deterritorialization refers to the elision of national boundaries and of the authority of states to enforce territorial codes and laws, then Harbinger depicts itself as the sovereign of this new spatial universe. Cyberspace defined this way, as an absence of national territories, foretells the end of a Weberian sociology based on the "legitimate use of organized force within a given territory."

Hardt and Negri argue that Capital's current historical stage can be understood as "deterritorializing and immanent" insofar as the governing mechanism shifts from fixed structures to the fluidity of a "set of equations and relationships that determines and combines variables and coefficients immediately and equally across various terrains without reference to prior and fixed definitions or terms" (2001:326–7). It is the same premise that we have already recounted with respect to Capital's imperative towards speed as a means of reducing circulation time. Just as friction reduces profit margins, so too does fixity – whether it be the fixity of traditions or the fixity of place or the fixity of nation-state boundary locations, or the fixity of capital. How is this aspect of deterritorialization represented in the Harbinger ad? There is unceasing movement in the ad – the peripatetic movement of feet and legs across this dark space, along with the numeric shadows that wander across otherwise blank eyes and face. The continuous flow of numerals symbolizes the perfect form of abstracted knowledge that permits relationships of general equivalence to be articulated and swept away so that the process can be repeated over and over again.

Writing over twenty-five years ago, Baudrillard wondered about the possible political consequences of changing representations of time and space.

The body, landscape, time all progressively disappear as scenes. And the same for public space: the theater of the social and theater of politics are both reduced more and more to a large soft body with many heads. Advertising in its new . . . dimension invades everything, as public space (the street, monument, market, scene) disappears. It realizes, or, if one prefers, it materializes in all its obscenity; it monopolizes public life in its exhibition . . . It is our only architecture today: great screens on which are reflected atoms, particles, molecules in motion. Not a public scene or true public space but gigantic spaces of circulation, ventilation and ephemeral connections. (1983:129–30)

Telecommunications and computer technologies have materially challenged traditional, and even modern, ways of experiencing time and space. Just as significantly, when joined to the digital reproduction of images, these technologies challenge the ways we represent and conceive of time and space. If we only looked at the Harbinger ad, we might readily agree with Baudrillard about the disappearance of "body, landscape and time," but looking across the many ads touting time–space compression this might be hyperbole. The Harbinger ad transformed landscapes into the architecture of screens, reduced public space to darkened margins illuminated by the power of Capital's eye, while shining Capital's eye on the cynosure of the most lucrative transactions. Everything else drifts towards the shadows. Just as the apparatus for reproducing images displaces landscapes, so too the self-motivated body is taken over by the technological capacity to digitize all relevant market information turns.

6

Deterritorialized and Reterritorialized: The Semiotic Architecture of Capital

Landscape has become a common-sense trope, a way of turning any topic to make it conceptually fit within our frameworks of seeing and knowing the world. In contemporary media culture, "landscapes" of popular music, sports, politics, industry, and religion abound. Faithful to traditional meanings of landscape, contemporary usage still connotes a panoramic view as surveyed from outside and above. Though our cultural history of landscape pictures has been heavily influenced by the painting and pho-tography of nature scenes, its adoption as a generalized metaphor for grasping the general disposition, or the entire "terrain," of any given subject matter, whether it be *terra firma* or the current organization of technologies, suggests that the concept has become unmoored from its prior relationship to Nature. We no longer restrict ourselves to conventional topographic and geographic maps, but now move on to map cultural geographies as well.

Sociologically, landscapes compose symbolic expressions of underlying social formations. As "ways of seeing," advertising-mediated landscapes are constituted via agendas of power; by deciphering them, we hope to reveal those relations of power. Through advertising, corporate capital frames symbolic representations of an emergent globally networked society. And yet these symbolic landscapes generally make sense only if we restrict our imaginations of landscapes to the most abstract spatial constellations of relations. In other words, the landscapes that we identify – or map, if you will – in the corporate ads are second-order landscapes, full of cartographic imagination, but weak in cartographic realism.

Ads turn landscape representations into symbolic portrayals of Capital.

These landscape representations sketch a polarity between place scapes and space scapes. These different kinds of semiotic constructs mythologize the landscapes of Capital – romanticizing place or fetishizing space. "Anthropological place is formed by individual identities, through complicities of language, local references, the unformulated rules of living 'know-how'" (Augé 1995:101). If, as Augé suggests, place designates the cultural geography of adaptation to locality, then non-place designates the landscape of supermodernity, where place succumbs to the abstracting, universalizing powers of Capital and technology and is converted into spaces that we pass through with a minimal sense of relationship, history, or identity. The expansionary logic of Capital and the diffusion of global electronic media, coupled with institutional imperatives for speed, threaten local economies, uproot organic communities, and transform cultural texts into commodity signs.

Through the lens of the spectacle, landscapes appear airbrushed to conceal social costs and political-economic contradictions. Abstracted, aestheticized, and decontextualized, the landscapes in corporate advertising have been cleansed of the ruin, havoc and dislocation that invariably seem to accompany capital accumulation – the shantytowns, unemployment lines, soup kitchens, polluted air and water, trafficking and addictions, or International Monetary Fund austerity measures and ensuing riots. But while power, exchange, and labor magically dematerialize in Capital's symbolic landscapes, traces of ambivalence and contradiction are less easily purged from these scapes. Advertising landscapes express tensions between market forces and the experience of sociality even as they try to gloss over frictions. As determinate structures, market forces and exchange relations rarely receive direct representational expression; instead, tacit assumptions of a universal market guide interpretation of the advertising landscapes.

Advertising produces imaginary landscapes. By imaginary we do not mean landscapes that are wholly fictitious, but rather that they are ideological in the sense that Althusser (1971) had in mind, "the imaginary relationship of individuals to their real conditions of existence." Indeed, these landscape representations speak to, and of, "a material existence"; as a politics of representation, corporate ads fashion landscape imagery that constitutes an imaginary of freedom and consensus – mostly as frictionless movement through space. And yet, imagery of the local, the nostalgic, and the authentic still carry considerable ideological weight as idealized landscapes that appear insulated from intrusions, free from restrictions and boundaries, from struggles over power, and, often, free of people. The imaginary does not work without alienated fantasy. These advertising landscapes labor to dissolve tensions between the universalizing logic of Capital and the politics of place. Ads for new technologies, transportation, communications, and financial institutions depict the freedom of futuristic open spaces in terms of reproducible and transferrable generic non-places – universal spaces that tend to be lonely and unpopulated.

If some ads ideologically distort the impacts of Capital – inverting the relationship between capital and geographies of place, such that capital appears not to dominate place, but to enhance it – many more offer idealized visions of non-places in capitalist globalization processes. These are not unlike the "heterotopias" that Michel Foucault (1986:24) identifies – "places of this kind are outside of all places, even though it may be possible to indicate their location in reality." In this way, the coordinates of time and space may seem to correspond to real geographies and historically locatable architectural formations; but though they are born of historical imagination, they are absent the social coordinates of actual relationships.

Abstraction and deterritorialization: flow and space

Television advertising accentuates scapes as flows. These images from a Verizon 2006 ad addressed local to global connectivity by picturing landscapes dedicated to flows. Image one addresses the speed of communications using speeded flows in an urban transit system. Image two put viewers into a POV position inside an information packet whizzing through the corporate world.

Arjun Appadurai (1996) linked globalization with deterritorialization, and affixed the suffix "scape" to create terms that reflect the flows of media, peoples, ideologies, technologies, and finances across national boundaries. Appadurai saw the global cultural economy as disjunctive – comprised of overlapping flows and ruptures that he labeled mediascapes, ethnoscapes, ideoscapes, technoscapes, and financescapes. Advertising portrays these flows by giving them an aesthetic coherence that hides the contradictions that structure them. From beams of light traversing the globe, to video editing practices that contribute to appearances of continuous streaming, to graphically drawn vectors that define the circulation of movement, the visual aestheticization of flow has become a defining feature of Capital's landscapes – its self-definition. "Representations of space encompass all of the signs and significations, codes and knowledge, that

allow [corresponding] material practices to be talked about and understood" (Harvey 1989:218).

In *The Rise of The Networked Society*, Castells (1996) argued that space organizes time in the networked society. He called this a "space of flows" in contrast to the "space of places" that organized earlier stages of modernity. How do "flows" and "places" differ in representations of social life? What visual metaphors of flow, place, and space tend to predominate? Is there a relationship between the flow of imagery through advertising's cultural circuits and how viewers conceptualize the spatiality of globalization in relation to everyday life?

Advertising landscapes of deterritorialized Nature frequently serve as stages for the new universal social subjects – individuals who are free to transcend the limits of race, gender, age, and place – because the spaces they occupy are unencumbered by structural impediments. In spaces of flow, individuals are apparently able to engage only those social contacts they choose. An early 1990s AT&T ad campaign was among the first to depict an era of corporate globalization, shrinking and collapsing spatial distance via its global communication network. Consumer-goods advertising routinely represents culture as autonomous and free-floating – unfettered by location, material production, or social formations. By photographically abstracting landscapes from all geographic coordinates, consumer ads treat culture as universal, yet only relevant at the level of the individual – a culture that worships at the feet of hyper-individuated consumers. AT&T inaugurated an approach that stitched together isolated snippets of cultural geography to compose the connective tissue between abstracted spaces. AT&T's network visually flipped separation into connection, linking dispersed spaces into a community of global space – thus permitting an eclectic mix of globalism and hyper-individualism.

Like so many other campaigns, the AT&T campaign hailed the uniqueness of the private consumer, while also addressing totem group identities based on cultural difference – "What makes us all the same is that we're all different." The linkage between globalism and the individual consumer had shifted – flexible, customized consumer packages offered a personalized corollary to flexible accumulation. The aura of telecommunications casts a happy glow over this, converting geographies of space into meaningful opportunities for personal growth. This is soft-Hobbes, preserving the self-calculating and self-moving appetitive being who seeks to maximize her or his value and utility, but jettisoning all that human-nature stuff about men being nasty and brutish.

Telecommunications ads visually conjure spells that exorcize political friction and economic conflict, envisioning instead frictionless staging spaces through which individuals effortlessly move without getting in one another's way. These campaigns picture a new global society composed of spaces distributed everywhere, but not located anywhere. Corporate advertising defines globalization through heavy decontextualization and visual abstraction. And while this robs its representations of specificity and depth of meaning, as a device for identifying the relations amongst privatized monads who pass to and fro across a global consumption landscape, such visual abstractions also reveal key symbolic assertions about global civil society. Set against a flattened background of depoliticization, the only shared attribute of the figures who make their way across this metaphoric landscape is their common access to the semiotic presence of the sponsoring corporations.

Abstraction is standard operating procedure on television, especially so in advertising where the cost of time is so great that messages must be compressed and abbreviated into highly charged signifiers. The tendency in television advertising is towards greater and greater time-compression, which in turn pushes abstraction further, compounding the already discontinuous moment inherent in photography. This moment isolated in time must be re-motivated – its meaning must be redirected.

In constructing landscapes of globalization, corporate advertisers select images for their abstract aesthetic and affective appeal rather than for the particular place they represent. An image's geographical place of origin becomes immaterial. Stunning photographs of isolated scenes are deposited in image banks; when withdrawn they can be resituated within any particular narrative and made to mean within the discursive framework of the advertising form (Machin 2004). Though in theory an infinite array of photographic signifiers could be appropriated, in practice fewer images get used repeatedly within the total body of corporate advertising, contributing to a familiar visual lexicon of spatiality.

Because our shared understandings of geography become more reliant on coding practices, the landscapes thus constituted are always subject to revisionism. In television advertising, decontextualized signifiers of landscape are all the more transitory, appearing for a split second, before being pushed aside to make way for other abstracted signifiers. Suturing photographic signifiers into edited landscape quilts appears simple enough, and yet this relentless plundering, mixing, and remixing of place and space creates simulacra of place/space that exist nowhere except in the ads themselves.

The digital era, above all else then, promises to make territory obsolete – unhinging the coordinates of time and space. Liquid modernity consists, in part, of a swirl of signs, images, and texts that have been freed from spatiality and temporality. Careening through the electronic circuits of the network society, signs of spatiality become disjointed from their material referents in what may be called the deterritorialization of signification. Amplified by the conditions of digital sign construction, the corrosive instability of the signifier–signified relationship made necessary by the continuous circulation of signs renders conceptions of a unified "Sign" and a unified "Territory" quaintly obsolete. Signifiers, once liberated from their sites of origin, are appropriated, aesthetically modified, and reharnessed to new signifieds. Celeste Olalquiaga has shown that, whereas "indexicality" rests on "pointing to first-degree references (objects, events)," the simulative system produces meaning intertextually (1992:6). Olalquiaga says the breakdown of spatial and temporal boundaries weakens cultural referents. Corporate advertising creates the illusion of heterotopias, with global landscapes made by mashing together spatial and temporal scales – leaping from the microscopic to macroscopic and back in the blink of an eye. The global and the local, the molar and the molecular, the cellular and the universal, all seem to exist side by side.

Berger and Mohr (1982) and Foucault (1986:22) each make the powerful argument that while "[t]he great obsession of the nineteenth century was . . . history . . . the present epoch will perhaps be above all the epoch of space." Television spatializes history. "We are in the epoch of simultaneity: we are in the epoch of juxtaposition, the epoch of the near and far, of the side-by-side, of the dispersed." The vertical axis of history that shaped modernist consciousness has been displaced by the lateral axis of a slipping and sliding spatiality. Technologies of high-speed transportation and communication aim at transcending the geographical limits of territory and the barriers of time. And by now territory has given way to the landscape. Where time and space have collapsed, the spectacle of the landscape rules; as the importance of territory diminishes, the abstractions of landscape grow more generalized.

From global panorama to electronic microscapes

The map is not the territory, the word is not the thing.(Alfred Korzybski 1933)

What do maps communicate when used as signifiers in commercials? Map images usually flash past us on the screen too rapidly to be considered in any great detail. Instead, we may simply recognize the category of "map" and attribute to it meanings of "map-ness." By contrast, early modern maps aimed at a specific functionality – maps gave direction and purposefully indicated routes to destinations. The map claims to direct the reader to a material geography outside the map. A still earlier

epoch's mythological maps pointed the viewer to no geographic place, but to a shared symbolic space. In a curious way
the map images that conceptualize spatiality in corporate ads
have returned to mythological mappings. Hints of geography
may linger, but geography in these maps is beside the point.
The object of the mapping disappears in favor of the representational image of the map itself. The map as simulation
becomes its own referent, pointing nowhere except to itself.

The transition from old-school geography to an electronic
global geography is a theme made explicit in the 1998 MCI
WorldCom inaugural ad that celebrates the world historical significance of the Internet transforming the globe into
a unified business space. The ad presents the early modern
mapping of geography and history via its retelling of how
the US transcontinental railway was built to unify the capitalist nation-state. This mapping tracks the relationship of
geographic space across time to create a narrative of comple-
tion and Progress. The ad establishes a semiotic opposition
between that now-archaic relationship between technology
and mapping, and the maps that orient a contemporary
system of globalization constituted via MCI WorldCom's
advanced optical fiber technologies. The flows shift from the
linear tracings that draw a historical route, to the less fixed

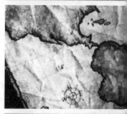

The representational construction of global spatiality draws
on referents to technologically mediated forms of viewing.
On the one hand, we are positioned outside the earth able
to peer down from the heavens. The satellite-like photo of
a populated region works as a marker of scientific/technical
rationality. The globe is mediated by superimposed grids,
veins, and electronic schematics. In each image, we recognize the nature of a map before we recognize where we are.
Each scene exists only to indicate the capacity to precisely
track spatiality. Without specialized training in how to read
such maps, it becomes evident that each abstracted map
has been turned into a second-order signifier. Each to some
degree signifies a beneficent panoptic that permits technological order and precision targeting. On the other hand,
entering the micro universe of the chip visually signifies a
technologically organized space. Conducting flows through
binary circuits on the computer chip has become a supreme
metaphor of rationalized socio-physical space.
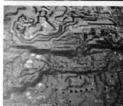

(but just as fetishized) orbital tracings of MCI WorldCom's iconic sign now unifying the globe. As territory becomes more abstract, and our means of representing it becomes more mathematized and rationalized, the means of representing it in image form becomes correspondingly abstracted.

New technologies modify how we represent a world out there; they also alter our ontological conceptions of maps. A 2007 ad for Epic Imaging, specializing in medical imaging technologies, offered a familiar narrative: "New technology can open our eyes and reshape our world in a heartbeat." The ad is organized as a visual narrative, coming down through the clouds to see a yellowed parchment map of the Americas that references voyages of exploration and discovery. This visually transitions to neural electrical impulses that encircle a globe "reshaping our world," before transforming into a detailed imaging scan of the human heart. The imaging scan is so real in its mapping of the human heart, it bridges the gap between referent and signifier. The heart morphs back into a radiant globe heralding the hegemony of Epic's medical imaging technology. This visual tour of the world abolishes previous notions of spatial scale, turning the macroscopic and the microscopic into equivalent spaces that morph back and forth into one another.

The micro-technology revolution that underlies advances in semiconductor chips, fiber-optics, biotechnology, and telecommunications has its own landscapes. Montage ads for technology companies string together "high-tech" signifiers anchored by scenes of complex microchip circuit boards to herald new landscapes of power. Embedded in this nascent architecture of space is the grand narrative of science and technology. Photographed to resemble a "panoptic" overview of a modern city, the mappings mimic the landscapes. The microprocessor as a visual metaphor for the city makes sense if we think of cities as "intersecting networks" and "a nexus of flows". "The oft-noted analogy between the layout of city grids and that of circuitry is here revealed as more than mere metaphor: cities are digital processors and digital circuits are cities, abstracted and shrunk on to silicon" (Harris and Taylor 2005:113). Scenes appear fleetingly in this high-tech landscape of miniaturization, vanishing as abruptly as they appear, flushed away in the stream of images that follow. This landscape signifier, however, recurs with such frequency in technology advertising that it became an important trope linking advanced technology to the architecture of urban space. Like the mapping signifiers mentioned above, the semiconductor landscape suggests a friendly panopticism – tacitly pointing to computer circuit boards as the new "ground" of a global unification of digital telecommunications.

The grids and networks that appear in these landscapes speak to the rationalized electronic and optical delivery of services and information. But if Virilio is right that territory becomes outmoded by the micro-electronics revolution, why construct a visual analogy between the technology and the territorial landscape? Microchips morph into jets, office towers, and even brand logos. The microchip connotes the deep infrastructure of the information society underlying creativity, development, organization, circulation and profit. Suffused with energy, the microchip landscape serves as trope for turbocharged economic vitality.

Circuit board landscapes coupled with network diagrams represent landscapes of speed and rationality. The inverse relation between speed and territorialization, however, immediately contradicts this reading. But perhaps it is precisely the latter tension that accounts for this type of symbolization. Turning microelectronics into landscapes may offer a modest reassurance about the stability of social forms. Mapping offers a way of ordering our world, and electronic forms of mapping offer the imaginary of a precision-ordered world. Maps are especially comforting when we feel lost, or out of control. As the watchword of commerce has become speed and more speed, a sense of bewildering dizziness may result – hence the need to give order to the chaotic feeling of spinning. The recurring presentation of microchip landscapes may represent a high-tech order committed to the interests of a reordered society.

Representing space

Augé drew attention to what he called non-places – e.g., airport lounges, superhighways, megastores – all spaces through which people pass. Non-places have since spread to virtual spaces such as social networking sites, online auction sites, and e-tailing sites like Amazon.com. Lamenting the loss of a world where the organicity of place prevailed, Augé argued that the barrenness of non-places created an emptiness and solitude for those who routinely occupy them.

> The only face to be seen, the only voice to be heard, in the silent dialogue [the individual] holds with the landscape-text addressed to him along with others, are his own: the face and voice of a solitude made all the more baffling by the fact that it echoes millions of others . . . Meanwhile, he obeys the same code as others, receives the same messages, responds to the same entreaties. The space of non-place creates neither singular identity nor relations; only solitude, and similitude. (Augé 1995:103)

This hyper-rationalization of space in corporate ads suggests a built environment perfectly suited to Capital's quest for

frictionless efficiency and profit. Photographically abstracted architectural spectacles provide the imagery of non-places in corporate commercials. To compete with NASDAQ's high-tech profile, the New York Stock Exchange (NYSE) ran a millennium campaign that celebrated a futuristic look of supermodernity. A pulsing techno beat framed the nearly deserted landscapes of hypermodernity with a sense of dynamism aggregated by investment capital. When not representing itself as a blur of energy jetting through fiber-optic networks, Capital is cast as a series of abstract, formal spaces designed for very specific functionalities – control rooms, clean rooms, biotech labs, computer server spaces, network centers, information screens, and trading arenas. These are the supposed value centers of the new global capitalism – indeed, these are the "the gateway to the global economy." To represent the open architectural flow of people and data, advertisers frequently turn to image bank photos of supermodern architecture, especially the abstractly shaped spaces found in contemporary airport design – precisely those supermodern sites that inspired Augé's designation of "non-places" because they function as spatial voids through which nomadic monads pass. The functionality of such spaces depends on their emptiness – or abstractness – which is represented as unobstructed flow, as freedom from social, political, economic, and cultural frictions. The aesthetic of supermodern architecture works well as a signifier of flow because it suggests streamlined and hollowed spaces that are mere conduits to value. This abstract, formal meaninglessness corresponds to Augé's thesis regarding the void of organic cultures in non-places. Sequenced together in rapid rhythmic succession, these fetishized spatial signifiers aim at representing "spaces of flows" – celebrating their anomic flatness as a necessary precondition for global economic vitality.

Corporate advertising's montage form routinely sequences these abstracted spatial signifiers into narratives of spatial overabundance, each image momentarily occupying an equivalent space. Without a voiceover or the syntax of music to guide the combination of these discrete structural elements, the overall meaning of these landscape narratives would be thoroughly arbitrary. Without such narrative direction, the random sequencing and the serialized editing of scalar relations yield an imagery of globalization that might be described as fractal turbulence.

Horizontal mash-ups of spatial scales suggest both a scalar and a non-scalar ontology of globalization. The ads themselves continue to invoke narrative assumptions of hierarchical scale, especially when visually chaotic arrangements of spatial scale culminate with a globe itself, and yet the actual scalar location of images within chains of signification displays a random – aleatory – character.

Advertising does not entirely separate images of place from non-place. When, in 2004, the NYSE confronted a controversy stemming from a $140 million pay package secured by its chairman, the campaign that followed addressed the theme of trust by buffering the cold emptiness of non-places devoted to exchange with hyperreal representations of authentic cultural places.

Optimism has always been celebrated with a bell
And every day when this bell rings it's a symbol of our pledge to serve the investor
With new standards, new leadership, and a renewed commitment to being the best market on earth
After all it's your market and there's only one trade that really matters here
– Yours
The New York Stock Exchange

To lend a populist tone to the circuits of capital, the spatial frames oscillate between modern and traditional signifiers, juxtaposing and unifying the relationship between the social spaces of the quotidian bells that represent organic cultural traditions (church bells and school bells) and the new master quotidian bell of our epoch – the bell that signals the NYSE trading day.

Interwoven with images of supermodern spaces and technologies, signifiers of place, daily life, family, and ethnicity dot and label the landscapes of non-places. But place has been no less liberated from geography, itself chopped up into ready-made, free-floating commodity signifiers. Nortel, Microsoft, Cisco, Oracle, GE, Siemens, ABB, and Boeing all depict their technologies' impacts on social and cultural life as if occurring in a distributed manner across a simulacrum of everyday life.

Nortel stamps its presence across a global landscape with omnipresent signs bearing the question – "What do you want the Internet to be?" – across a variety of landscapes paired as antipodal sites, on skyscrapers and in hayfields, inside fortune cookies and on melons in an Islamic fruit market somewhere far on the periphery of the global center. Urban skylines, rural landscapes, Eastern marketplaces, Western media, all appear unified by the shared emotional vitality of Nortel's symbolic presence – because its sign presence is its material presence, sharing ideas and connecting people on a global scale.

Ads like this construct global landscapes as choreographed visualizations of antipodes – connecting this territorial space with that cultural geography. Though such ads speak of a world in progress, the serially arranged placeless places that constitute the world seem to exist outside time (in a liminal zone between progress and nostalgia). The ad space itself constitutes a universal synchronic moment that witnesses the beginning of the utopian amid the seemingly mundane. Nortel framed its technology as spatially ubiquitous and spatially transcendent. Because every landscape is captured as a scene, from teeming Asian ports to the surface of a melon, every landscape turns into an equivalent representation of the same abstraction – a corporately mediated Internet encompassing all spaces without imprinting on them. All discontinuous spaces are thus transformed into a global quilt of meta-space that has the potential to be reterritorialized by corporate signs. The corporation positions itself as a global citizen because its services blanket geographically dissimilar referents with functionally similar activities.

Every surface that can be turned into a space that accepts the corporate sign can be granted "placeness." Corporate representations homogenize the world, taking the many differences that make up the world and unifying them by stamping their brand signature across them all. This turns difference into equivalence in the manner that Augé calls the "homogenization of diversity" (Augé 1995:32). In this kind of "spatial overabundance," we give meaning to everything, and yet attach limited significance to anything. The terrain of meaning becomes infinite in extension, but thin like crust.

Cyberspace

William Gibson's genre-making novel, *Neuromancer*, introduced the concept of cyberspace: "Cyberspace . . . A graphical representation of data abstracted from the banks of every computer in the human system. Unthinkable complexity. Lines of light ranged in the non-space of the mind, clusters and constellations of data. Like city lights, receding" (1984:51). Advertisers faced the challenge of making this "consensual hallucination" visually recognizable. A 1996 ad campaign for Digital Computers explicitly wondered what a "landscape of cyberspace" might become. Digital envisioned many imaginative possibilities, including a deliberately fake-scape cyberspace, an artist's rendition of a virtual, simulated landscape that may only exist in a corner of our brains with the benefit of special goggles. Drawn this way cyberscapes are an extreme abstraction of scapes – deliberately emptied to become a canvas on which human figures can be digitally cloned.

Visual efforts to represent dizzying barrages of data often yield imagery of distorted spaces that can be remedied and perceptually reordered by selecting the correct corporate vendor. USABancshares. com was a short-lived effort at tapping the venture capital market's desire to fund firms that would not carry the weight of brick-and-mortar overhead costs. Their television ad pronounced (tongue in cheek) the "end of the world," by which they meant the overcoming of material space, electronically. Representations of cyberspace are almost always linked with significations of speed and bending, curving architectures of information. Global Crossing imagined a giant transparent fiber-optic beam – a cyberspace Noah's ark carrying every species of information – zooming towards infinity while orbiting the Earth.

SAP's 1999 "City of E" campaign featured a blue-tinted holographic city floating above the Earth, ribbons of binary code feeding into it. Crystal-like imagery gives the appearance of a celestial magic kingdom. Translucent open architecture reveals three-dimensional planes of data that simulate a complex technical division of labor – everything taking place at once and in the same space. The virtual space contains a seamlessly integrated information network that spurs commerce and speeds exchanges.

There is a place on the Internet.
A virtual city built by SAP out of seamless information.
10,000 companies, every industry, millions of people your business linked to theirs in one easy step, shrink your work, expand your ideas.
You've got a business, we've got a city.

The crystal-like structures that form the "City of E" symbolize the SAP infrastructure that simulates markets. The defining feature of this compressed complexity of space is Speed – Speed that enables efficiency. Markets remain invisible here except in their form as flows of data across the internal computer-scape of the virtual City of E.

Layered planes of superimposed activities compose the City of E hologram – commodities, web pages, floating industries (fashion, automobiles), medical data, and streaming computer data. Three-dimensional holographic billboards bear the key concepts – Speed, Ease, Enjoy, Retail, e-business. SAP's "City of E" transforms chaotic disorganized markets into a unified information system. An enlightened businessman visits the "City of E" and gazes upward in amazement as futuristic "information flow" images stream past. Efficiency prevails in this paperless business environment. In spite of this, the City of E projects an atmosphere of alienated activity. If Weber's metaphor of the iron cage captured the experience of bureaucratic rationalization, perhaps now we should speak of the crystal cage of technostructural rationalization.

Vectors, gradients, and morphing

Advertisers use visual graphics to modify the representational landscapes of Capital. Latitude and longitude lines disappeared from advertising's representations of global maps in the 1990s, replaced by the schematic route lines of telecommunications networks that now connect the continents. Vectors – artistically styled – are another visual effect that redefines landscapes by superimposing visual scaffolding over geographical and spatial imagery. As a visual metaphor for information flows and force fields that connect spaces liberated from the constraints of geographic place and time, artistically mediated vectors map a network of connectivity that stresses the value of branded technologies traversing and transcending conventional landscapes.

Vectors impose layers of order and control over the external world, while also mapping for viewers trajectories of potentiality available to those who utilize the appropriate products. Vectors and gradients as spatial diagrams construct visual metaphors for the magnitude and direction of telecommunication and computing technologies. The agency or driver behind branded vectors is assumed to be the corporate sponsor. When the vector takes the form of a spatial overlay it suggests both an empowering capacity and the extent of corporate reach and power.

Representing a technology of knowledge/power as a vector implies that its power can be harnessed. Numerous technologies of knowledge/power are depicted as vectors: computational networks; electronic stock-trading technologies; 3-D modeling technologies; DNA double helices; binary codes. Especially with technologies that work at the atomic and molecular scale, the vector works as a visual abbreviation for technoscientific "discoveries." As a visual graphic, active, moving vectors symbolize the practical contribution of new technologies to the march of progress.

Paul Virilio has examined vectors as lines of power, particularly the "mobile stream of information or images or narrative without direction but filled with force" (During 1995). The vector locates abstract trajectories of movement through space and across territories – but no trajectory can exist without the action of prior forces. Virilio's study of vectors arose from concerns about how technologies of speed eclipse geographic space and time relationships. Vectors permit us to conceptualize power in a world where markets seem to eclipse territory as the ultimate object of control, and where electronic information flows have become a strategic pivot point in financial competition. They offer a way of conceptualizing the material impacts of accelerating information flows through, and across, the spaces of everyday life as well as the spaces of global markets.

Corporate advertisers visually conceptualize the importance of controlling information flows in a global economy by looking for tropes that evoke the transformation from a world grounded in modern institutions into one governed by digitalized flows of information. However, the ads often accomplish this with a twist that acknowledges and locates new planes of power, but without fully acknowledging the force, agency, or agendas that underlie such power. Curiously the vector offers an *enchanted* representation of rationalized forces – it celebrates the rationalization of the world by turning the representations of science and technology into force fields of magic.

As a means of producing and controlling space, advertisers' visualization of vectors "effectively represents a spatialized rendition of Marx's conception of fetishism" (Merrifield 1993:520). If the vector symbolically represents the capacity for organizing production systems, it does so minus the laboring subject. The agency of labor is erased by the action of the vectors, even as the vectors appear to serve both the broader interests of humankind and the specific needs of individual subjects. In the case of AT&T's (2004) network, the vector visually assumes a Cartesian human form ("it can think for itself") before it "transforms itself" and "grows into whatever the future demands."

Corporate advertisers artistically draw vectors as forces that civilize and organize landscapes. Defining scapes as flows, vector drawings represent the spatial movement of engineering, information, money, shipments, and energy. As a narrative device, advertisers use vectors to hide deeper relationships between knowledge and power, substituting instead the appearance of knowledge as the means of disinterested power. The knowledge that coalesces into technological discovery emerges as an ideological pivot on which these ads build because it represents a clean form of power motivated less by greed than by desires for transcendence, less by self-interest than by contributions to the greater good of humanity. Claims to global legitimacy by corporate sponsors now hinge on making claims to being special mediators of information via the organization of knowledge databases that empower the imagination.

Campaigns for computer-related corporations associate animated vectors with a vision of global capitalism in which domination evaporates because software technologies unlock production flows in everyday life. Like cyberspace representations, the vector metaphor assumes a dematerialized conception of economic structure. Endowed with agency, vectors sometimes, as in Microsoft's 2003 campaign, visualize and develop the imaginative potential that lies within every person. Turning vectors into animated extensions of human persona preserves their meaning of directional force (as applied by the tools of Microsoft), but channeled according to the dreams and imaginings of individuals.

Spaces organized by vectors are always unfettered by enclosures or limits. Rather than clarifying the lines of power, vectors signify a world where digital technologies vaguely empower all who wish to partake. In television ads the forces that stand behind the vectors' trajectories possess neither faces nor motives. Rather the motive force that makes possible the HP or Microsoft extension of technologies seems to emanate from a more universal plane where the interests of humankind supersede mundane concerns about market share or glory. To visually conceptualize the material force of networked electronic information technologies, the vectors pictured in ads contribute to a double disappearance – the evaporation of territorial boundaries and authority structures.

By superimposing a visual vector layer over both social and territorial spaces, the ads sketch out visions of a master narrative – information flows enable deliberative control over nature, and hence greater productivity – uniformly spread out across a world where there is no longer a significant differential between core and periphery. In a 2003 campaign, HP declared that its technology is "powering the engine of the world economy."

> Today hp technology is producing prodigies of speed, and discovering new directions in film (Sundance). It's investigating new worlds out there and in us, and it's making the global economy more global. For the world's great companies, thinkers, and doers, hp makes more things more possible.

Transformations in the mode of production contribute to altered modes of perception and representation. Televisual and telecommunication technologies have prompted significant changes in the dominant modes of representation that have been themselves subject to modification as digital technologies continue to fragment and reunify spatial representations. Just as the cultural construction of perspective coincided with the science of optics to develop photography as a technology of everyday seeing that transformed the epistemological convictions of those who call themselves modern, so the technology of digital video contributes to a new hegemony of seeing – the capacity for redefining the assumptions that we make about landscapes of time and space.

Video morphing techniques made possible by digital editing technologies are often used as transition devices. Because the morphing effect makes implausible claims of verisimilitude in these ads, viewers are encouraged to accept the metacommunicative premise that the morph is a metaphor for states of transformation. An HP campaign formulated around the theme "Solutions for the adaptive enterprise" adopted the morphing device to represent the necessity of flexibility in a rapidly changing business world. HP morphs corporate organizational spaces – the spaces of the built environment – into fluidly collapsible and mutable spaces. HP stressed the visual morphing of workspaces to stress the demand and capacity for rapid adaptation in the contemporary business environment. Morphing emphasizes "flow" and "change" as opposed to the fixity of older business structures. The morphing of one structure into an infinite array of possible configurations symbolically expressed the power of HP technology. HP calms the winds of change, turning them into a diurnal rhythm of continuous change as natural as the rising and setting of the sun. Whereas early modernists perceived the modern as a "whirlwind of change," these contemporary discourses of liquid modernity perceive change in less dramatic, but more continuous terms as ceaseless flow: "HP services and technology help the world's great companies face, manage, and love change."

The HP campaign visually braided vector imagery with the transformative imagery of morphing office spaces, desktop configurations, and built urban environment. Indeed, the sign of HP emerges out of the convergence point of colored vectors signifying totalizing control over all possible external forces that might otherwise disrupt the continuous flow of value producing activities. Corporate advertisers – via the master signifiers of the vector and the morph – demonstrate how change can be channeled and turned into a positive.

The semiotic architecture of capital

Capital has, from its inception, advertised itself through its architecture. Like the architecture of dominant economic classes throughout history, the architecture of Capital's built environment has been an exercise in power. The architectural backgrounds that predominate in corporate ads constitute "landscapes of power" (Zukin 1993). At the very least, these ads suggest a globalization of urban form with interchangeable architectural parts, an urban form defined by the homogeneous dispersal of supermodern formulae that characterizes "the geography of nowhere" (Kunstler 1993).

Corporate advertising visualizes an architecture that emphasizes appearance and design over structural underpinnings. Capital still aligns itself with the iconography of the modern skyscraper skyline and its streamlined vertical lines of ascent. Sassen (1991) calls the core capitalist cities of the planet – New York, London, Tokyo, Los Angeles – "global cities." Coupled with "regional" global cities like Hong Kong, Singapore, Sydney, Dallas, Chicago, San Francisco and Vancouver that Castells designates as "megacities," these centers connect globally integrated markets to commodified resources severed from local populations.

Megacities are the "*nodes* of the global economy, concentrating the directional, productive, and managerial upper functions all over the planet:
the control of the media; the real politics of power; and the symbolic
capacity to create and diffuse meanings" (Castells 1996:403–4).

Advertisers who help steer this symbolic apparatus have adopted
tightly abbreviated signifiers of the generic global city, like the imagery
of corporate skyscrapers and the supermodern skylines they give shape
to. Skyscrapers define the capitalist city and symbolically capture the
nodal concentration of "managerial upper functions" that organize
economies, even while rendering invisible the linkages between this
administrative functionality and the lives of local populations. When
coupled with traffic metaphors that point to the rapid movement of
data as well as people, the skyscraper skylines signify a spatial hub for
a corporate economy. Panoramic scenes featuring an imposing phalanx
of corporate towers seem apt symbols for the enormous concentration
of corporate capital and its condensation of space.

The relationship between the skyscrapers and the speeding flows of
traffic (data) captures a crucial dialectic between circulating and fixed
capital: "As circulating capital it fixates itself, and as fixated capital it
circulates" (Marx 1973:621). While the towers symbolize the power of
capital, they also represent the fixing of corporate capital into its static
material thing-form. However, to signify the ideal conditions of circulating capital, the towers must be visually linked to the spatial emptiness of
landscapes devoted to continuous circulation.

Ads abstract corporate towers from place, erasing their time and
space coordinates. Most skyscraper images no longer can be seen
occupying any ground. To be sure, a recognizable building shape peri-
odically appears that allows viewers to identify New York City (the
Chrysler Building) or San Francisco (the Transamerica Building). But
this only reinforces how generalized signifiers of global cities have been
abstracted from geographical location. Decontextualized, skylines have
been converted into Myth, second-order signifiers hollowed out of the
spatial relations of the capitalist city.

Establishing visual metaphors for the space of flows is crucial to its
signification. But which flows will be represented – flows of commodities, capital, and labor or the circuitry of information via high-speed
microelectronics and telecommunications? Capital mobility has moved
production around the planet – geographically dispersing production
and reorganizing it via supply chains – reshaping international labor
markets. Rather than dwelling on material flows of supply chains, the
ads stress the semiotic flows that represent the trading of capital.

Another way of representing urban nodes shaped by the "space of
flows" is to show how the global information city has been spatially

converted from ground transport systems to visual conduits of information and data flows. In scenes from the NYSE and Boeing, the architecture of bridges turn from carrying traffic into channeling information flows in and out of the capitalist city. Where bridges were once crucial to the flow of workers, consumers, and goods, they now carry broadband flows.

Global cities tend to monopolize "advanced producer services" that include heavily specialized capital functions – management consulting, accounting, legal services, marketing and advertising, product engineering and design, financial instruments, risk assessment, software programming, information management, and symbolic analysts (Sassen 1991:11). Corporate management has become a matter of coordinating the flows of supply chains via an infrastructure of computing networks. These functions are tacit, buried in the symbolism of

Signifying a global hierarchy of cities that form "command and control centers," towers of power are photographed from angles that abstractly accentuate the power wielded by the multinational businesses they headquarter. These images recur throughout corporate advertising because they anchor corporate conceptions of how the world has become ordered. Hovering above the horizon the modern office tower symbolically broadcasts phallic power.

> Metaphorically, it symbolizes force, male fertility, masculine violence. Here again the part is taken for the whole; phallic brutality does not remain abstract, for it is the brutality of political power, of the means of constraint: police, army, bureaucracy. Phallic erectility bestows a special status on the perpendicular, proclaiming phallocracy as the orientation of space, as the goal of the process – at once metaphoric and metonymic – which instigates this facet of spatial practice. (Lefebvre 1992: 286–7)

Capital claims the power to physically reshape the landscape. While power is present in these representations, the narratives constructed from these representations suggest it is used in benign and progressive ways. Moreover, representational abstraction and aestheticization ensure that the spectacle of celebratory monumentalism eliminates any sense of the destruction or devastation that might be the consequence of the logic of Capital.

office towers connected to the world by fiber-optic streams as the medium of information exchange.

Serene, impersonal, and imposing, this version of finance capital envisions an ability to manage the contradictions of a chaotic market economy. Capital can be shown presiding over society by sealing it off. Skyscrapers as citadels are insulated from the social problems associated with urban environments (poverty, violence, congestion).

The 1999 First Union ad campaign offered a carefully articulated link between architecture and the capitalist city. Capital dominates this landscape in its entirety, its function visible in its architectural style. And yet, in a world marked by the dollar sign, the preeminent tower appears like a shrine, comparing a banking empire to the new kingdom of God by wrapping the architectural monolith in an aura of radiant light and heavenly glow. Symbolical markings define these buildings – the dollar signs and upward-pointing arrows (male power and the power of capital seem once again to converge). This focal symbolism runs counter to the capitalist city that characterized the era of Fordism, a city whose corporate architecture became denuded of "symbolic embellishments" (Gottdiener 1987:26–7). First Union tried reversing this by visually capping the bank with a signifier of the dollar sign, thus reminding us that their tower stands supreme because its signifier elevates the code of Capital into a symbolic language about society.

Though the city skylines that appear in corporate advertising tend to be thoroughly divorced from locale, one particular skyline scene can no longer be viewed in this way. The New York City skyline, dominated as it was by the twin towers of the World Trade Center, is now fully invested with the meanings of September 11. Now, just as famous as the New York City skyline are the photographs of the towers being exploded and destroyed on that now infamous day. The symbolic aspects of the murderous attack on the towers cannot be avoided. We have already seen how reductively corporate advertising represents the capitalist city as a locus for corporate power. And while this may often seem facile because it has been so heavily abstracted from the relations of everyday life, the repetition of this symbolic order has nonetheless achieved its goal of familiarity. To those in the US, the towers stood for the ascendancy of American capitalism and a consumer way of life. To much of the rest of the world, being steamrollered by the expansion of capitalist globalization, the twin towers stood for the American hegemony exercised over them. If to citizens of the US the towers stood as a monument to civilization and its advances, to much of the rest of the world it stood for the monopoly of global power and oppression.

The World Trade Center towers exemplify symbolic power and how symbols become targets of antagonism and resistance. Especially following their destruction, the towers were cast as representing a place, New York City. Their destruction was interpreted more as an attack on New Yorkers than on global capital, more on America than on global capital. This demonstrates how much the State and Capital have become commingled in our society. The response is suffused with patriotic sentiments because, in the aftermath of September 11, the towers became a symbol of an imagined community of the United States.

It is worth recalling what Baudrillard wrote about the symbolic dimension of the twin World Trade Center towers several decades ago, observing then that the towers signified a "competitive verticality" characteristic of the capitalist city, while at the same time suggesting an end to that stage of development:

> The fact that there are two towers signified the end of all competition, the end of every original reference. Paradoxically, if there were only one, the World Trade Center would not embody the monopoly, since we have seen that it becomes stable in dual form. For the sign to remain pure it must become its own double: this doubling of the sign really put an end to what is designated. (Baudrillard 1993a:69)

Baudrillard (2002b) interprets the terrorist attack on the World Trade Center as a fulcrum for a new stage of the politics of the simulacrum. The irony, as Baudrillard presents it, is that the reductionism of Western power into abstracted symbolic form, though it initially depoliticized the power of Capital amongst domestic populations, has had quite the opposite long-term consequences, as it has fueled repoliticized antagonism towards US Capital throughout the world. Baudrillard saw the terrorist attack as marking a massive spike in the politics of the spectacle.

Spatial fetishism

> This abstract space took over from historical space, which nevertheless lived on, though gradually losing its force, as substratum or underpinning of representational spaces. Abstract space functions "objectally," as a set of things/signs and their formal relationships: glass and stone, concrete and steel, angles and curves, full and empty. Formal and quantitative, it erases distinctions, as much those which derive from nature and (historical) time as those which originate in the body (age, sex, ethnicity) . . . Differences, for their part, are forced into the symbolic forms of an art that is itself abstract. A symbolism derived from that mis-taking of sensory, sensual and sexual which is intrinsic to the things/signs of abstract space finds objective expression in derivative ways: monuments have a phallic aspect, towers exude arrogance, and the bureaucratic and political authoritarianism immanent to a repressive space is everywhere. (Lefebvre 1992:49)

Advertising assists in the cultural production of space. The drive to ideologically reterritorialize the landscapes of Capital is accomplished at the cost of spatial fetishism. As "apologists for a globalizing neo-liberalism," corporate advertisers visualized "the end of geography" (Merrifield 1993:103). This requires the treatment of space as homogeneous and empty, a "passive receptacle" to be occupied or filled (Lefebvre, 1992:90). In the case of corporate ads, this spatial fetishism goes hand in hand with commodity fetishism and technological fetishism.

The postmodern corporate city: Boeing's (2000) artful imagery of the city of the near future mixes postmodern architectural decoration with a landscape metaphor that highlights the movement of data at blurring speeds. The circulatory movement of highway transit flows defined by light streams signifies the self-regulating character of an economy organized around electronic flows. As a landscape for the information age, this shows postmodern citadels of corporate culture presiding over a smoothly functioning environment without need for external (political) intervention. A no less artful futuristic skyscape and landscape appeared in a 1998 ad from MCI WorldCom. Like the Boeing ad, the superfast flows of information are depicted as central to the information era, but here, in an alternative postmodern landscape, the built environment is unnecessary – a relic of the past. To be sure, the shrine-like representation of contemporary capital is the more common because it permits the corporation to celebrate its fixed hegemony at the center of the system, whereas MCI WorldCom wanted to locate its hegemony in the sphere of pure circulation (stemming from its technology that displaces the built environment). The third image belongs to GE (2010). The cityscape is present-day Shanghai. Here Oriental and Occidental architecture seamlessly blend, producing the new landscape icon for global capital.

Abstractions of deterritorialization and reterritorialization replace the historical contradictions within a political economy of capitalist deterritorialization and reterritorialization. The result is an ideological mystification in which social conflict played out across material landscapes disappears. As always, the same images can reveal multiple stories: the visualization of Capital in vector forms represents a superficial claim to the legitimacy of corporate rule as a non-invasive form of economic reorganization; at the same time, it reveals Capital's desire to be free of "relatively fixed and immobile territorial infrastructures" (Brenner 1998:461).

7

The Cultural Geography of the Corporate Imaginary

The concept of cultural geography in the age of deterritorialization seems doomed to self-contradiction. Geographies of representation usually presume a correspondence between maps and particular sets of place and time coordinates, but the cultural geography of which we speak has itself been deterritorialized. The routine of mechanically reproduced images has long since disrupted the expectation that every cultural image has roots in a set of geographic and historical coordinates. When mediated through advertising's machinery of sign making, signs of culture become detached from the geographical referents that once located them. By the time we see some of these images in ads our acquaintance with the signifiers has traveled through multiple circuits of signification, and may be loaded with meanings that have little to do with conventional cultural geography.

Spectators in the contemporary era have learned to navigate conceptions of territory through chains of imagery. Once decontextualized, the meanings of images are rearticulated according to the codes of advertising – in the semiotic geography of advertising location becomes both fluid and extensive along a commodity sign chain. Culture is rendered digitally into an assortment of second-order signifiers that can be recombined or reordered to suit the advertising narrative.

Corporate advertising routinely draws on stereotypical representations that imagine an exotic cultural past – clichéd visions of culture lifted from the legacy of colonialism. These clichés construct non-Western culture from a relatively limited list of reified visual signifiers that nostalgically imagine a pre-modern era. To advertisers, traditional sartorial displays in premodern landscapes stand for Otherness. In this way, corporate ads claim to celebrate the ethos of universal humanism by invoking a mythic multiculturalism.

Equating the exotic with non-Western cultures defines Otherness in terms of a binary relationship organized from a privileged Western perspective.

> The origin of the idea of culture as a distinctive way of life, then, is closely bound up with a Romantic anti-colonialist penchant for suppressed "exotic" societies. The exoticism will resurface in the twentieth century in the primitivist features of modernism, a primitivism which goes hand-in-hand with the growth of modern cultural anthropology. (Eagleton 2000:12)

Early anthropology situated culture as an outcome of geographical adaptation. Over time a people produced a system of norms, values, and beliefs that allowed a group to adapt to a physical environment. Underlying symbolic life is materiality; the production of language, ideas, norms, objects, and values is interwoven with the activity necessary to survive in one's environment. In this view, culture is spatially bound. For those who lost sight of the historical dimension, it became all too easy to essentialize cultures, and celebrate the spiritually indigenous and "authentic."

National cultural forms excluded and devalued regional and local cultural formations as a means of legitimating the State as modernizer. The transnational corporation, however, recognizes different interests. Its practices must fluidly pass across national boundaries as it seeks out raw materials, cheaper production costs, and emerging consumer markets. Among transnational corporations, the "management of diversity, presented as the new prerequisite for sustainable competitive advantage, effectively continues global colonialism" (Banerjee and Linstead 2001:683). Unlike the cultural forms promoted by the nation-state to erect bastions surrounding national character, identity, and morality, corporate ads prefer the inclusive look of multiculturalism and the apparent valorization of cultural diversity.

Advertisers follow a formula when they assemble colorful tributes to multiculturalism. Ads draw on photo databases to devise versions of multiculturalism by editing together arbitrary assortments of interchangeable cultural markers (a Bedouin face, a Kenyan tribesman). Advertisers thus press signifiers of multiculturalism into the service of exchange value, forcing "cultural" signifiers into homogenized equivalence along the signifying chain of a multiculturalism narrative. The specificity and history of any given cultural sign is hollowed out and the shell is transformed into a second-order signifier that points towards a universal category of Otherness (desire rather than resistance).

Ideologically recognized as "universal humanism," this homogenization is purchased via "an infinite fragmenting of the system. The global interconnection of networks is doubled by a dislocation of the fragments moving further and further apart from each other" (Baudrillard 2001). By so severely decontextualizing the markers of cultural Otherness (itself a universal category), the corporate ad annuls the "singularity" of culture in favor of "culture as difference, a multicultural organization" (Baudrillard 2002a). In this way these ads both ideologically mask the structural forces of globalization that pulverize the singularity of locality and utterly refuse to acknowledge the agonizing resistances to globalization, while simultaneously revealing the underlying logic of globalization – "the globalization of exchange puts an end to the universality of values" (Baudrillard 2001).

Corporate advertising constructs a scopic multiculturalism as if it is the natural outcome of a network economy built on advanced electronic technologies – a streamlined mode of organization made to appear antagonistic to older forms of political domination, while conducive to the spread of democratization and human rights. The spectacle of multiculturalism fashioned out of second-order signifiers seems to soften commodification, and translates market forces into aesthetic values. This version of multiculturalism serves a necessary double hegemonic function: it suggests the disappearance of racism as a relic of an immature stage of development, while also depoliticizing the market and erasing the last vestiges of inequality and domination as a result of globalization.

The corporate hymn to multiculturalism, however, points not to the decline of racism, but rather to its semiotic reconstitution within the framework of global capitalism. By deterritorializing and delocalizing cultural geography, the canvas of corporate representation fosters a spectatorial vantage point that is "a kind of empty global position." It continues to draw on the legacy of colonial imagery, "treat[ing] each local culture the way the colonizer treats colonized people – as 'natives' whose mores are to be carefully studied and 'respected'" (Žižek 1997:29). Advertising concocts a tourist vision of multiculturalism that is

> a disavowed, inverted, self-referential form of racism, a "racism with a distance" – it "respects" the Other's identity, conceiving the Other as a self-enclosed "authentic" community towards which he, the multiculturalist, maintains a distance rendered possible by his privileged universal position. Multiculturalism is a racism which empties its own position of all positive content (the multiculturalist is not a direct racist, he doesn't oppose to the Other the particular values of his own culture), but

nonetheless retains this position as the privileged empty point of universality from which one is able to appreciate (and depreciate) properly other particular cultures – the multiculturalist respect for the Other's specificity is the very form of asserting one's own superiority. (Žižek 1997:44)

Landscapes of cultural geography

A set of preferred signifiers predominates throughout these ads, in part because they visually stand out, in part because they are recognizable from prior mass-media uses. One cluster of recurring signifiers of cultural geography that appear in advertising montages includes pyramids, camels, Bedouin, and sand-dune desert scenes. These images are familiar from nature documentaries, commodity advertising, magazines like *National Geographic*, and Hollywood films. A metonym not just for Egypt but for the literary and cinematic romanticism of the desert, the pyramids ooze exoticism. The exotic stereotypes remain loaded with colonial fantasies of the Other, with overused images of faraway foreign places that magically capture difference, adventure and romance.

And yet while they are recognizable, they are not locatable except in the broadest regional terms – a camel refers to North Africa, a minaret to Asia, or a cardinal to Italy. Though each image has been selected as a stereotypical signifier of traditional ways of life, each image is itself a floating signifier, a particle in the flow of signs that has been accelerated to meet the needs of Capital. Strung together, these signifiers speak to the universalizing reach of technology, capital, and corporate practice.

Where once map pins marked spots on cartographic representations, the abstracted signifiers of camels, turbans, and pyramids now become the map pins of cultural geography that substitute altogether for the mapping representation. Shuffled into a mix of scenes lifted from other climatic and cultural regions from across the planet, the camel contributes to a corporate cartography of globalization.

Interpreting these images depends more on how they are positioned in the advertising montage that frames them than on any relationship they might have to referents of origin. By itself the camel or pyramid is an unconstrained signifier, so radically abstracted from context that it can be made to mean any number of things. But sew it together with, say, a scene of a hypermodern urban skyline and we have two sides of a global coin, permitting corporations to claim they span core (supermodernity) and periphery (cultural exoticism) of the world system. For Cisco, the recognizable Bedouin turban wrap joins other multicultural signifiers to suggest that Cisco technology links all peoples together into a universal technological unity.

In 2000, HP sought to rename and reinvent itself by reinvigorating the symbol of its origins: the humble garage of its founders as the site of their technological inventiveness. What begins as a narrative of rediscovery rooted in an ethos of craftsmanship and innovation – Hewlett-Packard's origins as an anti-bureaucratic, pro-innovation organization – migrates into a travelogue narrated by the new CEO, Carly Fiorini. The garage is posed – like a tourist – in front of architectural styles defined by cultural geography: a pyramid, Beijing palaces, Notre Dame on the river Seine, and Wall Street. The shadow of the camel and its rider across the garage posed in front of the pyramid testifies to the global presence and reach of HP. The overlay of signs is reinforced with each scene of cultural geography – the next scene shows the garage parked in front of a Chinese palace. Leaping from one site (sight) of cultural geography to the next is a stark reminder of the seductiveness of time–space compression, and that photographic reproductions actually negate the relationship of representation to place.

Stamped with the GE logo, a camel caravan punctuates a collage of global cultural geography that includes a Kenyan runner, an Asian rice farmer, an Italian cardinal, Chinese and African school-children, and a Greek Orthodox priest. Key words flash on the screen: *communications, power, medical, lighting, transportation, capital, and plastics*. GE supplies these products and services to global markets conceptually exoticized by signifiers of multicultural diversity. Traditional images are situated adjacent to the imagery and language of technological modernity, and framed by triumphal music that cements the mix, turns political economy away from power relations. When the GE logo and slogan ("We bring good things to life") frames the Bedouin crossing the Sahara by camel at dusk, the scene affirms an emotional desire that GE's benevolence will cover the entire planet.

As advertising signifiers of cultural geography, the camel and pyramid are made to testify that global corporations can spread the infrastructure of modernity anywhere while preserving the cultural signifiers of that place. Siemens positioned a camel-in-the-desert scene to signify that no place is too distant for the penetration of Siemens' technologies. Siemens brands itself as a company bringing an array of critical technologies to the entire spectrum of humankind. Overall, these images stand for corporate global reach into a periphery defined by the harshness of nature and the exoticism of non-Western cultural differences, rather than by poverty, inequality, or the fears associated with their spatial referents – resource catastrophes and internecine warfare. In ads that construct a cultural geography of multicultural imagery, signifiers of culture, ethnicity, and locality become invested in the circulation of capital instead of being perceived as obstacles to that circulation. Whereas the historical legacy of colonialism, imperialism, and now neo-liberalism has been that Capital's penetration into the hinterland comes at the expense of nature and community alike throughout the periphery, the semiotic reconstruction of traditional ethnicity turns branded Capital into the pivotal actor that makes possible both peace and progress.

Among the most prominent of the cultural geography signifiers used to compose landscapes of globalization are facial portraits of a culturally diverse cast of characters, but none of these portraits are labeled or identified. Instead, the specificity of each face is redirected to signify the persistence and authenticity of traditional cultures per se. Portraiture in these montages would seem gratuitous if we were looking for straightforward narrative continuity. But if instead we recognize these abstracted portraits as filling the gap between space and place, then their presence offers testimonials to the universalism of the corporate entity – "the negation of a particular identity transforms this identity into the symbol of identity and fullness as such" (Žižek 1997:29). As signs of cultural

geography, these faces suggest a proxy for the geographical coordinates of a corporate global presence.

Boeing surrounds its cultural geography of faces with the frame, "A jet that goes so far . . . it brings the world closer." Geography of place is not abolished; it must still be implied so that a grander signified can be revealed – the ability to span and unify space. The premise of place is requisite to Boeing's narrative, but it is a kind of place that lacks grounding. Fittingly, Boeing punctuates its ad with a landscape composed as a gridded mosaic of images meant to represent a global array of non-Western cultures, so that the brand and the map of the world become identical.

A utopia of equivalence

The idea of representation assumes an exact symmetry between the sign and its external referent. This premise is an exaggeration, a "utopian" fantasy, but it is necessary if we are to believe in, and act on, the conviction that there is a correspondence between the real and the signs we use to represent it. In the television era, simulation, however, threatens to overwhelm the principle of referentiality, substituting for it "the emancipation of the sign," so that signs can enter into infinite circuits of combination and recombination. Once the processes of "substituting signs of the real for the real itself" pick up speed, "the age of simulation thus begins with a liquidation of all referentials" (Baudrillard 1994:2). As much as any discursive form, advertising conforms to Baudrillard's premise of a "utopia of equivalence," for its framework permits the purest emancipation of signs from referents and allows them to be exchanged, substituted and combined in virtually any combination or order. A signifier interjected into an advertising montage is placed into relationships of commutability – convertible and exchangeable with other formally equivalent (by virtue of being placed in the same abstract, empty spaces) signifiers serially arranged and narrated.

Another Bedouin-in-the-desert scene shows up in a 2003 ChevronTexaco ad, keyed to mean "far from markets" with ensuing scenes of African women and a Chinese boy arranged to mean "across the globe." To ChevronTexaco, nature's geography – its oceans and deserts – has "locked" sources of value, "growth and promise" far from the non-Western communities (here conceptualized as markets) that constitute human geography. When ChevronTexaco merged, it triggered a global branding campaign entitled "Turning Partnership into Energy" – "to deliver energy and all the growth and promise that goes with it." ChevronTexaco covers continents and oceans, and appears to encompass a universal Spirit that has been fractured into, and reassembled from, innumerably framed photographic scenes. The ad relies on a photo mosaic technique that turns each photographic scene, abstracted from a culture somewhere around the world, into a distinct "framed tile image" arrayed in a flattened (two-dimensional) field of rows to form larger images. The field of tiles spins and tilts, each tile (a social relationship) becomes a pixel in the formation of a larger mosaic image. It might be difficult to find a more exact illustration of simulation as Baudrillard defines it – here signs truly are exchanged and mutated against each other. Each scene becomes a pixel, and each pixel becomes a data point in the "meta-image" of a global, universal boy whose face symbolizes the global community made possible by ChevronTexaco's promise of a global future predicated on partnership and growth.

The scenes that spark the visual transition from the simulated three-dimensional world of video snapshots to the flattened symbolic field repeat the primary theme in couplet form – people working in pairs. Each framed signifier repeats the ad's primary message – ChevronTexaco stands for building partnerships between Chevron and Texaco, between the faces of West and East, between modernity and tradition, between producers and "communities where we operate," between energy extraction and environmentalism.

> For us, corporate responsibility means being responsible stewards of the environment and constructive partners in the communities where we do business. It means respecting human rights, valuing people and embracing diversity in its broadest sense. (ChevronTexaco website)

Another 2003 campaign ad, "Prosperity," framed a global multicultural community covering "180 countries." To emphasize its global reach, ChevronTexaco translated the ad into Arabic, English, Angolan Portuguese, Brazilian Portuguese, Russian, and Spanish versions.

> *The world's growing quickly. So is its need for energy.*
> *That's why in over 180 countries, we're sharing technology and the skills to use it.*
> *Working together, we're developing energy faster.*
> *Developing people faster.*
> *And accelerating prosperity for all of us.*
> *ChevronTexaco. Turning partnership into energy.*

Time-lapse photography creates an arcing blur of color (energy) that speeds through a dawning urban landscape before morphing into a school bus of Japanese children. This unfolds into a narrated sequence of multiracial, multiethnic scenes that geographically span the global reach and presence of ChevronTexaco. Anchored in the universal imagery of an

Anchoring ChevronTexaco's stream of diversity images, this picture epitomizes a cultural geography composed of floating signifiers – indeed it is so severely abstracted that even anthropologists have difficulty locating or identifying it. We have several choices here – we might say that this is what happens when cultural geography becomes fully deterritorialized; or that this is a phantom referential. Either way, though this image invites us to inquire about the character's origins, it mostly encourages us to see her as something that she is not – the Universal Exotic Other – by placing her in a framework that substitutes the structural form of sign equivalence for the determinate social circumstances that may have produced her.

indigenous mother and baby, a series of smiling men and women of color, drawn predominantly from Africa and Asia, aims at over-representing peoples from the developing world. Each decontextualized and abstracted photo carries the same weight and significance – each becomes a signifier of ChevronTexaco's respect and support for global multiculturalism. ChevronTexaco claims to exercise technically enlightened and gentle command of a political economy of energy – a benevolent paternalistic hegemony that will serve the diverse constituencies of the world.

The structural law of value – whereby all values are exchangeable as signs and all signs are exchangeable as values – governs this sequence of cultural representations. By contrast, monetized commodity relationships disappear from view. Even though contractual relations may be the shifting ground that motivates ChevronTexaco's every move, such old-school exchange relations seem strangely unnecessary in the world of corporate branding. Money rarely changes hands, and commodification barely registers as a structuring force. Indeed the narrative emphasizes the sharing of energy technologies (both products and knowledge) as a vehicle for "Developing people faster. And accelerating prosperity for all of us." The stress on partnerships rather than divisive conflicts with environmentalist opponents ("NGOs like the World Wildlife Fund, The Nature Conservancy, or the World Business Council for Sustainable Development") leads ChevronTexaco to conclude on its website "that partnerships help turn values into value for all of us." Gone is the specter of expropriation; gone is the market hegemony of a vast combination of capital. In their stead this merged combination of capitals stands for global community and environmental sustainability by renouncing a Hobbesian marketplace in favor of entrepreneurial partnerships.

The visual effects that form the ad's concluding scene draw attention to the layers of representation that constitute Capital's vision of itself in relation to global communities. Abruptly, the frame pulls back from a strikingly exotic woman to reveal hundreds of tile images of people, tankers, oil rigs, and landscapes that then swirl together before morphing into a pointillist mosaic of a dark-haired woman looking adoringly upon her smiling baby swaddled in a colorful blanket. We call her the ChevronTexaco Madonna – she is framed as Capital's meta-image, its brand image – a morphing swirl of abstracted images of cultural geography, technologies, and peoples that momentarily coalesce into the symbolic warmth of the Other's loving, nurturing smile. But then her image too is absorbed into the gravitational field that forms a vanishing point inside the first "O" of ChevronTexaco.

Baudrillard's general critique of advertising sees it as an uber-discourse that translates "all original cultural forms" and absorbs all other "modes of expression" into a depthless machine of signification that is both "instantaneous and instantaneously forgotten" (1994:87). Like other corporate ads that rely on the montage form, the ChevronTexaco ad houses a signification process that rests upon a process of fracturing cultural meaning into "the smallest common denominator of all signification." ChevronTexaco's visual technique actually draws attention to the way in which atomized bits of signification are treated as floating signifiers that can be recombined to form hybridized signifiers. The act of appropriation energizes these floating signifiers – they are re-motivated by the narrative frameworks and agendas utilized by any given ad campaign. No sooner than the Madonna's image is given significance, her image is again pulled into the decomposition of meaning and returned to what she had been – a particle of meaning – one among thousands of undifferentiated frames that have been absorbed into the vortex of meaning at the center of ChevronTexaco.

Produced from a mix of other similarly emptied signifiers, ChevronTexaco's Corporate Madonna is a computational feat visually constituted from the shadings of a thousand photographic surfaces. She is a feat of technical artistry, a composition emptied of depth, so ruthlessly dissociated from any personal cultural biography that her mosaic representation can no longer even perform the function of cultural geography. For this brief instant, her mosaic representation is undifferentiated from the map of the whole. What we see here in an "unarticulated, instantaneous form" is the visual premise of the mosaic form – that her image is a composite of the universal diversity of similar biographical tiles.

And yet her instantaneous significance as "Madonna" can only occur if we recognize her likeness (her similitude) in a symbol that has profound religious depth in our cultural history. Here is one of the oddities of contemporary sign culture – in the midst of the "Triumph of superficial form, of the smallest common denominator of all signification, degree zero of meaning, triumph of entropy over all possible tropes," symbolic depth of meaning can re-erupt, if only to fall back again a nanosecond later into a fused stream of fleeting, and disintegrating, signifiers (Baudrillard 1994:87).

Advertising of this sort exposes a fundamental contradiction at the heart of a sign economy – a dialectic of acceleration and entropy. The faster images circulate through the sign economy the more they break down the possibilities of meaningful belief. The "degree zero of meaning" is easy to engineer – even the worst advertiser can do it – but as the signifiers tumble out of sight, the logic of advertising demands that they be replaced by others and still others and, as the process speeds up, the insincerity of signification mounts with the endless looping of the "degree zero of meaning." This is the larger cultural framework within which the ChevronTexaco ad contrives its hyperreal global community. And so all the belief that might have been summoned on behalf of the charged symbolization of the ChevronTexaco Madonna disappears a moment later in a stream of assorted, and now blurred, images. What remains is an aesthetic sensibility – an eye-catching simulation necessary to induce an instantaneous recognition corresponding to the velocity of televisual flows. The "value" supposedly conjured by ChevronTexaco is a clichéd emotional signifier of traditional culture – the simulated Madonna and her baby smile away the power relations of gender, race, and class constituted by capital, religion, and nation.

Globalizing the imagined community

Benedict Anderson (1983) coined the concept of the "imagined community" to make sense of the nationalist sentiments shared by those who, though they may never have met one another, identified with a nation-state. For transnational capital, the imagined community extends globally beyond national boundaries, where imagined communities form around branded products and services. When compiled together, ethnic difference as signified by dress and language is made to point towards a universal humanism *à la The Family of Man*. In this kind of montage, nationalism disappears, and the corporation stamps this vision of humanity with its logo. The national flag is replaced by the corporate brands that serve as a totem for a global citizen based on participation in the cultural economy not on human rights. These multicultural representations celebrate global interconnectedness.

A 1996 IBM ad elevated the imagined community to the transnational scene where the binding force includes the "language" of IBM itself. Under the tagline "Solutions for a Small Planet," IBM ads in the mid 1990s self-consciously featured English subtitles to narrate IBM's global universal presence amongst the diversity of cultures on planet Earth. By allowing people to speak in their native tongues, the IBM ads demonstrated a respect for diversity, while also claiming to provide the means of bridging ethnic, nationalist identities and language communities through its computing technologies.

> *1st African man: Something magical*
> *. . . is happening to our planet.*
> *European children: It's growing smaller.*
> *European woman: Every day the global web of computers. . .*
> *2nd African man: weaves us more tightly together.*
> *Asian woman: Join us.*
> *A group of young scholars: Wander through a distant library.*
> *Icelander man: Turn your corner store . . .*
> *into a mini-multinational.*
> *European man: Curious?*
> *German man: IBM can get you there.*
> *Young American woman in a rowboat: Just plug in . . .*
> *1st African man: . . . and the world is yours.*

The common thread among otherwise linguistically diverse peoples that turns them into an "imagined community" is their ability to recognize IBM. Suturing together phrases from many languages, subtitled in English (perhaps because it is still the master language, or simply because the primary target audience for this is in the US and not the rest of the world), creates the impression of a shared global discourse. Weaving together this community of discourse parallels the metaphor of "weaving" people together via a "global web of computers," and it would appear to be a community based not on exclusion, but on universal access to the new means of production – IBM tools.

Collapsing and preserving binaries

A tripartite spatial layering – a core, a semi-periphery and a periphery – became an enduring feature of the capitalist world system. That order corresponds to common-sense understandings about the penetration of modern forms: the core characterized by speed, motion, and constant change; the semi-periphery by rustic stubborn ethnicity; the periphery by backwardness. Corporate advertising highlights these divisions to show how a process of globalization driven by network technologies preserves the cultural distinctions, while abolishing economic disadvantages. Because traditional cultural signifiers suggest spatial distance from the center of the world system, as well as historical distance (the past) from the leading edges of technological and market innovations, stereotypical significations of traditional culture thus indicate the capacity of Capital to integrate both the near and far and the past and present within a global system.

During the 2000 Olympics, an IBM ad told an amusing story about a group of Scottish fishermen gathered on the North Sea's remote rocky shoreline. Their quaint spot is identified as the site of a traditional fish market in a semi-peripheral region of the world system. Even out here on the edge of the Old World, unseen forces threaten to reshape traditional markets.

> *Male voiceover: "The sea is a harsh mistress. No one knows this better than the men who fish the Firth of Forth, bringing back their catch each morning to sell in the old market."*
> *Group of fishermen:*
> *1st man: "Where's Eric then?"*
> *2nd man: "He never misses a market."*
> *3rd man: "There was a bad squall last night."*
> *4th man: "Wretched."*
> *5th man: "Maybe he ran up on some rocks."*
> *4th man: "Maybe he was swept overboard."*
> *2nd man: "Maybe he drowned."*
> *3rd man: "Or sharks"?*
> *Whole group: "Ah sharks, sharks," they echo.*
> *A younger man standing away from the group: "Maybe he already sold his catch, online, from the boat. Maybe we're on the cusp of something so big we don't even know it. Virtual marketplaces, frictionless economies, the invisible guiding hand of capitalism manifesting itself, even here." He turns and walks away.*
> *The group of older men: [pause] "Sharks. Sharks. Definitely sharks."*
> *Female voiceover: "Now you can sell anything, from anywhere. Wireless e-business from IBM."*

The "shark" joke, performed in the fishermen's thick accents, positions these men as superstitious, stubborn, and set in their ways, the doubting Thomases of the technological revolution. Their way of life has changed little over the centuries and they still must bring their catch to the "old market." IBM's joke depends on tone of delivery – their laconic, measured lack of affect frames their speculations about the possible misfortunes that may have befallen their comrade, thus exaggerating a stereotype of men hardened by a life at sea.

Are these fishermen stuck in their old ways because they are so spatially removed from the modern world? While their ethnicity again signifies their traditionalism on the edge of the world system, it symbolically points to all who have stubbornly refused to learn how new technologies can make their livelihoods easier and more profitable. This ad, more than most, articulated the macro-theoretical issues swirling about us all – "Virtual marketplaces, frictionless economies, the invisible guiding hand of capitalism manifesting itself, even here," on the spatial and economic fringe of the global system.

Like IBM's other commercials, this suggests that advanced technologies can fit into any cultural setting and improve economic efficiency while leaving the culture intact. IBM depicts its wireless service advantageously linking the fisherman (small businessman) to the global market and simultaneously "liberating" him from the local market. Ironically, IBM also captures the unintended social privatization likely to follow from their vaunted structural change in how markets are organized. Eric no longer need go to the old market to sell his fish and can thus disengage from the face-to-face social relations tied to the fish market. Where, if not here, in the basic social relations of the region, is the production of culture located? Perhaps the butt of the joke isn't just the old fishermen prone to idle speculation, but rather insular business cultures that enable narrow-minded habits rather than forward thinking.

The relationship between systems of capital and locality is a recurring motif in this advertising genre. Whether it's the serial montage mixing together decontextualized traces of locality or the ethnographic montage that focuses on just one locality, both approaches legitimize the penetration of capital into more and more spheres of social and cultural life, reconceptualized as networks. These ads also split social formations into the systemic scale and the particular scale. The systemic consists of technological, financial, informational, and service networks that span the globe as an undifferentiated totality – represented as visual abstractions (grids, light beams, schematics) and personal relations (handshakes, shared screen texts). The particular, on the other hand, is dislocated in a place signified by ethnic identifiers – dress, customs, language, and accent. At the global scale, Capital imagines landscapes as pure systems space; at the scale of the local, it conjures landscapes as affect.

Landscapes of networked seriality

Advertising for information sector corporations like Cisco, Oracle, Microsoft, and IBM aims to craft fluid, mobile, yet civil and moral landscapes. They draw transnational landscapes as consensual landscapes of universal inclusion and unification. These serial social landscapes take shape within a video architecture that assembles clipped utterances made by multiracial (signified by skin color), multicultural (signified by clothing styles), multi-accentual (accented English), and multiregional (rural and urban, core and periphery backgrounds) speakers. Cisco's millennium campaign presented each speaker as a node in a global network of communication, and each voice continued or completed the utterances of prior speakers as if together they constituted the single voice of an imagined community. The device of a recurring phrase that repeats, punctuates, and unifies the utterances lends these serial discourses a ritual feel – almost like a liturgical form that successively invokes a common response at the end. The serial editing of spatially and socially separated discursive acts creates the illusion of speech that is social – a form of speech that can only occur where there is already a shared bond. This device *simulates* the discursive voice of the multitude. For the communication technology industries it supports the metanarrative that free, open, and fast communication eliminates all discriminations associated with race, gender, ethnicity, and social positioning. Instead of hierarchies of wealth, power, and labor, there are differences of cultural geography: "The multitude is a grouping without unity. People come together in the multitude, on the basis of what they have in common; but without becoming One, without subordinating their singularities or negating their differences" (Shaviro 2004).

Stringing together markers from diverse cultural settings maps a simulated new material reality upon which acceptance of cultural difference might be hung, while also fostering the impression that the particular corporation operates fluidly across transnational settings. Imagined community exists in these corporate technology ads on the premise that a global network has been built to conduct commerce as a way of organizing social life. The network infrastructure offers the scaffolding for these serialized chains of imagined community. This new social formation appears to be organized around the flow of information coupled with a shared sense of global citizenship, a social philosophy of multiculturalism, and an unlimited horizon of social and technological progress.

The first advertisement in Cisco's 1999 campaign opens with a Chinese youth arriving by boat. Standing amidst a densely urban pedestrian throng, he speaks the first words of what will be a world narrative.

"There are over 800,000 job openings"
A young man of indeterminate nationality stands atop a wall in the middle of nowhere: "for Internet specialists. Right now."
Two young African boys, arm in arm, declare in unison: "Three million more in the next five years."
A ten-year-old European boy in a swing: "By the time I'm eighteen,"
A preteen female echoes the same phrase: "By the time I'm eighteen, over a billion jobs will require Internet skills."
Asian girl: "Are you ready?"
American girl leaning out of truck window: "Are you ready?"
Company voiceover: "Virtually all Internet traffic travels across the systems of one company. The same one sponsoring thousands of networking academies. Cisco Systems, empowering the Internet generation."
The two African boys: "We're ready."
Chinese girl: "Are you?"

The Internet economy beckons youth from around the planet, telling them that future jobs belong to those who possess Internet skills. Not only is Cisco at the material heart of this emerging Internet system, they also "sponsor" networking academies where youth from all over the world can acquire the training that will prepare them for a promising work future in which computer networking skills will make them mobile. Mobility means here more than upward occupational movement and social success and higher status, it also means being spatially mobile (free labor) to take work in the emerging global economy. Migration in pursuit of Internet employment will become routinely transnational with the promise of a more affluent life: a young man flying a kite against a brightly tinted sky symbolizes opportunities for well-being – leisure time and personal choice.

Their multi-accentual statement fosters the impression of something that is not stated, but implied – that the Internet economy will bring with it, not only jobs, but relative egalitarianism as well, along with a world discursively unmarked by power relations. Absent from this world are signs of domination or even authority relations. There appears to be no ranking by race, gender, nationality, or age. Social rank seems to play no discernible role in how this string of utterances has been arranged. This impression is, in part, a function of how the ad has been crafted – the serialized discourse casts all relationships as lateral and horizontal relations, as opposed to vertical (authority of rank) relations.

Serial relations are portrayed as borderless amongst this Internet generation, a sensibility reinforced by backgrounds that appear to continuously drift on the horizontal plane within each frame. Though the speaking subjects address the camera, they almost appear to float in relationship to the drifting landscapes behind them. Though Cisco's ad wanders from continent to continent, national culture to national culture, it tends to be China-centric. This is where the Cisco ad begins – in a sepia-tinted Chinese harbor where the young migrant coming off a boat points to new opportunities – and where it ends, with a young girl asking if "you" are ready. The passage from sepia atmospheres to a pale blue may symbolically alert us to a transition that is taking place from dirty industrial economies to uncongested new economies – from relatively primitive forms of modernity to a now-digitized, and, hence, ubiquitous form of modernity; from an authoritarian state (China) to a less authoritarian capitalism (China)?

Ads like this construct a curious amalgam of place and space. Assumptions about location are built into the emphasis on signifiers of cultural geography, and yet location cues are rarely sufficient to precisely identify particular places. Though inferences about place identification may be surmised from photographic codes, most of these "place-markers" are situated in hard-to-define spaces because a spatial indeterminacy is essential to the logic of abstraction that makes ads like this work. Instead of situated places, these ads offer utopia as deterritorialized spaces. Place is only important here as an index of varied origins (poverty, lack of opportunity, etc.), as the flipside of where the Internet generation is going. What irony – a utopia that originally meant "no place" (because it was an impossibility) is now made to refer to the weightless anyplace of the networked society.

Cisco's ad arranges a discourse about a new mode of production and distribution – transnational systems of computers connected by the telecommunications network known as the Internet – and its impact on a Global Society. And yet, the ad either leaves out, or veils, all of the crucial relations that make up this new system of global markets. Markets are assumed but unmentioned, while a future of wage labor is not cast as grueling workdays, but as a utopian ideal. While the assumption of networked computer technologies animates and gives meaning to the ads, those technologies make almost no appearance in the video. Naturally enough – this is after all an advert – technology must be translated from material force into signifying force. But the Cisco ad avoids this technological materiality even in its status as signifier by avoiding its visual presence. Its spiritual presence is far greater, an aura of hope evoked by the abbreviated referent of the "Internet." Never mind what kinds of deskilled factory jobs this new economy of tomorrow will generate, or what kinds of labor migration will result. Never mind who will own and control the technological infrastructure that Cisco is selling. Here, in Cisco's serialized landscape of cultural geography, all that matters is the anticipation of a new era of prosperity and relative affluence for all, mediated by the promise of Internet technologies.

Cisco's "Are you ready?" campaign embraced a genuine and unfeigned tone of voice. The serene, therapeutic background music consists of an Enya-esque new-age soprano that frames the scenes with an ethereal peacefulness. The music lends the ads their metacommunicative axis – an aura of hopeful sincerity, peaceful and purposeful, frames the discursive landscape of the emergent global civil society. Lovingly paced, there is no hint of anti-social speed in this world mediated through the Internet, but rather a sense of undisturbed connection. In this framework, the montage sews together the dispersed, but serialized speech acts into a unified discourse – to produce the "monologue" of a global community.

The edited string of sound bites from speakers of varying nationalities and ethnicities envisions a landscape of the post-nation-state, as speakers from China, Russia, Spain, Vietnam, India, Italy, and North Africa serially constitute a transnational imagined community. The subject of their imagined conversation concerns the growth of e-commerce across the Internet – an economy expanding so rapidly that it will soon be the glue that binds us all. To be sure, this is the imagined community of the electronic telecommunications era – the new digital era – and not the kind of imagined community rooted in the nationalist newspaper. The imagined community that marked the transition into modernity was a necessary precursor for the emergence of the nation-state. The difference of locality (language, customs, and history) had to be homogenized into a simultaneously political and cultural entity. By contrast, in the imagined community that accompanies global capitalism, "We, the people" must now include others with radically different cultural histories. Corporate discourse evokes a utopian imagery of harmonious cultural difference that thrives under the umbrella of the globalized network of technocapitalism.

In this landscape there are no authoritarian intrusions, no limits on freedom, no maneuvering for power. Cisco's "Are you ready?" campaign imagines a new world order, a global marketplace tied together by its Internet infrastructure. Conversely, Cisco hails a new global marketplace freed up from the political maneuverings, intrusions, and inefficiencies of governments and bureaucracies. Projecting from the expansion of the Internet economy, Cisco's community of speakers envision the coming demise of "paper money" as a liberating moment in human history. Paper currencies are situated as the product of State power and their enforcement within territorial boundaries. Dissolving the interventions and restraints government imposes on free exchanges in the marketplace, the system of transactions that runs through Cisco's universal system heralds a new era of freedom and possibility. Cisco imagines a landscape of non-power relations, a landscape free of restrictions, domination, or oppression. On this boundary-less landscape, Cisco projects a quiet revolution from the obtrusive authority of the nation-state to the unobtrusive capacity of interconnected computer technologies to organize the whole of everyday life via markets. Cisco depicts a global Internet economy and the imagined community of transnational multiculturalism as transcending the State and the hegemony of paper currencies. Instead, the newly unfettered, free-market computer technologies seem to lead inexorably to the eclipse of paper money and its replacement by digital cash.

These ads rhetorically reproduce glimpses of Cisco's philosophical goals and direction. Cisco is heavily invested, not just in terms of capital expenditures, but also rhetorically, in depicting the new Internet economy as "level[ing] the playing field by providing access and opportunity for lifelong learners of all ages in any location." Conceptualizing the links between education, jobs, and society, Cisco offers this vision at its corporate website: "As society makes large digital leaps in teaching and learning, it is increasingly important that no one be left behind. The Internet has the power to serve as a great equalizer."

Towards a social ontology of simulation and virtuality

The Who's "Baba O'Riley" framed Cisco's 2006–7 "Welcome to the human network" tour across the landscape of networked globalization. With an energetic and enthusiastic rock 'n' roll beat and rhythm, Cisco imagines a global landscape where space–time compression has been achieved. The ad catalogues a list of positive social possibilities that accompany space–time compression, as Cisco offers an ideological account of emancipation and empowerment that corresponds to a stage of global society oriented around a networked infrastructure of computer technologies. Sketching out an ontology of social life, the ad first extends the premises of universal humanism to all who have been historically relegated to the status of the Other – equality regardless of race, ethnicity, or gender becomes a distributed resource in an age of universal network access. Second, it reconceptualizes society as a "human network." Third, it redefines "place" as a site of shared meaning, so that "place" can be relocated anywhere in virtual or simulated time and space. Fourth, it depends on an aesthetic of cultural geography to signify the vitality of social life. Fifth, it requires that we entertain the possibility that the virtual reconstitution of the social provides a more equitable basis for allocating quality-of-life resources.

This validates corporate globalization as a means of democratizing progress. A young girl's slightly breathless voice, full of wonder and anticipation, narrates the tour through a colorful montage of 108 scenes of multicultural faces and geographies that highlights the budding forms of social relations in a global society governed by the invisible hand of technology. Rather than the homogeneity and monoculture critics associate with globalization, Cisco's global society envisions heterogeneity and difference, regardless of the space one occupies.

Welcome. Welcome to a brand new day.
The new way of getting things done.
Welcome to a place where maps are re-written and remote villages are included.
A place where body language is business language.
Where people subscribe to people, not magazines.
And the team you follow now follows you.
Welcome to a place where books re-write themselves.
Where you can drag and drop people wherever they want to go.
And the phone doubles as a train ticket, plane ticket or lift ticket.
Welcome to a place where a wedding is captured and recaptured again and again.
Where home video is experienced everywhere at once.
Where a library travels across the world.
Where businesses are born.
Countries are transformed.
And we're more powerful together than we could be apart.
Welcome to the human network.

Cisco declares a new paradigm in human history, the dawn of an enlightened globalization and the rise of a global society rooted in the shrinking of space. Technologies of video conferencing, mobile computing, smart phones (not just voice, but data, maps, and video), all eclipse geographical distance and offer a "new way of getting things done," creating new kinds of relationships between people. Well-designed technology

No matter how remote the space or place – culturally or geographically – Cisco claims that its tools for the global network have eclipsed the limits of distance, both spatially and socially, making everyone part of the human network. Semiotically, the point can be made by turning to exaggerated signifiers of Indigenous Otherness.

facilitates undistorted communication across spaces, languages, and cultures, permitting global business to proceed without friction or disruption. Wireless handheld devices – networked and decentralized computing technologies – will allow dispersed individuals to spatially reorganize their way through everyday life. Unobtrusive technological devices also enable individuals to socially connect with others, instead of the orbits of consumer privatism (magazine subscriptions) that have colonized our desires. And when home video can be "experienced every-where at once," simultaneity makes possible the instant viral cultural product that appears as the end-game of democratization. None of the old dichotomies need be continued – the division between private and public spheres of discourse is bridged in a single digital stroke and Andy Warhol's snide insight about the ephemeral nature of commodified celebrity turns into a utopian moment that enables every one of us to be noticed and appreciated. The dialectic of recognition that underlies the arduous history of the master–slave dialectic resolved just like that.

Cisco's landscapes portend stories of enhanced productivity and the emancipation of human potentiality because the network constitutes "a place where people can collaborate face-to-face" even when they are on separate continents. In this new day, every person – even the most indigenous, even the poor – can be considered the moving center of the world. Remote villages are just as much a part of the new world system as global cities because networked mapping changes perceptions and experiences of geography such that there is no more periphery in a technologically unified global society. With the right tools, geography and social barriers are fluidly transcended; imagined communities can exist in space, and amongst dispersed individuals across places. All of the old hierarchical barriers seem to vanish – race, age, gender, class, education, nationality – none can stand up to the liberating force of network technologies. When knowledge becomes accessible to every-one, regardless of class, race, or geographic location, there will be no more knowledge-underprivileged and everyone can participate in the production of knowledge across time and space. If knowledge is power, then we are bound for an era that is domination free.

Across Cisco's landscapes, wireless technologies permit convergence and frictionless movement without the inconvenience of currency trans-actions or bureaucratic rules; all modes of governance become seamless. Transnational businesses unfettered by the regulatory rigidities and territorial politics of nation-states can operate on any scale, trans-forming backwards regions and countries into vistas of supermodern urban splendor and wealth. Wirelessly distributed network technologies evolve a new division of labor that unites people, rather than divides them – capitalism and the nation-state are each neatly sublated by the presence of a network technology that is not concerned with reproducing power.

A profusion of children's images lend the network a human face while also marking the colorful confluence of multiracial and multicultural formations within the global society. This presence of children is a standard feature in corporate montages – the strategy of exaggerating children's presence stresses the *nascent* quality of global synergies necessary for a new society of equal opportunities for all. When coupled with the upbeat scenery and hyperreal photographic styles, the over-representation of children's faces feels hopeful. Consequently, ads that signify inspiration, imagination, or creativity are strewn with images of children constructed as naturally curious and enchanted with learning.

Mixed with images of children is a second set of cultural markers – skylines, towers, basilicas, and mountains. These highly aestheticized representations of architectural styles point outward to the global rather than downward towards a specific socio-historical place.

Cisco's advertising portrays a global society whose primary axis is the Internet – a ubiquitous, but invisible, network of communication tools that bridges distance and connects persons with other persons, with groups, with businesses, and with mediated information. The emergent world imagined by Cisco is profoundly social, sometimes even communal, and not at all subject to the isolationism of hyper-individuated privatism that sociologists see as the undoing of community.

The sharing that connects, rather than separates, takes place via monitors that proliferate across Cisco's landscapes, from cameras and handheld devices to the jumbo screen that covers the side of a Times Square skyscraper, deterritorializing culture while also universalizing and normalizing its spectacular form. Digital technologies organized through the Internet also soften the profile of commodification – in these landscapes commodification has become universal, but its integration into digital technologies makes it less visible and less overt, ruled now by the logic of reason rather than greed. With the disappearance of money, commodification is no longer an end in itself, but merely a means to the freely chosen desires of unimpeded individual movement and empowerment.

Miniature screens themselves signify at once the flexible mobility and utility that network technologies bring to the architecture of everyday life. Mobile communication technology extends the penetration of networks into civil society, "deepening the presence of a culture dominated by a pervasive system of electronic communication made of text, images, and sounds in a relentless interactive exchange" (Castells et al. 2007:258). Blogs have changed the landscape of political discourse. Twitter and text messaging are changing the language of interaction. Wikipedia redefines and democratizes (for better or worse) the meaning of the encyclopedia, and the sociology of smart phones will take years to play out. Google Maps married to Geographic Information Systems has revolutionized mapping, while Facebook and other social media have fundamentally reshaped the architecture of everyday life for youth across the continents. But none of these has yet abolished the capitalist division of labor or made less precarious the nature of wage labor amongst the multitudes.

The "drag and drop" metaphor taken from desktop computing visualizes a profoundly different materiality to social life as a way of signifying the possibilities of mobile interconnection across the world of everyday business. The transfer works only as a metaphor since there is as yet no material equivalent to dragging and dropping someone in everyday life. Still, it is an evocative metaphor for the possibilities of a virtual social life. When a female executive drags and drops a file on her screen, it visually materializes into a videophone connection with a young man in transit. His visual genesis as a file begins to suggest relationships based on the flow of intertextual signs. Scenes such as this imagine relationships between bodies as relationships between signs. Cisco's narrative tells of empowering people via their connection to "the network" and the technological machines that they hold or to which they are tethered. To become part of "the human network" is to become a cyborg.

The human network becomes a landscape turned into a chain of signification. Its productivity is rooted almost exclusively in symbolic labor. Even though these signs all point ultimately to social life organized around networks of commodities, in another sense the signs erase commodity relationships, particularly the commodity chains that link producers with sites of distribution and consumption, as well as the outsourcing of production to subcontractors relying on cheap labor to fuel a labor-intensive factory model.

In Cisco's narrative, computerized globalization marks a dramatic departure from earlier stages of modernization that sought to diminish traditional cultures in everyday life, but preserve them in museums. With the tools of digital communications, ethnic groups can now be seen retaining their cultural traditions and practices and still becoming integrated into a global community that participates in the pleasures and desires of consumerism. This is illustrated by a vignette of an Indian wedding recorded and then shared over the network with relatives and friends throughout the world who emotionally watch the video on handheld devices and computer screens. Meet the global extended family distributed geographically around the world, united by global computer networks.

Though a diasporic culture has been deterritorialized across the network, its visual signifiers remain dominated by colorful traditional attire. Cisco's narrative shows how a system of wireless handheld devices integrated via network technology can permit members of culturally identified ethnic groups to retain their authenticity and identity by maintaining contact, no matter where they have become geographically dispersed. Where diasporic communities once maintained solidarity by cloistering themselves in urban enclaves and separating themselves from mainstream society, the Cisco infrastructure suggests an unprecedented range of choices – individual migrants can appreciate the benefits of modern society while maintaining the bonds of their clan, and escape assimilation into the nondescript culture of the metropole. Distance no longer separates – a kin group distributed in gatherings around the world shares the immediacy of the wedding and its emotional vibrancy. Of course, the choice of a joyous wedding stacks the deck a bit. Suppose instead that the event was a Palestinian funeral and the same technology was used to share a politics of rage and grief among their globally dispersed numbers. Would not the same technology of connecting people permit groups to bond for purposes of war as well as love? Would there not then be moaning about the shrinking of our world – that there is no longer a safe "here?"

The Indian wedding ceremony demonstrates the social and cultural benefits of collapsing space–time coordinates, while digitally replicating the place–time experience as often as is desired. The event exists in real time in as many places as there are people to view it, and the event is preserved so that it can be enjoyed again. Here is a global social landscape in which distance is overcome not by nullifying time, but by digitally preserving it and reproducing it. "Instantaneity (nullifying the resistance of space and liquefying the materiality of objects) makes every moment seem infinitely capacious" (Bauman 2000:125).

The wedding scene strikes a visual symbolic balance between modernity and tradition. As a semiotic device, the image of a young man digitally recording the wedding registers a binary opposition between business suit and turban head-wrap. The recording he makes is transmitted and received by a young woman (friend or family) in another city. The gadgetry of high-tech modernity meshes seamlessly with premodern cultural practices. The celebratory ritual event is beheld as easily by the individual whose migration choices have taken her away from family and friends, as by a gathered kin group who thus observe the wedding collectively from afar. For them the virtual event is no less social because it is consumed via the computer screen. With a webcam mounted above it (so the events in this auxiliary location can be shared at the wedding site), a screen has been carefully situated on a bureau, flanked between framed photographic portraits of the young couple as teens. The virtual event already takes its place in a pantheon of memories of familial significance. The computer screen flanked by the photos creates an altar, a shrine with depth of meaning. Never mind that the materials from which it is made are silicon and fiber-optic, these are easily ingested by the receiving culture – it is not the Otherness of ethnic choices that is to be assimilated, rather it is the flexibility of the technology engineered to accommodate itself to any and all cultural preferences. The inventions of supermodernity do not dissolve traditions of shared ritual practices, but rather turn the far-flung spaces of globalization into a virtual village. Cisco defines the serial networked combinations of spatial locations as the *new place*.

This is certainly not the same social and cultural world envisioned by critical theorists considering the transition to globalization. Cisco's vision reads as the inverse of Baudrillard's who feared that "the expansion of the commodity production system is the triumph of signifying culture and the death of the social." Cisco's account denies the death of the social part, claiming instead to rejuvenate the social through wireless networks. The Cisco ad has assembled an "'aesthetic' hallucination of reality," a colorful, dazzling photographic reconstitution of signs and images of the social. Yet where Baudrillard argued that "an endless cycle of the reduplication and overproduction of signs, images and simulations leads to an implosion of meaning" (Featherstone 1995:19), Cisco theorizes the opposite: "Welcome to a place where a wedding is captured and recaptured again and again," thereby amplifying shared meanings.

Though it rehashes a thoroughly modern ideology of universal humanism with its "family of man" clichés, the Cisco ad also normalizes a postmodern cultural condition. In contrast to those who hold on to the singularity of time and place as the *sine qua non* of organic culture, the ad turns simultaneity and duplication (digital reproduction) from threats to authenticity into the means of authenticity.

One could easily interpret Cisco's hyperreal landscape of multicultural geography as a visual argument against even the possibility of cultural hegemony. Even the concept of hegemony appears outmoded here: an anachronism from another historical era, ironically made unnecessary by a military technology (the Internet) produced at the center of global power. What is the relationship between the symbolic and the material? Have all labor relations floated into the symbolic realm? Though the advertising landscape itself is a product of symbolic labor, it is also a cultural formation with a material referent, the promotion of corporate capitalism in all spaces and all spheres, across all boundaries. What labor relations lie behind these global landscapes? Just as the bourgeois way of seeing embedded in the landscapes of the eighteenth and nineteenth centuries conveniently occluded the role of labor and the coercion that permitted the extraction of surplus value, so too the global landscapes of companies like Cisco choose to leave out moments of coerced exchange and how surplus is generated across the network (Cosgrove 1985).

Simulating the multicultural

The cultural landscapes of corporate advertising portray the world as a financially and electronically interconnected economy as well as a distribution of humane communities in which the materiality of the global economy supports traditional cultural forms as well as hypermodern forms of cultural hybridity. Materiality takes form in technological advances, financial services, and transportation systems, or what we might refer to as integrative services. We see the wonders of Capital without seeing Capital itself, for Capital has returned to its mythological liberal roots as the "invisible guiding hand" – only now this needs to be rephrased as the "invisible guiding brand." Thus, there is no moment of exchange – much less unequal exchange – between local communities and providers of integrative services. Behind these landscapes the institutions of corporate capital are presumed to operate in a taken-for-granted manner, the "disembedding" mechanisms of modernity: expert systems and symbolic tokens (Giddens 1991). To give these systems substance, meaning, and affect, signifiers of locality and ethnic specificity are necessary. Such signification strategies comprise what Giddens calls the "face work" of global capital. The scapes thus imagined are stripped of the economic realities of class and denuded of the politics of national, ethnic, and religious identity. Indeed, the very conditions of cultural production and reproduction disappear – culture as a set of relationships disappears, visually rematerializing instead like museum artifacts.

The distinction in the world of advertising between multiculturalism and traditional cultures is generally one of semiotic nuance – the same signifiers can lead in either direction. Multiculturalism is made to signal the historical future of global capitalism – the utopian moment that supposedly accompanies the universal extension of commodity relations and networked technologies. Traditional culture is turned to signify Capital's newfound respect for the past – the recognition that creative destruction is not the only way forward, but that, armed with the latest and greatest technologies, market forces can be (as if there is a choice) imposed without structurally dislocating former ways of life. In either case, the result depicts landscapes of cultural life arrayed on the horizontal plane as a "network that connects points and intersects with its own skein" (Foucault 1986:22). This method of spatially visualizing gobalization has an effect of dispersing critique. The technique of connecting spatially dispersed figures scattered across cultures and societies on the horizontal plane imagines all the virtues of the "network" without any of the "skein" – we are denied access to the complexity of the knotted and tangled coils created by networks of fibers.

As the cultural act of "producing locality" comes under increasing pressure from the nation-state, diasporic flows, and electronic communities (Appadurai 1996), it follows that group identities may be rearticulated in translocal spaces (e.g., Cisco) or in the resurrection of stereotypical signifiers of traditional identity. "The singularity of the idea of *place* is increasingly difficult to maintain, however; at the same time, it remains irreducible to an autonomous logic of globalism" (Rajagopal 2001). As networked technologies collapse time and space, bridging distances between core and periphery, we find ourselves dispersed across landscapes of "simultaneity," ever more in need of ways of signifying the unity of opposites (the collapsing of binaries). Hence we find that, within the framework of globalization, precisely as "the production of locality" wanes, "the representation of locality" waxes in importance in corporate branding landscapes.

In order to signify "traditional culture," there must be retained at least some tiny sliver of reference to history and yet this becomes such an abstracted sliver that the very concept of history becomes as static and reified as the concept of culture itself. History and tradition become nothing other than the abstraction of the past, while simulated multiculturalism becomes the abstraction of the future. With both simulated multiculturalism and traditional culture, cultural signifiers become reduced to a visual alphabet used to signify global market penetration and good corporate global citizenship.

8

Mapping the Terrain in a Sign Economy

As we have analytically mapped corporate advertising's landscape representations of a globalizing
society, we have pondered Celeste Olalquiaga's concluding thoughts about postmodern cultural forms
in *Megalopolis:* "We are faced with a transitory landscape, where new ruins continually pile up on each
other. It is amid these ruins that we look for each
other" (Olalquiaga 1992:94). We must now turn to
an exploration of contradictions in the landscapes of
commodity culture.

Even in the transitory landscapes premised on continuous cycles of
creative destruction, we have found elements of corporate landscape
representations relatively easy to identify: the primacy given to communications networks and, more generally, to science and technology;
the disappearance of the state and bureaucracies; the demise of divisive
categories of class in favor of the harmonious imagery of multiculturalism; the collapse of material distance in favor of instantaneity. And we
can identify the preferred images that compose the lexicon of corporate
advertising – the transparent acrylic markerboards, the orange-robed
monks and camels, the spiral stairwells, satellite dishes, wind turbines,
and speed blurs. But what shall we make of the mappings themselves
– the montages of decontextualized and floating signifiers? Do such
mappings/landscapes offer an appropriate way of apprehending the
system they purport to represent? Or are such landscapes truly a simulacrum – out in front, preceding a world that is in the throes of an
unrepresentable transition? Perhaps these are pseudo-scapes, neither
true nor false, but rather the product of a medium – television and
video editing – that pushes beyond the conventions of representation by
routinely violating the historical conditions of time and space.

What can we learn from corporate advertising about globalization, capitalism, and cultural formations? How does the representational world of advertising imagine the time–space relations associated with global capitalism? Referencing the transitional epoch labeled as post-Fordism, advertising representations of time–space coordinates oscillate between nostalgia for relationships that were never quite real and a yearning for a utopian future that will not be quite real.

Advertising is a system of producing sign values, and its relationship to the wider political economy of global capitalism is more than simply ideological window dressing: it also forms a crucial system for reproducing value as capitalist systems mature. As capital races to reduce circulation time and expand the total domain of exchange values, the issues of time, space, and speed become more than simply external matters for representation; they also become leveraged to the continuous search for exchange values in both material and sign forms.

Advertising as a system of sign production plays a dual, if contradictory, role. On the one hand, to the extent that advertising contributes to the accelerated construction of sign values, it becomes part and parcel of the forces that must be represented as blurs in space rather than as figures in place. A political economy of sign production is a culture-hungry machine that relentlessly abstracts, displaces, and devours meaning in pursuit of the appearances of use value (Goldman 1994; Willis 1994). On the other hand, as Capital moves into a second phase of post-Fordism where networks spiral both inward and outward (or as Thomas Freidman popularizes it, the "flattening of the earth") sign production takes on a stabilizing force. TV ads as cultural texts anchor capital formations and the markets that organize them, at the same time that they destabilize cultural formations. This is the classic tension between accumulation and legitimation; capital's contradiction between motion and fixity.

If we tweak just slightly Baudrillard's theoretical framework of the simulacrum, the simulacrum does not simply signal the end of political economy as Baudrillard argued, but rather represents the necessary other side of an already developing phase of political economy that seeks to eclipse territory, compress time and space, and virally reproduce the commodity form and its sign form.

Rather than view ads as producing a map (a representation) of the territories of the time–space coordinates of global capitalism, the map has come to precede the territory. That is, these mappings have a material force – though some may think of them as arbitrary, their arbitrariness is over-determined by the forces of necessity that structure a political economy that is visible to most only in its simulated state. For those dependent on the media, the simulacrum offers the only vision they may have of the territory. Paraphrasing Baudrillard, we might suggest that "globalization never happened" even though we know that something has happened / is happening "out there." If "ideology is the meaning *made necessary* by the conditions of society [and political economy] while helping to *perpetuate* those conditions" (Williamson 1978:13), we can begin to see the system of sign value as both a material and ideological force in reproducing both simulacrum and political economy while simultaneously blocking the recognition, as Baudrillard puts it, that we can no longer tell the difference between the representations that form the map and the territory.

Phrases such as zero gravity, weightlessness, hybridity, and floating signifiers all seek to describe a so-called "postmodern" regime of cultural production in which there is an apparent separation of culture from a material base (Jameson 1984). Our analyses of 2,400 TV ads suggest that, while weightlessness, hybridity, and floating signifiers are empirical features of spectacular culture, we must be careful not to let their appearance confuse us. In actuality, these cultural representations are deeply determined by the material base, even as they float. We must interrogate this dialectic of decontextualized meaning and over-determination as we turn to the relationship between the landscapes of a sign economy and the corporate political economy of global capitalism.

The logic of the network and representational stability

Harnessed to the relentless competitive search for higher rates of profitability, technological innovation has spread the logic of electronic information networks across the globe. These electronic networks contribute to an acceleration of market dynamics – this global informational economy operates in real time (global simultaneity) – such that the more successful corporations are those able to confront rapidly shifting market conditions by adopting the dynamic and flexible tools and strategies that rely on the extension of network logic. The goal of speed via optoelectronic circuits is to facilitate the continuous flow of signals that represent data, money, and commodities. Optimizing and coordinating these flows becomes a technical matter, but making processes of creative destruction continuous also piles up wreckage. In this political-economic space, organizational stability relies as much on brand integration as bureaucratic organizational structures. In the flux and flow of globalized corporate transactions, brands provide a stable interface between consumers, clients, employees, and the corporation (Lury 2004).

Castells argues that successful corporations in the contemporary world system are those that position themselves competitively in networks. But that alone does not explain which firms achieve market dominance in capital markets. Competition invariably begets consolidation and the processes of corporate consolidation take place via the mechanisms of merger and acquisition. The churn that this generates in capital markets and in the names of the key corporate players can be disorienting. Here "the world of mythical representation (of self-serving image-making by management consultants)" begins to take precedence over "the institutionally bounded realities of the world economy" (Castells 1996:192).

These are the intersections between "economies of signs and space" – the relationship between an infrastructure of "flows" and its self-reflexive productions (Lash and Urry 1994). The latter, in the world of corporate advertising, invariably take the form of myth as Barthes conceptualized it, where abstracted signifiers indexically supersede the empirically complex relations existing in the referent world that they point to, but displace. In advertising, these productions are motivated by the dual search for value and legitimation. Where truly "all that is solid melts into air" – where Capital must be open to a continuous revolution of the tools (and content) of production – Capital must train its capacity for signification on mutually contradictory goals. Because a political economy of signs has become a centerpiece of capital accumulation, Capital must be open to a continuous revolution in the sphere of signification (it is after all now just another tool of production). This very process signals the demise of the transcendental signified (all that is holy melts away) and it is ever more imperative that corporate entities also seek representational anchors for volatile, shape-shifting market arrangements based on contingency rather than principled convictions.

When meaning and discourse are driven by the speed of competition in capitalist markets, one consequence is the degradation of signification and the dissolution of rational discourse (Agger 1989). Advertisements composed of over-used aphorisms, visual clichés, authoritative voiceovers, and affect-laden musical abbreviations are designed and tested to hail audiences in targeted ways – corporate recognition, practice legitimation, or product or service sales. When meaning can be disassembled and reassembled in the semiotic assembly line of advertising, discourse becomes oriented around how advertisers aesthetically spin and differentiate their particular combinations of floating signifiers. In the sign economy this process of continual refracting meaning shapes a public sphere of discourse. In such a sign economy all is reduced to signifiers; images, music, words, narration, intonation – all of it becomes subject to an intensely motivated process of semiotic fracturing into discrete signifiers that can be arranged to mean in the service of producing and reproducing sign values. Every seme becomes loaded with meaning, but doing so tends to spread meaning thin. The very same process that has become essential to articulating an economy of values threatens to negate the condition of value itself, because value is predicated on differentiating that which has value from that which does not. The greater the churn of the valuation process, the more superficial and insubstantial are the values produced, and the more fragile the very category of value itself. And so the process races along, the semiotic circulation process of advertising must soon run as fast as the commodity circulation process that it was designed to stabilize.

Where once critical theorists distinguished commodification and legitimation processes, these have become ever more blurred in this semiotic whirlwind. While many of the corporate ads in our database can be conceptualized as hegemonic smokescreens – superficially diverting conceptualization of poverty, disease, pollution, and violence – even this form of legitimation is itself subject to the half-life of the image, rather than to depth of argument or conviction. That is, legitimation must be continuously reconstituted as an aestheticized sign system rather than as a discursive system.

The most immediate versions of these signs are brand images. In 2005, SBC acquired AT&T. Though SBC was the acquirer, the SBC name and iconic imagery possessed relatively less sign value – or brand value recognition – than AT&T. SBC achieved its gargantuan capitalization via a series of acquisitions, in the process adopting an abbreviated version of its original regional name, Southwestern Bell. By contrast, though it had been swallowed, AT&T had a history dating back to Alexander Graham Bell. In the years preceding the merger, AT&T's "Boundless" campaigns focused on adding value to its icon, the globe. AT&T took the sphere and logo-ized it by stripping it of all geographic referents and giving it a metallic look. Each ad in the campaign visually morphed the globe to demonstrate a range of functions, services, and practices. The pleasure of the text involved deciphering the morph itself. While each ad signified a specific dimension of AT&T's communication network – reliability, speed, integration – the creative use of the icon signified innovation and flexibility as qualities associated with this corporate giant. Dubbed the "Death Star" by corporate insiders because of its visual similarity to a seemingly indestructible weapon of the Empire in the *Star Wars* saga, the AT&T sign contained contradictory meanings. Ironically, the newest chapter in this corporate icon's history seems to mimic its referential source – despite the demise of AT&T (the corporation), the icon plus the AT&T name continues because it offers a recognizable brand value. Aptly, this "new" telecommunications corporation uses the AT&T "death star" icon to represent itself. As the corporate organizational structure mutates, shifts, merges, or downsizes, the abstract signifying representation, ephemeral though it may be, provides corporate identity. The "death star" is a black hole of myth – it absorbs any and all second-order signifiers.

The SBC/AT&T campaign constructed an upbeat montage of a seamlessly integrated social world to signify the power of a newly merged corporate universe. The ad imagines a time–space totality that accommodates and binds together a curious amalgam of otherwise disparate and disconnected images – a helicopter approaching corporate towers; kids in a vintage, homemade soapbox derby car; coffee at an old-school Americana diner counter with the addition of laptop computer; a cowboy riding through snow-covered mountains; an ornate spiral stairwell; women discreetly passing a handheld device in a meeting; a woman using sign language; a child speaking to a New York City policeman/guard; a high-tech lab with screens of computed tomography (CT) scans swathed in the blue fluorescent signifying light of science; satellite dishes on a roof channeling a basketball game into a penthouse living room; farmers framed next to a truck at sunrise; and Cirque du Soleil acrobats – all brought together under the slogan "Your world. Delivered." What could possibly have motivated this set of images? When recounted as we have done here, this image sequence borders on the absurd: though these images are clearly motivated, how many other photographic scenes could be substituted for these? What do these

images have to do with the mythology of the new AT&T? They define society! How do they define the territory presided over by the regime of AT&T? When narrated by the grandiose music, however, these images speak to privatized, "unique" combinations of commodified lifestyles all made available by "the most complete and secure network on earth." This is, further, a territory composed of freedom-enhancing technologies and traditional ways of life, the latter not only preserved, but enhanced. While the ad stresses that the structure of this merger of capitals creates an integrated network that facilitates instantaneity and globality, it does so by resituating the glories of time–space compression at the personal level. The velocity at which information circulates, which is the selling point of this grand historical merger of capitals, is buffered by privileging the appearance of sociality.

The commercial ends with an act of semiotic magic, the fusion of SBC/AT&T into a redesign of AT&T's "death star." Despite the merger and the apparent flow of incongruent images, the brand sign punctuates the narrative to assure representational stability along the grand, global horizontal axis constituted by the corporate network. An almost identical process of sign merger is accomplished in a recent Verizon ad that celebrates the merger of Verizon and MCI. Here again, the power of the sunspot seals the union of corporate icons into one.

Fractal value

Baudrillard's inquiries into the relationship between signification and value trace the relationship of sign to referent from reflection to dispersion. Baudrillard conceptualizes sweeping, highly generalized historical stages of signification. First, there was the realist order of Feudalism, in which symbols correspond to external reality. The image, like a map, appears as a direct reflection of reality. It also corresponds to a fixed social position for all strata. This is followed by the "Counterfeit" period, from the Renaissance to the Industrial Revolution. As stratification systems weaken, so does the relationship of signs to their referent: "In this moment the arbitrary sign appears. It no longer links two persons in an unchanging relationship." In the industrial period signs become mass-produced by machines according to the rules of exchange value. Uniqueness and authenticity are undermined by serial production. The technologies of photography and cinema released signification from the coordinates of socio-historical location, necessitating overarching codes driven by the "structural law of value" that have led in turn towards an epoch of simulation (see Kellner 1994). When signifiers and signifieds are routinely split, these codes grow in importance as a means of organizing and valuing the infinitude of recombinations that are possible. In the order of simulacra, the simulation precedes its referent so that "the very definition of the real becomes that of which it is possible to give an equivalent production." This is the age of hyperrealism. While Disneyland and Las Vegas may appear to be examples par excellence of the hyperreal, Baudrillard viewed the hyperreal as spreading across the social itself: "today, reality itself is hyperrealist" (1993a:74). Not only does the mechanical reproduction of culture dislodge signs from organic genesis, spurring along "nostalgia for the natural referent of the sign" (1993a:51), but new technologies (that extend and speed up circulation) in transportation, telecommunications, electronic networks, integrated satellite networks, and digital communication networks extend the hyperreal into everydayness. The technologies of computers, video, and networks also "give us the language and images that we require to reach others and see ourselves" (Olalquiaga 1992:93). This is crucial to understanding how the landscapes of Capital reflect the network ontology that technologically underlies and mediates those scapes.

In *Fatal Strategies*, Baudrillard (1990) adds a new stage that he calls the "fractal," where simulations seem to infinitely extend in all directions, produced at what seems an accelerating pace and spiraling outward, cross-breeding, fragmenting, connecting, and layering. In *The Transparency of Evil*, Baudrillard situates the fractal stage in relation to the political economy of sign value. He calls the "fractal" "a new particle" in the "microphysics of simulacra" (1993b:5).

> Fractal (or viral, or radiant) stage of value, there is no point of reference at all, and value radiates out in all directions, occupying all interstices, without reference to anything whatsoever, by virtue of pure contiguity. At the fractal stage there is no longer any equivalence, whether natural or general. Properly speaking there is now no law of value, merely a sort of epidemic of value, a sort of general metastasis of value, a haphazard proliferation and dispersal of value. Indeed, we should really no longer speak of "value" at all, for this kind of propagation or chain reaction makes all valuation impossible. (1993b:5)

In the transition from the sign as industrial commodity "to the reproduction of forms *'conceived* according to their reproducibility' from their model" (1993b:56), the condition of equivalencies in constructing sign values is violated. The systematic modeling of equivalence exchange produces a seismic-like

> Sliding of the referential. The end of the infrastructure. Nothing remains but shifting movements that provoke raw events. We no longer take events as revolutions or effects of the superstructure, but as underground effects of skidding, fractal zones in which things happen. Between the plates, continents do not quite fit together, they slip under and over each other. There is no more system of reference to tell us what happened to the geography of things. (Lotringer and Baudrillard 1986:141)

Slippage between sign and referent and between materiality and ideation is replaced by the infinite reproduction and dispersion of meanings. Lost is the "referential guarantee" (Merrin 2001:91) that supported the mirage of certainty and the illusion of equivalence exchange that buttressed liberal conceptions of value and justice. Signifiers multiply, replicating so quickly that the value conferred via equivalence exchange dissolves just as swiftly. Value becomes perceived as less and less substantial, and more and more what it always has been – a market fluctuation. This fractal stage is a self-contradictory consequence of the political economy of sign value. Here we encounter Baudrillard's second metaphor for the fractal – cancer. "Instead of metamorphosis we get metastasis, not the eternal return, but the return of the infinitely small (the fractal)" (Wernick 1993).

The fractal metaphor captures the internal contradictions of a sign economy. Just as was the case for material commodities and services, so too for commodity signs there is a tendency for investment and competition to flow to the highest rates of return. This, in turn, leads to diminishing rates of profit, which prompts even more strenuous investment in the construction of brand values and boosting the rate of commodity circulation. The faster this circuitry spins, the more cluttered the sign marketplace becomes, the more saturated the product categories, the more desperate the need for differentiated signs. Speeding up circulation while simultaneously extracting value is the formula for contemporary capital. But doing so introduces the logic of Capital into processes of signification (Goldman and Papson 1996). Repetition and speed in the circulatory orbit of commodified semiosis has a deadly impact on the categories of meaning – it annuls the possibility of the transcendental signified, while elevating in its place the dislocated grand signifier. The grand signifier becomes the brand signifier. Hence the obsession with the brand signifier – whether it is the Cisco brand sign or the AT&T brand sign or the Dow brand sign – and the hope that it will be recognized long after the floating signified of the moment has been forgotten or displaced by the momentary signifying angle of the next ad. This is the cancer of commodification in which exchange value is infinitely extracted and signifiers' primary economic function is to speed up infinitesimally smaller exchanges. The fractal is reflected in the viral character of the network.

In this symbolic universe, social relations concentrate on the individual and the family, but mostly neglect intermediate social institutions. Indeed this seems to be a society with a minimum of institutions – a social body hollowed out of materially situated institutions. The advertising narratives offer a corporate version of society as a "body without organs." But what then constitutes the macro-forces that organize the whole of society? The corporate narrative envisions Society organized by two sets of forces, each equally unobtrusive and invisible: a free, unregulated, market and a network that consists of hidden nodes and flows. This is the "catatonic" body without organs that Deleuze and Guattari (1987) refer to, characterized by pure flows, always passing through spaces, and never terminating. And this is where the corporate vision of a body without organs encounters its own negation – pure flow requires an unlimited and continuous reservoir of value to keep circulation in motion. This demand for reproduction becomes unceasing, no longer an end in itself, but a means to replicating exchange value. Replication out of control becomes metastatic, ultimately destroying the social body.

More often than not, in the discourse of television ads, images merely

mean that they mean. Hence the spiral staircase does not prompt significant reflection when we encounter it in the AT&T ad or later in the Morgan Stanley ad. The crisis of the fractal order is that such signs as markers are no longer really referential, and no longer really indexical. They point, they refer, but to what? Because they are transient in a sea of signification, available to the eye for but a split second, they are consumed in a process of infinite reproducibility. Because every image is now recognized as arbitrary, viewers look to other semiotic, narrative cues to re-motivate the meaningfulness of that image, recognizing even as we do so that its meaning will have to be re-motivated again the next time it is seen. The already mutable signifier turns into the floating signifier. It may seem odd then that we could argue that the floating signifier becomes the only thing that has duration, while the act of myth production takes place in the blink of the eye, and must be performed over and over again.

The 2006–7 Cisco campaign discussed in chapter 6 offers a stark illustration. The ad spectacularly collapses time–space relations to signify

how the computer network can seamlessly reintegrate the world's peoples and places. Given the immediacy of the network and its connective powers, temporality is turned into extensibility that corresponds to spatial pluralism. In this advertising context, signs of cultural geography become the primary ingredient for producing the second-order signifiers of a global civil society. Here the imagery of orange-robed monks, or Chinese children traditionally garbed are exemplars of the fractal – its reproducibility turned to metastasis, its meanings hemorrhaging out.[1]

From these signs "exchanged against each other" the Cisco ad assembles a hyperreal imaginary of organic culture freed up from social location, and reorganized along the lines of networks. This is not simply an ideological trope disguising the real relations of production in a capitalist world system; it also aims at pure simulation.

The Cisco ad evokes warmth of meaning, but it does so by fracturing time, space, and culture into a dispersed array of ghostly referentiality. The referential and the simulative become impossible to differentiate in the circulatory recycling of images. As Celeste Olalquiaga observes, referentiality becomes contingent on intertextuality – the reference to orange-robed monks now relies on our having seen these figures in other texts, and not on our encounters with them. Every image has a referent, but every referent is another text.

The aestheticization of landscapes must not go unremarked. The more that corporate ads deterritorialize, the more they dislocate culture from geography, the more they seek to translate cultural symbols into marketable signs, the more they rely on aesthetic fascination and fetishism.

> For me it's useless to attempt to artificially perpetuate a system, because culture became a system of values, it's no more an organic, symbolic organization of sociality, now it's a system of market values, but of aesthetic values, not so much economic values. As a system of aesthetic values it is a very antinomic proposition, because culture perishes from this mixture of the symbolic and of values. The symbolic order of culture is not value, value is an economic structure. With infiltration or contamination of signs by an aesthetic circulation, and the rise of cultural goods as aesthetic goods, that's the beginning of the end. (Baudrillard 2002a)

We need not agree with Baudrillard's conclusion about this being "the end" to recognize how the stress on style depoliticizes landscapes, elevating fascination and desire as the floating signifier of culture. While the intent of such ads is surely to appropriate the vitality and color of cultural life and turn these into the surface of our landscapes, the unintended consequence is that culture is transformed into packaging – into the appearance of use value. When Cisco makes the spatial backgrounds interchangeable equivalents, we can no longer differentiate real ecologies, or historical differences. While exchange value may start with the labor process, market value is now contingent on transforming cultural geography into aesthetic values.

Where Cisco translated the spectacularized collapse of time and space into the fractal iconography of cultural geography, Dow's "Human Element" campaign illustrated the philosophical consequences of discourses organized around fractal signification. Dow's campaign conjured up the sincerity of universal humanism. It oozed depth of thought and conviction, and yet when it is analytically dismantled we see it consists of nothing more than aesthetic codes arranged together in montage fashion. The appearance of a grand narrative about the human condition has become embedded in the aesthetic codes that hail a cosmopolitan subject.

The flexibility of the montage structure can accommodate any collection of decontextualized signifiers, no matter how disparate. Touting empowerment coupled with a credo of universal humanism, corporate ads put the montage to the task of ideologically legitimating corporate power. The montage framework lends itself to fluidly weaving together representations of how financial capital, science, and technology transform the world into a new imagined community based on global multiculturalism, universal humanism, and social progress. But while the montage aims to engineer meaning on the model of equivalence exchange, the often dazzling array of imagery that floods through it also contributes to a fractal disorder in which simulated value flies in all directions.

The 2006 Dow "Human Element" campaign exemplifies this fracturing and reassembling of signifiers. Anchoring that campaign was a ninety-second montage of nature photography interspersed with images of isolated individuals situated in abstractly deterritorialized spaces. Slow smooth camera pans and dissolves produce a visual poem choreographed together by a soothing Cape Breton fiddle waltz while a voiceover gives meaning to these seemingly unrelated images by making them seem to be part of a story line. Framed this way, arbitrary image choices appear to be motivated and immanent – part of a totalizing relationship between subject and object in a state of nature that may always have been there, but is only now fully realized.

The musical aesthetic coordinates and frames the elements of nature photography that flow in slow motion, prompting a sense of fascination in the timelessness and beauty of nature's patterns. Mixing scales of magnitude, the scenes flow from lush nature scapes of volcanoes and waterfalls to electrical impulses and neural synapses. The effect is the appearance of landscape-like images that present a not-quite decipherable hermeneutic puzzle, requiring that we listen to the spoken words if we are to make sense of this admixture. Viewers can never be quite sure whether they are looking down from the heavens (or satellite) or through a microscope. Either way, the optic of hyper-magnification so thoroughly decontextualizes and abstracts these picturesque scenes that it becomes impossible to speak of recognizable referents, only of the repetition of patterns. The only scale that matters is shaped by aesthetic form and desire.

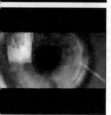

A soothing paternal voice narrates the ad, while the soft harmonies of the waltz therapeutically lull interpretation into a dream-like state that invites the translation of the serenely empty landscapes into open canvasses of potentiality and possibility for all human subjects. For each of us there is a moment of discovery.

We turn a page, we raise a hand
And just then in the flash of a synapse
We learn that life is elemental
And this knowledge changes everything
We look around and see the grandness of the scheme
Sodium bonding with chlorine
Carbon bonding with oxygen

Hydrogen bonding with oxygen
We see all things connected
We see life unfold
And in the dazzling brilliance of this knowledge
We may overlook the element not listed on the chart
Its importance so obvious
Its presence is simply understood
The missing element is the human element
And when we add it to the equation
The chemistry changes
Every reaction is different
Potassium looks to bond with potential
Metals behave with heartened desire
And hydrogen and oxygen form desire
The human element is the element of change
It gives us our footing to stand fearlessly and face the future
It is a way of seeing
It gives us a way of touching
Issues Ambitions Lives
The human element
Nothing is more fundamental
Nothing more elemental

The Dow ad fashions a variant of the Creation Myth with a modern twist. Primal elements of fire and water take on meaning in the periodic table. The world is ordered by natural laws that chemistry documents – nature fits together in amazing combinations: "We look around and see the grandness of the scheme." In this modernist account, however, there is no tension between God and science. Whereas the Genesis version of the story ousts humans from the garden because of our pursuit of knowledge, here the "dazzling brilliance of this knowledge" permits the possibility of overcoming the alienation between object and subject. The self and the landscape become one. And knowledge of the world allows human beings to intervene in the world – to create the world and ourselves simultaneously. Science, in this grandest of narratives, does not foreclose on subjectivity, but makes it the crucial variable in shaping the world and ourselves.

Supplanting oxygen (O) at number 8 in the periodic table, Dow designates the human element (Hu) as the missing element that drives change and desire. Such an affirming story of human potential taking place in a world without boundary limits requires only that we forget about Capital (or by extension any other structuring institutions such as the State) and the relationships that it has structured.[2] How ironic also that, in order to acknowledge human agency, Dow chose to kick oxygen off the periodic table, and with it the planet's means of survival. But if we retell this story in terms of what is omitted from Dow's history, a very different story emerges. We must always begin with the images left out. Even a cursory account of Dow's history would acknowledge the unintended consequences of mastering nature's laws of chemical bonding – consequences that reverberate through ecosystems because, indeed, "We see all things connected." Similarly omitted are the human costs when the domination of Nature and economic systems converge. The more grandiose myth becomes the more it flees from historical reality. Where is the historical experience of Bhopal or the legacy of environmental degradation entailed by dioxin contamination of Lake Huron? Where might we find Dow's continued efforts to avoid responsibility for cleaning up spills that disproportionately impact the have-nots of a global society? Dow can leave out its role as capital in the production of inequality, just as it can omit the decision-making logic imposed by market forces on the direction and development of science, because the discursive form of the montage makes irrelevant the referent of history and includes the referent of nature only for its aesthetic visual value.

The montage as representational structure

While the particular landscapes fashioned by the Dow ad are less an expression of emergent infrastructural forms than a nostalgic desire to rescue a vision of humanity from the ruins that history now confronts, the method of their construction is characteristic of corporate advertising. The montage has become the preferred means of landscape representation in television advertising, and has evolved as the representational structure par excellence of fast capitalism. The montage annihilates historical time–space relations, substituting for these relationships leaps of aesthetic imagination, unbound by laws of gravity or motion.

Photographic decontextualization is the nature of the medium. The fundamental starting point of discourses organized around the reproduction of photographic images is, as Berger and Mohr observe, that "All photographs are ambiguous. All photographs have been taken out of continuity . . . Discontinuity always produces ambiguity" (1982:91). The "shock of discontinuity" must thus be re-narrated – that is, each image must be returned to meaningfulness, even if that meaning now involves a new or different story. The narrated montage is just such a tool that nonetheless works to conceal that discontinuity when it feeds viewers streams of images – "certainty may be instantaneous; doubt requires duration" (Berger and Mohr 1982:89). When put to work in ads, the thematic montage permits corporations to insert themselves in the form of logos and icons into the mix of disparate images it has elected to narrativize. The resulting signified is transferred to the brand by associative equivalence. The formula is simple: choose signifiers from image banks and/or film a series of very short shots, decontextualize them from their historical location, aestheticize them, recontextualize each signifier in the flow of other decontextualized signifiers – such as narration and a musical score to create the desired affect – complete the meaning with a slogan, and transfer the value thus constituted to the corporate brand.

As semiological process, the Dow landscapes are thus little different from the Cisco landscapes or those depicted by GE, AT&T, Siemens, or Boeing. Yet, as representations of the spaces of global capitalism, corporate representations of landscapes are plural and mutable. The plurality is partly a function of firms competing to produce differentiated visual imagery for their sign values. It turns out that there are many ways to express time–space compression – a multiplicity of scapes and flows differentiated by aesthetic nuances. While it may become ever more important to find ways to signify a mutable landscape given the political-economic push for flexible accumulation, it is also the case that the ungrounded landscape is a function of the televisual form through which it is expressed – the montage yields mostly deterritorialized landscapes, governed by ontological assumptions of instantaneity and the disappearance of spatial separations.

Constructed from sequences of incommensurate frames, each photographically stylized to add value and momentarily capture attention, the montage becomes an elaborate device for generating equivalence exchange and thus gives apparent (superficial) order to a fractal universe. Quicker edits seamlessly tied together by narration and music yield a "world-taken-for-granted" of how transnational capital works. The montage as landscape form is predicated on acceptance of the flow of television – unless we slow it down, pause it, freeze frames, and separate musical codes and narration from image, critique is overwhelmed by representational velocity.

Even the tranquil pacing of the Dow ad makes reading specific images improbable. What we read are the aesthetic codes, and their Gestalt guides interpretation of landscapes defined by perceptual traces of flows, shapes, colors, and compositions. Scrutiny or reflection upon the meaning of any particular image is short-lived, as viewers struggle to keep up with the fascination with the following image. As the specific photographic signifiers speed past, what remains is the blurred ideological background of global capital. The very repetition, however, of a relatively small set of preferred signifiers registers disproportionately in defining these landscapes – e.g., beams of light, globes, trains, monks, nuns, eyes, handshakes, children, camels, rockets, satellites. The montage ultimately yields a landscape defined by the second-order signifiers.

Time–space compression as political-economic landscape

David Harvey's discussion of global capital treats deterritorialization as the result of space–time compression. Geographies and national borders become less important as finances, cultural texts, technologies, and persons flow across these boundaries. These flows are driven by capital and its contradictions. Capitalist competition has always entailed races to market, and over time that competition has relied ever more heavily on technological advances. Such technological competition, as Marx observed long ago, tends to reduce the rate of profit (now known as profit margins), while at the same time technologies that aim to diminish the limits of time and space are put into play to offset the tendencies towards declining profit margins in maturing markets. The faster the flow of commodities and commodity signs, the more profit is to be made. Profit is extracted from circulation all along the network. In the contemporary world of capital, boundaries translate into friction and have a logic all their own (e.g., homeland security). When boundaries are not porous, they slow down circulation and profit.

Deterritorialization also implodes ethnology, and makes irrelevant unified organic cultures, replacing these with signs of ethnology and cultural geography. Electronic information networks, commodity networks, and tourism penetrate the periphery, prompting both defensive rearguard actions and postmodern cultural forms. Under this model cultural signifiers are released from their socio-historical moments of production and enter the over-stimulated circulatory apparatus of capital. Fragmented, decontextualized, accelerated, and usually aestheticized, these signifying fragments are attached to commodities and organizational entities to either produce sign values or grease the paths of value production. But this system of semiosis is voracious – no sooner are these bits and pieces of meaning put to use than they are discarded and replaced by other sets of signifiers. While this separation of cultural texts from point of production is not new to global capitalism, texts are now appropriated and disassembled at "chop shop" speed, signifying a radical break between culture and materiality. Modernist institutions such as advertising and marketing, when pushed faster and faster, mutate into postmodernism or hypermodernism, depending on your theoretical preference.

The Holy Grail for Capital in the current period is the ability to compete in "real time." Speed in the world of transportation means that the constraints of distance (space) can be minimized. But the more significant revolutions in speed in recent years have been in the sphere of electronic communications, transforming the landscapes of Capital. The capacity to transact currency or commodity trades instantaneously across the globe has also transformed conceptions of time and space as they become compressed. Drawing on Harvey's notion of space–time compression, Ben Agger notes that the velocities of all types of circulations (texts, commodities, information, work process, consumption) are speeding up; consequently, boundaries (home/work, public/private, reader/writer, child/adult, expert/amateur, the spectacle / everyday life) break down. Especially at the height of the Internet bubble, in corporate ads each of these forms of boundary breakdown and space–time compression received imaginative expression. Bricks and mortar (signifying fixity of costs and location) trembled in the face of competition from amorphous electronic entities that seemed to hold the advantage in flexibility and speed. Speed became the currency of democracy and egalitarianism – trading stocks could be accomplished in the blink of an eye and dirt cheap if you simply jettisoned that smug, aristocratic broker in his corner office. The average guy could become heroic and compete anywhere in the world – witness IBM's cyborg commodities trader who works out of a space in a European public square. At the corporate level we have seen ads for Microsoft, AT&T, Cisco, etc., extol the extent to which a utopia of information systems can replace humans in their decision-making networks, reducing costs and transaction times via a faster and smarter corporate network.

A 2007 Morgan Stanley ad articulates a grand narrative that attempts to encompass the whole of the global economy from the perspective of Capital. The spoken narration offers the equivalent of a table of contents for an expert consideration of how to assess the global economy. Morgan Stanley's reflexive visual account of an integrated world system also functions as a primer on factors of production in a post-Fordist global economy where space–time compression has become taken-for-granted. All the buzzwords and categories are here. Morgan Stanley's use of the montage is relatively unusual insofar as the montage aims to simulate the logic of Capital in the contemporary world system. By contrast the montage used by AT&T, Cisco, and Dow spectacularizes, and denies, the logic of Capital.

Accompanying the narration as it starts off slowly and deliberately, the piano has a monotonic, metronomic quality. Even as the pace of narration quickens to signify complexity and overlap, the background rhythm remains a steady punctuating beat. While the visual narrative

seems almost to double back on itself, suggesting an iterative dimension to the world economy, the voiceover slows again to stress with the last three words, "the future, the wisdom, the world," that the strewn array of planes and axes actually contains a circulatory logic that, once deciphered (from on high), can yield profit.

The world
The markets
The technology
The borderless economy
The friction free state
The flow
The rate of change
The rate of interest
The rate of return
The deals
The mergers
The flow of capital
The flow of commerce
The flow of knowledge
Culture
The value of talent
Opportunity
Information
Insight
Growth
The flow of resources
The flow of goods and services
The political reality
Reputation
Knowledge of the consumer
Your investments
Knowledge of the marketplace
Your economic reality
Your portfolio
The practical reality
The future
The wisdom
The world

The Morgan Stanley montage sutures together camera tilts, pans and tracking to create the impression of a global economy that consists of a multiplicity of spatial planes connected by the narrative of investing. Rather than looking down on the globe from afar to conceptualize it as a whole, viewers are positioned by the camera's point of view to share the panoptic eye that Morgan Stanley has mastered, and is advertising.

Unlike the Cisco and the Dow ads which fashion a subject-centric set of landscapes, landscapes defined in terms of how they enable subjects to realize themselves, purporting even to show how subjects can themselves shape the scapes of their existence, the Morgan Stanley landscapes envision instead the otherwise determinately abstract flows of the geopolitical-economic forces that shape portfolios. Here, the color palette is toned down, a cold gray emotional tone washes out the space of the social.

By zooming in, tilting, panning, rotating, and zooming out, the ad changes perspective continuously, still suggesting an axis of fused continuity and interconnection. Morgan Stanley positions itself as an investment firm able to see the world economy operating at both a nuts-and-bolts level – a ground level that still seems to reference objects of production, transit, trade – and a theoretical level that indexes how spatial perspective must now be integrative. The textual narration of the ad references the necessity of grasping relations as higher-order abstractions in order to achieve mastery over the practice of capital gains. And what are these relations? The ad opens by surveying the space of a vast Asian factory cafeteria where there is no room for individuation or customization. A similar shot elsewhere in the campaign reveals comparable women in a comparable space working at sewing machines. There is no distinction between cafeteria and assembly plant – the former is unsentimentally what it is, a space for the feeding of laboring machines. The camera pans and viewers are transported to a different space that illustrates the "technology" of manufacturing and reveals relatively few blue-collar laboring figures. A moment later, the camera finds the space of "deals," a high-angle shot revealing a sea of white-collar workers in front of row after row after row of blue computer screens – a space of commodities transactions staffed by nameless and faceless technicians. In this way the ad sketches out the global division of labor – from the faceless, proletarianized Asian women to proletarianized white-collar males – and yet even here, these scenes *qua* signifiers, remain deterritorialized, abstracted, and un-locatable. The ad is about movement and axes of connectivity – Capital equals flow, and yet this flow is entirely self-referential. "World Wise" as a slogan suggests that Morgan Stanley understands the connections of the disparate elements that comprise the global economy.

Morgan Stanley thus addresses a political-economic landscape that it implies can be neither assembled nor understood from a lay perspective.

This landscape is so spatially dispersed that it requires symbolic reintegration. Without the interpretive presence of Morgan Stanley, this might be a landscape obscured by the very flows (scapes) that compose it. But by positioning itself (via its reflexive camera-work) to penetrate, reveal and reconnect each sphere, Morgan Stanley appears to move across physical barriers as if they were virtual. This is achieved through the graphic suturing of transitional shots that turn spaces into seamless functional planes. The ad visually creates a sense of both vertigo and flow that ostensibly replicates the flow of capital, and its equivalent forms, across and through the global economy. Morgan Stanley's peripatetic camera eye passes through borders as readily as we move from one structural plane to another – in this way the visual technique suggests a global panopticism, while also simulating the capacity of Capital to penetrate and permeate all spheres of existence. Morgan Stanley has harnessed the camera eye and the power of video editing to reframe a scattered array of spaces into a coherent sequence that makes sense as Capital. Despite Morgan Stanley's construction of itself as panoptic and omnipresent, as capable of theorizing the whole of globalization, Morgan Stanley remains subject to the same macro-economic forces to which it gave representational form in its ad. In September 2008 Morgan Stanley stock plummeted. Like Goldman Sachs, its status as an investment bank was changed to a more regulated bank holding company. By the end of the year, it lost its place as a member of the S&P 500.

Landscapes of sign territory

After examining the 2,400 corporate commercials in our dataset, a few generalizations come easily. Corporate ads offer a vehicle for producing

a legitimating mythology of global corporate capitalism. While each particular corporation tells stories to valorize itself, when these stories are taken together they tell a de-historicized story about Capital in a world that has become laterally arrayed. In this mythology, Capital has no apparent source; it exists in the form of grand signifiers that appear to be autonomous in every sense, except for their relationship to the individual subject.

In this mythology, Capital seeks not power or even excessive profits, but rather the greater good; Capital does not stand in relation to society, *it appears as society* via the imagery of a network of markets integrated by telecommunications and cool new technologies. In this mythology, Capital does not discriminate by gender or race or age, nor does it discriminate spatially or geographically – all spaces are equally abstract: the urban, the suburban, the natural all are within equal reach.

Taken from the Council for Biotechnology Information, GlaxoSmithKline, the New York Stock Exchange, Boeing, Siemens, and IBM commercials, these images point to a future being designed by capital and technology. Here we find not only technologies such as wind generators and satellite dishes and the high-tech landscapes of research labs and clean rooms, but also a layer of data superimposed on the faces of scientists and engineers. Whether it be space biotechnology, or communications, signifiers of information technology undergird Capital's vision of the future.

As we might have expected at this stage of transnational globalism, the nation-state and its boundaries have all but vanished. Corporate branding furnishes a protective shield from the political. Since the fall of socialism, Capital's only enemies are those forces that slow the flow of investment and the production of surplus. Theorizing the corporate sign economy in relation to a material referent, we must take into account the growing disparity between the global rich and poor. In corporate ads, inequality and exploitation have disappeared – the global poor do not exist – and poverty, hunger, war, disease, and pollution are absent as signifiers, apparently erased by the abundance made possible by the corporate direction of technology. These then are landscapes of possibility.

There is no unitary landscape of Capital; these landscapes come in a variety of ideological flavors. Nevertheless, there are some overarching features, the most significant of which is that Euclidean geography of space–time coordinates has been all but abolished, replaced by the aestheticized signifiers of cultural geography. But it is just as likely that this approach to landscape representation corresponds to the decoding presuppositions of montage editing in television, rather than a response to the transnational logic of Capital and its impact on people and place. This raises again a fundamental question. How much are the landscapes we have explored representations of an imaginary world out there – a.k.a. the globalizing economy and society? How much are they really mappings of the sign economy that has become a perquisite to the reproduction of all that lies beyond it? We have suggested that perhaps we must redefine "the real relations in which [individuals] live" (Althusser 1971:155) to

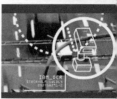

include the sign economy anchored by advertising. Perhaps, we must now invert the sensibilities of historical geography and ask if advertising landscapes are in fact the territory they represent?

Landscapes of capitalist communism

Across the advertising landscapes of Capital we have observed that the State has disappeared; that the materiality of labor in the production of value has become minimal, the source of value now seeming to emanate from science, technology, and manipulation of knowledge; that exchanges of labor for the means of consumption are no longer necessary; and that markets have grown so ubiquitous that commodity exchanges no longer need take place – instead of exchanges, there are transfers of value. Taken together, these, of course, are key features of what Marx anticipated would occur with the transition to communism. We can transpose Paolo Virno's (2004:108) observation that post-Fordism is the "communism of capital" to the imagined social landscapes of corporate advertising.

Here in its public relations discourse, post-Fordist multinational capital imagines a future social landscape that resembles communism – we'll call it capitalist communism. Indeed, we can look at this in several ways. On the one hand, we must admit that it is empirically untrue: alienated labor remains the norm; the capitalist state perseveres to protect capital, to sustain it, and to protect the rest of us from it (still an impossibly contradictory project); and with neoliberalism the hegemony of commodity exchange extends production time into every facet of our existence. On the other hand, as a representation it exposes the fundamental historical contradiction of capital – the replacement of labor with scientific knowledge as the means of expanding productivity and generating value. "As soon as labour in the direct form has ceased to be the great well-spring of wealth, labour time ceases and must cease to be its measure, and hence exchange value [must cease to be the measure] of use value" (Marx 1973:705). And this is precisely the picture one gets from these advertising landscapes: the mechanism of commodity exchange dissipates and in its stead the structural law of value assumes dominance – that is, value produced via the exchange of signs rather than the exchange of material goods.

Ah, but this is not communism; this is a simulacra of communism.

But communism in any shape or form would require equality, and this, capital is incapable of providing. Post-Fordism therefore can only satisfy the demands of a virtual communism. A communality of generalized intellect without material equality. How "communistic" can that be? (Lotringer 2004:17)

As we have observed, these landscapes reflect a vision of a social life so completely occupied by the commodity form that exchange becomes frictionless and hence unobservable (invisible). This can occur, or so the advertising narrative goes, because the twin logics of technoscience and networking have reorganized daily life, making the conditions of daily life wholly rational. These landscapes appear vacated of people because they move so fluidly through these spaces that relationships of hierarchy and power appear unformed. Spaces appear to favor the individual and small group by being self-sufficient and self-governing spaces, animated by the invisible hands of the commodity form and the technology form – making the State form of power appear unnecessary.

Notes

3   Landscapes of Fictitious Capital

1 Investopedia (www.investopedia.com/terms/s/securitization.asp) defines Securitization as: "The process through which an issuer creates a financial instrument by combining other financial assets and then marketing different tiers of the repackaged instruments to investors . . . Mortgage-backed securities are a perfect example of securitization. By combining mortgages into one large pool, the issuer can divide the large pool into smaller pieces based on each individual mortgage's inherent risk of default and then sell those smaller pieces to investors."

4   Representing the Social Relations of Production in the Network Economy

1 To contextualize, Allison Schieffelin, employed by Morgan Stanley from 1986 to 2000, filed an employment discrimination case against Morgan Stanley with the Equal Employment Opportunity Commission (EEOC) in 1998. In 2001 the EEOC found "reasonable cause to believe that [Morgan Stanley] discriminated against [Ms. Schieffelin] and a class of similarly situated females. . ." The EEOC filed an additional complaint against Morgan Stanley in Federal Court, alleging "unlawful employment practices" against women officers and retaliation in the workplace against the plaintiff. The EEOC filing alleged "Morgan Stanley systematically denied opportunities for equal compensation and advancement to a class of professional women." Prior to trial in July 2004, Morgan Stanley settled the sex discrimination lawsuit for $54 million with the usual language that they were not admitting to the allegations (Ackman 2004, and www.forbes.com/work/careers/2004/07/07/cx_da_0707topnews.html and www.forbes.com/2002/10/24/cx_aw_1024fine.html; accessed January 9, 2005).

8 Mapping the Terrain in a Sign Economy

1 Cisco has been heavily criticized for their role in supporting censorship and surveillance by providing technology used to filter information from Chinese citizens. See Gutmann (2004).

2 Dow's description of its campaign is as generalizing as its commercial. Emptied of all substance, its function is to produce a Dow mythology. "This is more than an ad campaign to our company. It is a statement to the world and, more importantly, to ourselves about the future direction of our business," said Patti Temple Rocks, Dow vice president of global communications and reputation; "It will be our calling card to people around the world who care about the future relationship between businesses, society and the environment. It reflects our intention as a company to prioritize the things we do to advance innovation and focus the people and resources of Dow on solving human problems" (Dow News Center, June 20, 2006: news.dow.com/corporate/2006/20060619c.htm; accessed July 2006).

Bibliography

Aberley, D. 1993. *Boundaries of Home: mapping for local empowerment.* Gabriola Island, BC: New Society.

Ackman, D. 2004. *Morgan Stanley and the Women.* Available at: www.forbes.com/work/careers/2004/07/07/cx_da_0707topnews.html. Accessed May 1, 2006.

Agger, B. 1989. *Fast Capitalism: a critical theory of significance.* Urbana: University of Illinois Press.

Althusser, L. 1971. *Lenin and Philosophy.* London: New Left Books.

Anderson, B. 1983. *Imagined Communities.* London: Verso.

Anderson, S. and Cavanagh, J. 2000. *Field Guide to the Global Economy.* New York: The New Press.

Appadurai, A. 1996. *Modernity at Large: cultural dimensions of globalization.* Minneapolis: University of Minnesota.

Augé, M. 1995. *Non-Places: introduction to an anthropology of supermodernity.* London: Verso.

Banerjee, S. B. and Linstead, S. 2001. "Globalization, Multiculturalism and Other Fictions: colonialism for the new millennium?" *Organization*, 8, no.4: 683–722.

Barthes, R. 1972. *Mythologies.* New York: Hill & Wang.

Baudrillard, J. 1983. "The Ecstasy of Communication," in H. Foster (ed.), *The Anti-Aesthetic: essays on a postmodern culture.* Port Townsend, WA: Bay Press, pp. 126–34.

Baudrillard, J. 1990. *Fatal Strategies.* New York: Semiotext(e).

Baudrillard, J. 1993a. *Symbolic Exchange and Death.* London: Sage.

Baudrillard, J. 1993b. *The Transparency of Evil.* New York: Verso.

Baudrillard, J. 1994. *Simulacra and Simulation.* Ann Arbor: University of Michigan Press.

Baudrillard, J. 2001. *The Global and the Universal.* Available at: www.egs.edu/faculty/jean-baudrillard/articles/the-global-and-the-universal/#. Accessed January 24, 2007.

Baudrillard, J. 2002a. *Between Difference and Singularity: an open discussion with Jean Baudrillard.* Available at: www.egs.edu/faculty/baudrillard/

baudrillard-between-difference-and-singularity-2002.html. Accessed January 24, 2007.

Baudrillard, J. 2002b. *The Spirit of Terrorism and Requiem for the Twin Towers*. New York: Verso.

Bauman, Z. 1998. *Globalization*. New York: Columbia University Press.

Bauman, Z. 2000. *Liquid Modernity*. Cambridge: Polity Press.

Beaud, M. 2002. *A History of Capitalism: 1500–2000*. New York: Monthly Review Press.

Beck, U. 1999. *World Risk Society*. London: Blackwell Publishers.

Bell, D. 1966. *The End of Ideology: on the exhaustion of political ideas in the fifties*. New York: Free Press.

Belson, K. 2005. "WorldCom's Audacious Failure and Its Toll on an Industry," *New York Times* (January 18).

Berger, J. 1974. *The Look of Things*. New York: Viking Press.

Berger, J. and Mohr, J. 1982. *Another Way of Telling*. New York: Pantheon.

Bernanke, B. 2009. *Testimony: acquisition of Merrill Lynch by Bank of America*. Before the Committee on Oversight and Government Reform, US House of Representatives, Washington, DC. June 25. Available at: http://federalreserve.gov/newsevents/testimony/bernanke20090625a.htm. Accessed August 10, 2009.

Best, S. and Kellner, D. 1991. *The Postmodern Turn*. New York: Guilford Press.

Blackburn, R. 2002. "The Enron Debacle and the Pension Crisis," *New Left Review*, 14 (March–April): 26–51.

Bogard, W. 1996. *The Simulation of Surveillance*. Cambridge: Cambridge University Press.

Bourdieu, P. 1984. *Distinction: a social critique of the judgment of taste*. Cambridge, MA: Harvard University Press.

Braverman, H. 1976. *Labor and Monopoly Capital: the degradation of work in the twentieth century*. New York: Monthly Review Press.

Brennan, T. 1993. *History after Lacan*. New York: Routledge.

Brennan, T. 2003. *Globalization and its Terrors: daily life in the West*. New York: Routledge.

Brenner, N. 1998. "Between Fixity and Motion: accumulation, territorial organization and the historical geography of spatial scales," *Environment and Planning D: Society and Space*, 16, no.5: 459–81.

Brenner, R. 2000. "The Boom and the Bubble," *New Left Review*, 43 (January–February): 33–59.

Brenner, R. 2003. *The Boom and the Bubble: the US in the world economy*. New York: Verso.

Brenner, R. 2004. "New Boom or New Bubble? The trajectory of the US economy," *New Left Review*, 25 (January–February): 57–90.

Brenner, R. 2006. *The Economics of Global Turbulence*. New York: Verso.

Browning, J. and Reiss, S. 1998. "Encyclopaedia of the New Economy: redefining business for the 21st century," *Wired*, 6, no.3: 105–14.

Busch, L. 2007. "Performing the Economy, Performing Science: from neoclassical to supply chain models in the agrifood sector," *Economy and Society*, 36, no.3: 437–66.

Castells, M. 1996. *The Rise of the Network Society, the Information Age*, Vol. I. Oxford: Basil Blackwell.

Castells, M., Fernández-Ardèvol, M., Qiu, J. and Sey, A. 2007. *Mobile Communication and Society*. Cambridge, MA: MIT Press.

Castoriadis, C. 1997. "Recommencing the Revolution," in D. A. Curtis (ed.), *The Castoriadis Reader*. Oxford: Blackwell Publishers, pp. 106–39.

Cosgrove, D. 1985. *Social Formation and Symbolic Landscape*. Totowa, NJ: Barnes and Noble.

Davis, M. 2006. *Planet of Slums*. New York: Verso.

DeLanda, M. 1991. *War in the Age of Intelligent Machines*. New York: Zone.

Deleuze, G. and Guattari, F. 1987. *A Thousand Plateaus*. Minneapolis: University of Minnesota.

Douglas, M. 1966. *Purity and Danger: an analysis of concepts of pollution and taboo*. New York: Praeger.

Dow News Center. 2006. *Dow Chemical Launches "The Human Element Campaign,"* http://news.dow.com/corporate/2006/20060619c.htm. Accessed May 10, 2007.

Duhigg, C. 2009. "Stock Traders Find Speed Pays, in Milliseconds," *New York Times*, July 23. Available at: www.nytimes.com/2009/07/24/business/24trading.html. Accessed January 19, 2010.

During, S. 1995. McKenzie Wark's Virtual Geography (review), *Journal of International Communication*, 2, no.1. Available at: www.mnstate.edu/gunarat/jicreviews2-1.html. Accessed May 25, 2006.

Eagleton, T. 2000. *The Idea of Culture*. Malden, MA: Blackwell.

Eichenwald, K. 2002. "For WorldCom, Acquisitions Were Behind Its Rise and Fall," *New York Times*, August 8. Available at: www.nytimes.com/2002/08/08/business/for-worldcom-acquisitions-were-behind-its-rise-and-fall.html. Accessed August 2, 2009.

Elliott, A. and Lemert C. 2006. *The New Individualism: the emotional costs of globalization*. New York: Routledge.

Featherstone, M. 1995. *Undoing Culture: globalization, postmodernism and identity*. Thousand Oaks, CA: Sage.

Feldstein, D. 2002. "Special-Purpose Vehicles Used to Control Market, Credit Rating," *Houston Chronicle*, January 28. Available at: www.chron.com/disp/story.mpl/special/enron/1228645.html. Accessed May 20, 2005.

Florida, R. 2002. *The Rise of the Creative Class*. New York: Basic Books.

Fort Worth Star Telegram. 2006. "Enron Executives Spun Off What Has Become an $18 Billion Enterprise," *Fort Worth Star Telegram*, January 29. Available at: www.redorbit.com/news/science/373104/enron_executives_spun_off_what_has_become_an_18_billion/index.html. Accessed August 6, 2009.

Foucault, M. 1986. "Of Other Spaces," *Diacritics*, 16, no.1: 22–7.

Friedman, T. 1999. *The Lexus and the Olive Tree*. New York: Farrar, Straus & Giroux.

Friedman, T. 2006. *The World is Flat: a brief history of the twenty-first century*. New York: Farrar, Straus and Giroux.

Gibson, W. 1984. *Neuromancer*. New York: Ace Books.

Gibson-Graham, J. K. 2006. *The End of Capitalism (As We Knew It): a feminist critique of political economy*. Minneapolis: University of Minnesota Press.

Giddens, A. 1991. *Modernity and Self-Identity*. Stanford: Stanford University Press.

Gold, J. and Revill, G. 2003. "Exploring Landscapes of Fear: marginality, spectacle and surveillance," *Capital and Class*, 80 (Summer): 27–50.

Goldman, R. 1994. *Contradictions in the Political Economy of Sign Value*, Current Perspectives in Social Theory 14. Greenwich, CO: JAI Press, pp. 183–211.

Goldman, R. and Papson, S. 1996. *Sign Wars: the cluttered landscape of advertising*. New York: Guilford.

Goldman, R. and Papson, S. 2006. "Capital's Brandscapes," *Journal of Consumer Research*, 6, no.3: 327–53.

Gottdiener, M. 1987. "Space as a Force of Production: contribution to the debate on realism, capitalism and space," *Journal of Urban and Regional Research*, 11, no.1: 405–16.

Gray, J. 1998. *False Dawn: the delusions of global capitalism*. New York: New Press.

Gutmann, E. 2004. *Losing the New China: a story of American commerce, desire and betrayal*. San Francisco: Encounter Press.

Hardt, M. and Negri, A. 2001. *Empire*. Cambridge, MA: Harvard University Press.

Hardt, M. and Negri, A. 2004. *Multitude: war and democracy in the age of empire*. New York: Penguin Press.

Haraway, D. 1991. *Simians, Cyborgs and Women: the reinvention of nature*. New York: Routledge.

Harris, J. and Taylor, P. 2005. *Digital Matters: theory and culture of the matrix*. New York: Routledge.

Harvey, D. 1982. *The Limits to Capital*. Chicago: University of Chicago Press.

Harvey, D. 1989. *The Condition of Postmodernity*. Cambridge, MA: Basil Blackwell.

Hegel, G. W. F. 1967. *The Phenomenology of Mind*. New York: Harper Torchbooks.

Henwood, D. 2003. *After the New Economy*. New York: New Press.

Hoopes, J. 2006. "Growth Through Knowledge: Wal-Mart, high technology, and the ever less visible hand of the manager," in N. Lichtenstein (ed.), *Wal-Mart: the face of twenty-first century capitalism*. New York: New Press, pp. 83–104.

Houston Chronicle. 2004. "The Fall of Enron." Available at: www.chron.com/news/specials/enron/glossary.html#barges. Accessed May 20, 2005.

Information Technology Association of America. 1997. *Help Wanted: the IT workforce gap at the dawn of a new century*. Arlington, VA: Information Technology Association of America.

Investopedia. 2009. www.investopedia.com. Accessed August 1, 2009.

Jameson, F. 1984. "Postmodernism, or the Cultural Logic of Late Capitalism," *New Left Review*, 146, July–August: 53–92.

Jameson, F. 2004. "The Politics of Utopia," *New Left Review*, 25 (January–February): 35–54.

Jha, P. 2006. *The Twilight of the Nation State: globalization, chaos, and war*. Ann Arbor, MI: Pluto Press.

Kellner, D. (ed.) 1994. *Baudrillard: A Critical Reader*. Oxford: Basil Blackwell.

Klein, N. 2007. *The Shock Doctrine: the rise of disaster capitalism*. New York: Metropolitan Books.

Korzybski, A. 1933. "A Non-Aristotelian System and its Necessity for Rigour in Mathematics and Physics," paper presented at meeting of the American Association for the Advancement of Science, New Orleans, December 28, 1931. Reprinted in Korzybski, *Science and Sanity – an introduction to non-Aristotelean systems and general semantics*. San Francisco: San Francisco International Society for General Semantics, 1995, pp. 747–61.

Kunstler, J. 1993. *The Geography of Nowhere: the rise and decline of America's man-made landscape*. New York: Simon and Schuster.

Lash, S. and Urry, J. 1994. *Economies of Signs and Space*. London: Sage.

Lefebvre, H. 1971. *Everyday Life in the Modern World*. New York: Harper.

Lefebvre, H. 1992. *The Production of Space*. Oxford: Blackwell.

Lipovetsky, G. 2005. *Hypermodern Times*. Malden, MA: Polity.

Lotringer, S. 2004. "Forward: we the multitude," in P. Virno, *A Grammar of the Multitude*. New York: Semiotext(e), pp. 7–18

Lotringer, S. and Baudrillard, J. 1986. "Forgetting Baudrillard," *Social Text*, 15 (Autumn): 140–4.

Lury, C. 2004. *Brands: the logos of the global economy*. New York: Routledge.

Lyotard, J. 1984. *The Postmodern Condition: a report on knowledge*. Minneapolis: University of Minnesota Press.

Machin, D. 2004. "Building the World's Visual Language: the increasing global importance of image banks," *Visual Communication*, 3, no.3: 316–36.

Macpherson, C. B. 1962. *The Political Theory of Possessive Individualism: from Hobbes to Locke*. Oxford: Clarendon.

Marx, K. 1967. *Capital*, Vols. I, II, III. New York: International Publishers.

Marx, K. 1973. *Grundrisse*. New York: Penguin.

Marx, K. 1975. *Wage-Labour and Capital*. New York: International Publishers.

Marx, K. and Engels, F. 1978. "The Communist Manifesto," in R. Tucker (ed.), *The Marx–Engels Reader*. New York: Norton, pp. 473–91.

Merrifield, A. 1993. "Place and Space: a Lefebvrian reconciliation," *Transactions of the Institute of British Geographers, new series* 18, no.4: 516–31.

Merrin, W. 2001. "To Play with Phantoms: Jean Baudrillard and the evil demon of the simulacrum," *Economy and Society*, 30, no.1: 85–111.

Mills, C. W. 1959. *The Sociological Imagination*. New York: Oxford University Press.

Mitchell, D. 2000. *Cultural Geography: a critical introduction*. Malden, MA: Blackwell.

Mitchell, W. 1994. *Landscape and Power*. Chicago: University of Chicago Press.

Nye, D. 1997. *Narratives and Space: technology and the construction of American culture*. New York: Columbia University Press.

Office of the Comptroller. 2008. *OCC's Quarterly Report on Bank Trading and Derivatives Activities Fourth Quarter*. Available at: www.occ.treas.gov/ftp/release/2009-34a.pdf. Accessed January 22, 2009.

Olalquiaga, C. 1992. *Megalopolis*. Minneapolis: University of Minnesota Press.

Petrovic, M. and Hamilton, G. 2006. "Making Global Markets: Wal-Mart and its suppliers," in N. Lichtenstein (ed.), *Wal-Mart: the face of twenty-first century capitalism*. New York: New Press, pp. 107–42.

Rajagopal, A. 2001. "Technologies of Perception and the Cultures of Globalization," *Social Text*, 68 (Fall): 1–8.

Salerno, R. 2003. *Landscapes of Abandonment: capitalism, modernity, and estrangement*. Albany: SUNY Press.

Sassen, S. 1991. *The Global City: NY, London, Tokyo*. Princeton: Princeton University Press.

Schiller, D. 1999. *Digital Capitalism: networking the global market system*. Cambridge, MA: MIT Press.

Schiller, D. 2003. "The Telecom Crisis," *Dissent*, 50, no.1: 66–71.

Schivelbusch, W. 1986. *The Railway Journey: the industrialization of time and space in the nineteenth century*. Berkeley: University of California Press.

Schumpeter, J. 1975. *Capitalism, Socialism and Democracy*. New York: Harper.

Sennett, R. 1999. *The Corrosion of Character*. New York: Norton.

Shaviro, S. 2004. "A Grammar of the Multitude," *The Pinnochio Theory*. Available at: www.shaviro.com/Blog/?p=363. Accessed April 2010.

Shiller, R. 2005. *Irrational Exuberance*. Princeton: Princeton University Press.

Simmel, G. 1950. "The Metropolis and Mental Life," in K. Wolff (ed.), *The Sociology of Georg Simmel*. Glencoe: Free Press, pp. 409–24.

Smith, R. 2003. "Baudrillard's Nonrepresentational Theory: burn the signs and journey without maps," *Environment and Planning D: Society & Space*, 21, no.1: 67–84.

Soros, G. 1998. *The Crisis of Global Capitalism*. New York: Public Affairs.

Spence, J. 2007. "Wachovia Sees Higher Loan Losses," *Marketwatch*, November 9. Available at: www.marketwatch.com/story/wachovia-sees-11-billion-drop-in-value-of-asset-backed-debt. Accessed January 25, 2009.

Spiro, L. 1997. "Commentary – WorldCom: Paper tiger?" *Business Week*, October 20. Available at: www.businessweek.com/1997/42/b3549101.htm. Accessed May 25, 2007.

Strange, S. 1986. *Casino Capitalism*. New York: Blackwell.

Tett, G. 2009. *Fool's Gold: how the bold dream of a small tribe at J. P. Morgan was corrupted by Wall Street greed and unleashed a catastrophe*. New York: Free Press.

Thrift, N. 2005, *Knowing Capitalism*. London: Sage.

Urry, J. 2003. *Global Complexity*. Cambridge: Polity.

US Department of Justice. 2000. *United States of America v. WorldCom and Sprint*. Available at: www.usdoj.gov/atr/cases/f5000/5051.htm. Accessed January 25, 2009.

Virilio, P. 1995a. *The Art of the Motor.* Minneapolis: University of Minnesota Press.

Virilio, P. 1995b. "Speed and Information: cyberspace alarm!" In A. Kroker and M. Kroker (eds.), *CTHEORY: Theory, Technology and Culture,* 18, no.3: 30–9.

Virno, P. 2004. *A Grammar of the Multitude.* New York: Semiotext(e).

Wachovia News Room. 2002. *Wachovia Introduces New Brand,* March 14. Available at: http://wachovia.com/inside/page/0,,134_307_348_1270_3392^795,00.html. Accessed February 10, 2007.

Waters, M. 1995. *Globalisation.* London: Routledge.

Weber, M. 1947. *The Theory of Social and Economic Organization.* New York: Oxford University Press.

Wernick, A. 1993. "Baudrillard's Remainder," *CTheory.net.* Available at: www.ctheory.net/articles.aspx?id=233. Accessed June 12, 2007.

Williamson, J. 1978. *Decoding Advertisements.* London: Marion Boyars.

Willis, S. 1994. *A Primer for Daily Life.* New York: Routledge.

Wood, D. 1992. *The Power of Maps.* New York: Guilford.

Žižek, S. 1997. "Multiculturalism, or the Cultural Logic of Late Capitalism," *New Left Review,* 225 (September–October): 28–51.

Žižek, S. 2005. "Revenge of Global Finance," *In These Times,* May 21. Available at: www.inthesetimes.com/site/main/article/2122/. Accessed January 2, 2008.

Zukin, S. 1993. *Landscapes of Power: from Detroit to Disneyworld.* Berkeley: University of California Press.

Index